A
CONFIDENT
PEACE

A CONFIDENT PEACE

LETTING REVELATION CHANGE THE WAY YOU LIVE

DR. MARK BECTON

AMBASSADOR INTERNATIONAL
GREENVILLE, SOUTH CAROLINA & BELFAST, NORTHERN IRELAND

www.ambassador-international.com

A Confident Peace
Letting Revelation Change the Way You Live

© 2013 by Mark Becton

Printed in the United States of America

ISBN: 978-1-62020-234-0
eISBN: 978-1-62020-332-3

Book design and typesetting: Matthew Mulder
E-book conversion: Anna Riebe

AMBASSADOR INTERNATIONAL
Emerald House
427 Wade Hampton Blvd.
Greenville, SC 29609, USA
www.ambassador-international.com

AMBASSADOR BOOKS
The Mount
2 Woodstock Link
Belfast, BT6 8DD, Northern Ireland, UK
www.ambassadormedia.co.uk

The colophon is a trademark of Ambassador

Dedication

This work is dedicated to the many who encouraged it with their words, time and prayer. Thank you, loving church family of Grove Avenue Baptist Church. Your hunger for God's Word fulfills my passion to teach it. God, in His gracious wisdom, has allowed us to share life together around His word. It continues to be a transforming adventure with God and you.

A heart-felt thank you to my assistant, Elaine Wilson. Her tireless efforts repaired fragmented sentences, verified references, and corrected the ever surfacing typographical errors. As your red pen colored each page, you made the message clear and respectable.

A special thank you goes to the Barbara Baranowski, Angela Dilmore, June Kramer, Rebekah Robb, Elaine Wilson, and my wife Loree. As the "Writing Group," your honest comments and earnest prayers encouraged the completion of this work. Your persistent help allowed it not to get buried beneath other responsibilities.

Above all, this work is dedicated to my wife, Loree. For thirty years you've been my loudest encourager. You are not only in some of the stories in this book, but you are in every word. As Genesis 2:24 states, the two of us are one. I'm so glad that's true, for I'm stronger and better because of you.

TABLE OF CONTENTS

CHAPTER 1
PULLING BACK THE CURTAINS — 11
REVELATION 1

CHAPTER 2
SEVEN URGENT MEMOS — 25
(Part 1)
REVELATION 2

CHAPTER 3
SEVEN URGENT MEMOS — 41
(Part 2)
REVELATION 2:18–3:6

CHAPTER 4
SEVEN URGENT MEMOS — 57
(Part 3)
REVELATION 3:7–22

CHAPTER 5
THE THRONE — 73
REVELATION 4

CHAPTER 6
THREE PHOTOGRAPHS — 91
REVELATION 5

CHAPTER 7
THE UNAVOIDABLE TALK — 107
"The Second Coming of Jesus"

CHAPTER 8
GOD'S TOUGH LOVE — 125
REVELATION 6

CHAPTER 9

GOD'S ABSURD GRACE − 141
REVELATION 7

CHAPTER 10

THE EARTH IS THE LORD'S...PHYSICALLY! − 157
REVELATION 8

CHAPTER 11

THE EARTH IS THE LORD'S...SPIRITUALLY! − 171
REVELATION 9

CHAPTER 12

SOMETHING EXTRA FOR THE EXTRA-STUBBORN − 187
REVELATION 10

CHAPTER 13

THE PLAN WORKS...IF YOU WORK THE PLAN − 203
REVELATION 11:1-14

CHAPTER 14

GOD WILL MAKE EVERYTHING RIGHT − 221
REVELATION 11:15-19

CHAPTER 15

SURVIVING THE WAR − 239
REVELATION 12

CHAPTER 16

BEWARE THE GREAT COUNTERFEITER − 255
REVELATION 13

CHAPTER 17

IT'S YOUR CHOICE − 273
REVELATION 14

CHAPTER 18

BETTER, OR BITTER? − 291
REVELATION 15, 16

CHAPTER 19

GOD'S EULOGY FOR RELIGION — 311
REVELATION 17

CHAPTER 20

WEEPING FOR HUMPTY DUMPTY — 329
REVELATION 18

CHAPTER 21

YOU'VE ALREADY WON! — 347
REVELATION 19

CHAPTER 22

A SECOND CHANCE AT EDEN — 365
REVELATION 20

CHAPTER 23

WHAT WOULD YOU PAY FOR HEAVEN? — 385
REVELATION 21

CHAPTER 24

HANG ON, I'M COMING! — 403
REVELATION 22

CHAPTER 1

PULLING BACK THE CURTAINS

REVELATION 1

[1] The revelation of Jesus Christ, which God gave him to show his servants what must soon take place. He made it known by sending his angel to his servant John, [2] who testifies to everything he saw—that is, the word of God and the testimony of Jesus Christ. [3]Blessed is the one who reads the words of this prophecy, and blessed are those who hear it and take to heart what is written in it, because the time is near.

— REVELATION 1:1 3

GENESIS, THE FIRST BOOK OF the Bible, opens with a sentence quoted by believers and nonbelievers alike: *"In the beginning, God created the heavens and the earth."* Unknowingly, believers and nonbelievers have been repeating the first sentence of the last book of the Bible as well: *"The revelation of Jesus Christ, which God gave him to show his servants what must soon take place."* I realize that this line in Revelation doesn't sound as familiar as the one in Genesis. That is because many have condensed Revelation 1:1 into one word: apocalypse. Now, "apocalypse" is a word most people are used to hearing.

To be fair, we get our word "apocalypse" from the title of the book and the opening phrase, *"The revelation of Jesus Christ."* The Greek word for "revelation" is *apokalupsis.* However, the word "apocalypse" projects chilling images of plagues, wars, and evil.

Though those are some of the images the word "apocalypse" reveals, that's not what the word means. It refers to an unveiling, and the book of Revelation unveils so much more than the horrors of the end times. In fact, Revelation 1 unveils answers to questions that have been asked for thousands of years.

Think for a moment of what such a gift from Jesus can mean. Imagine Jesus walking you into a room where each wall is covered by a large curtain and above each curtain is a question. Eagerly, Jesus turns to you and says, "If you want to know the answer to any of these questions, ask. I'll pull back the curtain and show you the answer." When you read Revelation 1, it's as though Jesus has put His hand on the curtains of four historic questions. One at a time He pulls them back to unveil the answer.

CURTAIN #1
Is the Bible God's Word?

The question above the first curtain could be, "Is the Bible God's Word?" A reading of Revelation 1:1–2 and verses 9–11 reveals that it is.

Verse 1 identifies God as the primary source of the Bible. It reads, *"The revelation of Jesus Christ, which God gave him."* Verse 1 also explains the inspirational process behind writing the Bible. It states, *"He (Jesus Christ) made it known by sending his angel to his servant John."* That was God's process for writing the book of Revelation, and it's similar to God's process for writing the entire Bible. 2 Peter 1:21 explains, *"For prophecy never had its origin in the will of man, but men spoke from God as they were carried along by the Holy Spirit."* Though different individuals may have held the pen, it was God who inspired them to write.

The fact that God wrote the Bible is impressive—even for a first grader. I heard of a mother sitting with her first grade daughter in church. Staring at her mom's open Bible, the first grader whispered to her mom, "Did God really write that?" When her mother answered, "Yes, He did," her daughter's eyes widened as she said, "Wow! He really has neat handwriting."

Though the pens may have been in the hands of others, God inspired each of them to write. The Bible is the result of God's handwriting. What is also impressive about the book of Revelation was the one God chose to hold the pen.

Verses 1–2 identify the Apostle John as the individual inspired by God to write the book of Revelation. When you read some of his story in verses 9–11, you get a feel for why this book is so special.

> ⁹ I, John, your brother and companion in the suffering and kingdom and patient endurance that are ours in Jesus, was on the island of Patmos because of the word of God and the testimony of Jesus. ¹⁰ On the Lord's Day I was in the Spirit, and I heard behind me a loud voice like a trumpet, ¹¹ which said: "Write on a scroll what you see and send it to the seven churches: to Ephesus, Smyrna, Pergamum, Thyatira, Sardis, Philadelphia and Laodicea."

John identifies himself as a *"companion in the suffering."* By the time God inspires John to write Revelation, he is the last of the original twelve apostles. All the others have been martyred. Like the others, he was arrested for preaching Jesus. Tradition says they tried to execute him by placing him in a pot of boiling oil, but he did not die. Therefore, they exiled him on the island of Patmos in the Aegean Sea, southwest of Ephesus. Now an old man, the apostle John, whom Jesus often called beloved, is asked to write what he sees. He's asked to write what is "unveiled" before him.

What is unveiled by God in the book of Revelation ties together everything else God said in the Bible. God also did this with the first book of the New Testament: Matthew has 92 Old Testament references. Furthermore, the book of Hebrews has 102. Yet the book of Revelation has over 550 Old Testament references.[1] This seems only right when you consider the history of the Bible. The Bible begins when God inspired Moses to pen Genesis while living in a wilderness. Around 1500 years and 40 authors later, God completes His work by inspiring John to write what he sees while in exile on the island of Patmos.

If you question whether the Bible is God's word, consider this: Around 40 authors of various cultures, countries, and languages, writing over the span of 1500 years, have produced a work that has:

- outlived those who wanted to kill it.
- changed lives that once challenged it.
- outlasted those who called it outdated.
- defied the odds, by prophesies fulfilled.
- reformed lives that once rejected it.
- produced peace, by promises kept.
- delivered one message understood by all.

---

1   James T. Draper Jr., *The Unveiling* (Nashville: Broadman, 1984), 12.

Only God could have written the Bible. Therefore, when you read Revelation or any other book of the Bible, God is saying, "I wrote this. You can trust Me."

CURTAIN #2
Is Jesus the Ultimate Authority?

As you move through Revelation 1, imagine Jesus moving to a second wall with a curtain. Above the curtain you read, "Is Jesus the Messiah?" Reaching for the curtain, He turns to you and asks, "Would you like to see the answer?" For you, the answer is unveiled in verses 12–16. John writes,

> [12] I turned around to see the voice that was speaking to me. And when I turned I saw seven golden lampstands, [13] and among the lampstands was someone "like a son of man," dressed in a robe reaching down to his feet and with a golden sash around his chest. [14] His head and hair were white like wool, as white as snow, and his eyes were like blazing fire. [15] His feet were like bronze glowing in a furnace, and his voice was like the sound of rushing waters. [16] In his right hand he held seven stars, and out of his mouth came a sharp double-edged sword. His face was like the sun shining in all its brilliance.

Verse 11 explains that John is writing all this with seven churches in mind. The seven golden lampstands in verses 12–13 represent those churches. But the lampstands are probably not what's most important to John at this moment. Turning to see who was behind him, talking to him, was most important: it was Jesus.

I remember reading of a woman who noticed actor Paul Newman standing in line behind her at an ice cream store. She thought to herself, "I'll not bother him. I'll just get my ice cream and leave." She stepped outside the store, took a breath and then wondered, "Now, where did I put my ice cream?" Suddenly Paul Newman walked up to her and said, "Lady, if you're looking for your ice cream, you put it in your purse."

John wasn't looking at a mere celebrity. He turned to see Jesus, adorned majestically, in a white robe that reached the floor and with a golden sash across His chest. In both the Hebrew and Greek versions of the Old Testament, only prophets, priests, and kings wore full-length robes, and sashes were worn only by priests. Seeing white hair on a white head is what Daniel saw in his vision in Daniel 7:9. It was his vision of God, and Daniel describes Him as "The Ancient of Days."

If that was where John's description ended we would have a picture of Jesus as God, who lived among us as a prophet proclaiming God's truth, as a priest reconciling people with God, and as a king with full authority.

It was hard for many in Jesus' day to see His divine authority: for them He was simply the carpenter's son. Many in our day, however, can't see His divine authority: for them He is just a good man, a moral teacher, or a prophet in the line of prophets. John's further description of Jesus unveils His authority—authority that most people can't or don't want to acknowledge.

John saw Jesus' eyes of fire and feet of bronze. Both qualities point to His authority to judge. The thrones of kings were elevated so that people approached at the level of the king's feet, thus distinguishing their authority to judge. The fact that Jesus' eyes were like a fire indicates His ability to judge perfectly. As Hebrews 4:13 states, *"Nothing in all creation is hidden from God's sight. Everything is uncovered and laid bare before the eyes of him to whom we must give account."* Thus, every lie is burned away by His gaze.

His voice, like the sounds of rushing waters, befits His authoritative power: each word thunders like Niagara Falls. As verse 20 explains, His right hand holding the seven stars reveals His authority over angels. From His mouth comes a double-edged sword as He wields the authority of truth (Heb. 4:12). Just as His eyes burn away every lie, every word from His mouth is truth. His face shining like the sun is a reference to the glory of God upon Him (2 Cor. 4:6). It answers the skeptic's question, "Who gave Jesus His authority and ability to judge?" God did!

In this unforgettable moment, I'd like to think that John was able to link together other unforgettable moments in his life. In Matthew 17:1–9, he saw Jesus transfigured. He was given a small glimpse of Jesus' heavenly greatness. Then in Matthew 27, he saw Jesus crucified. Yet in Matthew 28, he saw a risen Jesus ascend to heaven. Just before He did, John heard Jesus say, *"All authority in heaven and on earth has been given to me."* (Matt. 28:18) Now John fully sees what Jesus had said. He knows there's no authority greater than Jesus.

In a day when people view personal rights as more important than personal responsibility, and in a time when people think they're entitled to everything and accountable to no one, John's image of Jesus stands out as a stark reminder: Jesus is the ultimate authority. If you live your life thinking that what happens in Vegas stays in Vegas, think again. Nothing escapes the eyes and authority of Jesus Christ.

That's why it's important to ask yourself the question posed by pastor and author H. Dale Burke:

Whose voice is most important when everyone has a different opinion?[2]

For all of us, the answer should be clear. I want to hear and obey the voice of Jesus Christ. He alone is the ultimate authority.

CURTAIN #3
Is full surrender to Jesus worth it?

This experience for John is even more telling when you place it in the context of his life. John is an old man. All the other apostles have been martyred, His brother James among the first. John himself had been tormented and now was living in exile for his faith. Needless to say, full surrender to Jesus had not been easy. That's why I'd like to picture Jesus stepping toward a third wall, where above the curtain John reads, "Is full surrender to Jesus worth it?" What is unveiled in Revelation 1:17–20 provides a compelling answer.

> [17] When I saw him, I fell at his feet as though dead. Then he placed his right hand on me and said: "Do not be afraid. I am the First and the Last. [18] I am the Living One; I was dead, and behold I am alive forever and ever! And I hold the keys of death and Hades.

> [19] "Write, therefore, what you have seen, what is now and what will take place later. [20] The mystery of the seven stars that you saw in my right hand and of the seven golden lampstands is this: The seven stars are the angels of the seven churches, and the seven lampstands are the seven churches."

---

2   H. Dale Burke, *Less is More Leadership* (Eugene, OR: Harvest House, 2004), 48.

If you remember, John was the only one of the twelve who followed Jesus all the way to the cross. It was there Jesus asked him to take care of Mary, His mother (John 19:27). With Jesus' face beaten beyond recognition, His body mauled, bloodied, and crucified, John saw Jesus take His last breath. What an indelible picture of how the people regarded Jesus and His message.

Though John is old, that image hadn't changed. He wasn't present at the death of the other apostles, but I'm sure John wept each time he heard how they died. Then, in verse 20, Jesus asks John to *"Write, therefore, what you have seen, what is now and what will take place later."* The "now" had been painful for John as well.

There has been some discussion concerning when John wrote Revelation. Some believe it was during the reign of Nero. Nero's sadistically creative execution of Christians is well documented. Yet the early church fathers, the theologians of the first five centuries of the church, wrote that John penned Revelation around 94–96 AD, during the reign of Domitian, which was actually worse for Christians. Though Nero was creative in his executions, Domitian's persecution was extensive.

Anyone with a series of losses over a short period of time knows how one's view of life is affected. The portrait of life once painted by bright colors now carries the brush strokes of dark shadows.

Did John, surrounded by the deaths of so many of those surrendered to Jesus, wonder, "Is it worth it?" If so, can you imagine the dramatic swing of emotions when John sees Jesus in all His majestic glory (verses 12–16)? It would be impossible to describe his experience in verses 17–18 as he feels Jesus place His hand upon him and say,

"Do not be afraid. I am the First and the Last. I am the Living One; I was dead, and behold I am alive forever and ever! And I hold the keys of death and Hades." In short, Jesus was saying, "John! I won!"

Bernard Travaieille wrote that while in seminary, he and others got together to play basketball at a nearby school. The janitor, an old black man with white hair, waited patiently until they finished playing, often reading his Bible. One day Travaieille asked him, "What are you reading?"

"The book of Revelation," he answered.

Surprised, Travaieille pressed, "The book of Revelation? Do you understand it?"

"Oh, yes," he replied.

"You understand the book of Revelation?" Travaieille continued. "What does it mean?"

Very quietly the old janitor answered, "It means that Jesus is gonna win."[3]

To the surprise of many, the book of Revelation is God's message of hope to those who now suffer because of their surrender to Christ. Your parents may have disowned you. Your children may want little to do with you. Your friends may now avoid you because of your surrender to Christ. You might lose a job or a chance for promotion—all because of your surrender to Christ. There are even more believers being martyred today because of their surrender to Christ than there were in the days of John.

Yet no matter how you may suffer because of your surrender, Revelation reminds you that Jesus has already won. In NASCAR, the drivers speed around the track with the hope of winning the race.

---

3   James S. Hewett, *Illustrations Unlimited* (Wheaton, IL: Tyndale, 1988), p. 45

When a driver wins, he drives his car to the winner's circle. There his pit team, crew chief, sponsors, and all who have been in the race with him wait for him to step out of the car and take a drink of milk so the celebration can begin.

The message of Revelation is that Jesus has won the race. When He won, His followers won. We just haven't yet joined Him in the winner's circle, when the celebration will begin. Until we do, Revelation reminds us of the celebration to come; and, yes, surrendering your life to Jesus is worth it.

CURTAIN #4
Is time really short?

John was an old man, but even old men can grow weary with suffering. You may be at the prime of your life, or young and strong, and yet when you suffer for Jesus, you, too, want to know: "When will Jesus come? When will the celebration in heaven begin?"

It seems that since the time of the apostles, believers have been saying, "Time is short; Jesus is coming soon." According to some of the statements found in Revelation 1, it appears that Jesus has placed His hand on the curtain that answers the question, "Is time really short?"

The book of Revelation records the events leading up to the second coming of Jesus Christ. The book opens in chapter 1, verse 1, stating, *"The revelation of Jesus Christ, which God gave him to show his servants what must soon take place."* An alert reader might ask, "How soon?" Verse 3 gives a quick answer, saying, *"Blessed is the one who reads the words of this prophecy, and blessed are those who hear it and take to heart what is written in it, because the time is near."*

Skeptics would interject that since Jesus' resurrection, His follow-ers have said, "Time is short." And, they would be right. The Apostle Paul told believers in Rome that the day of the Lord was near (Rom. 13:12). James wrote, *"...be patient and stand firm, because the Lord's com-ing is near."* (James 5:8) Peter preached, *"The end of all things is near."* (1 Pet. 4:7)

The apostles, however, were not seeing Jesus' return as a date on the calendar, but as a change in seasons. In verse 3, when John writes that *"time is near"* he uses the Greek word *kairos* for time instead of *chronos.* If he had used *chronos,* he would have been referring to a mea-surement of time. By using *kairos,* he was talking about epochs of time. Epochs of history act much like seasons in a year. You know a change is coming because the signs are evident, but only after the change has occurred can you accurately date it.

Believers today, like the apostles then, should understand that we are in the season right before the change. This is our season to take the message of Jesus to the world; this is the season right before Jesus comes. We have no idea when the seasons will change and Jesus will return; only God knows (Matt. 24:36; Acts 1:7). The signs of a change in seasons grow stronger with time—and so should our urgency both to share Christ and to endure.

Author C. S. Lewis had a way of making complex theology clear, and I like what he said about the Second Coming of Jesus Christ.

The doctrine of the Second Coming teaches us that we do not and cannot know when the world drama will end. The curtain may be rung down at any moment. . . . This seems to some people intolerably frustrating. . . . We do not know the play. . . . The Author knows. The audience, if there is an audience (if angels and archangels and all the company of heaven fill the pit and the stalls) may have an inkling. . . . When it is over, we may be told. We are led to expect that the Author will have something to say to each of us on the part that each of us has played. The playing it well is what matters infinitely.[4]

Lewis is right. God, the author, decides when the play ends. As believers, we are not responsible for how and when God ends the play. We are responsible to fulfill our part in the play each day until Jesus comes. Time is short. As someone wisely said, "Live as though every day were your last—and someday you will be right."[5]

YOUR CURTAIN
Do You Trust Jesus?

In your imaginary room, there are so many more walls with curtains and questions. In fact, besides questions regarding the end times, the book of Revelation answers questions such as "How is Jesus Seen in Heaven?" "How Important is Holiness to God?" "What is Worship like in Heaven?" and "What Do Angels Do?"

Yet the real question to ask is "Why?" Why would God see it as important to write the book of Revelation? Why would He take the time to unveil the answers to these questions? To me, the answer is clear. God has done all this to assure you that you can trust Him. Think about the curtains and questions of Revelation chapter 1 alone.

---

4   Edythe Draper, *Draper's Book of Quotations for the Christian World* (Wheaton, IL: Tyndale, 1992), entry 9911.

5   Croft M. Pentz, *The Complete Book of Zingers* (Wheaton, IL: Tyndale , 1990).

Is the Bible God's Word? Revelation 1 affirms it.

Jesus says, "You can trust what I've said!"

Is Jesus the ultimate authority? Revelation 1 confirms it.

Jesus says, "You can trust who I am!"

Is full surrender to Jesus worth it? Revelation 1 reinforces it.

Jesus says, "You can trust that I've won!"

Is time short? Revelation 1 emphasizes the urgency of it.

Jesus says, "Trust me. Time is short!"

Going back to the imaginary room of walls, picture Jesus taking you to one more curtain. Above it you read the question, "Do You Trust Me?" Here, Jesus looks at you and explains,

> "All the other curtains answered questions you have of me. This is my question for you. Do you trust me? This time when I unveil this curtain, it will unveil your life. Your life will reveal if you trust what I've said. Your life will show if you know and fully surrender to who I am. Your life will show if you trust me when I have said time is short. However, before I pull back the curtain and show you what I have seen, why don't we sit down and talk. Let's talk about living as though you really do trust me."

CHAPTER 2

SEVEN URGENT MEMOS

(Part 1)

REVELATION 2

I STRONGLY DISAGREE WITH THOSE who see churches as corporations, but the following statement does highlight one area that churches and corporations have in common—they both need clear communication. As the Ford Motor Company says,

> At Ford Motor Company, communication with employees is a priority. Communication lets them know both good news and bad. And by knowing, they become part of it for better or worse.[6]

Apparently, Ford believes that their success depends upon clear communication—not just of good news, but of bad news as well. Ford also believes that if every employee is informed, then every employee is responsible. They are responsible to celebrate successes and to fix failures.

Revelation chapters 2 and 3 reveal that good communication was God's policy long before it was Ford's. In these two chapters, God communicates with seven churches in Asia Minor (modern-day Turkey). Since God has preserved what He wrote, He wants churches

---

6   Joe Griffith, *Speaker's Library of Business Stories, Anecdotes and Humor* (Paramus, NJ: Prentice Hall, 1990), 58.

from every generation to hear and take responsibility for what He has said.

Therefore, Revelation chapters 2 and 3 should be read as seven urgent memos from God to churches today. Some of the memos give us reason to celebrate. However, most of them inform us of areas that need fixing.

MEMO #1
God likes Responsibility, but not without Romance

God sends the first memo to a church in Ephesus. Like a memo from many supervisors, it begins with praise (Rev. 2:1–3).

> [1] "To the angel of the church in Ephesus write:
>
> These are the words of him who holds the seven stars in his right hand and walks among the seven golden lampstands: [2] I know your deeds, your hard work and your perseverance. I know that you cannot tolerate wicked men, that you have tested those who claim to be apostles but are not, and have found them false. [3] You have persevered and have endured hardships for my name, and have not grown weary."

Both the city of Ephesus and the believers living there had good reputations. The city was located on a major Roman highway and had one of the premiere seaports of that day. Thus this multi-cultural city of over 300,000 called itself, "The Vanity Fair of the World."

The city had a reputation for doing things right, and so did the believers. In verses 2–3, God praises them for what they are doing, saying, *"I know your deeds, your hard work, and your perseverance."* He also commends them for what they refuse to do. They refuse to follow false teachings. Finally, He applauds them for staying faithful, even though it's been hard.

Any church would love to receive such compliments from God. Yet every church should remember there is a difference between doing things right and doing the right things. As God continues His memo, it's clear that the church in Ephesus was so proud of doing things right that they neglected the one right thing God wanted most from them—their love. Verses 4–6 state,

> [4]"Yet I hold this against you: You have forsaken your first love. [5]Remember the height from which you have fallen! Repent and do the things you did at first. If you do not repent, I will come to you and remove your lampstand from its place. [6] But you have this in your favor: You hate the practices of the Nicolaitans, which I also hate."

Churches today can build right and be proud of their beautiful buildings. They can believe right and be proud of their unwavering convictions. They can do right and be proud of all their benevolent ministries and mission trips. They can stand right for a long time and be proud of their long history. In their own eyes, they can be living right for God, but unless their love is right with God, their life won't be right with God.

That is why God gives to Ephesus and churches like her three steps to correcting the problem. Step one, remember! Remember the height of love from which you have fallen. Step two, repent! Turn from simply doing things right and focus on doing the right thing— be infatuated with God again. And if you have forgotten how to live infatuated with God, remember what you did when you were, and take step three—repeat it! Verse 5 says, *"Repent and do the things you did at first."* [7]

I have found that though being responsible is good, it can blind you from what is best. While dating my wife Loree, I looked for reasons to be with her, and if I couldn't be with her, I found some way to tell her I loved her—like slipping notes on the windshield of her car. Once we were married and could spend more time together, some of the creative dating waned. Over time, responsibility can slowly replace romance in a relationship. When our boys were born, we were serving growing churches, so there was always a place to be and a need to meet. We have learned through the years that if we are not careful, our sense of responsibility to do things right will blind us of our need to do the right thing, which is to spend time together and love each other.

When a church is born, there is a sense of romance with God. But as ministries grow, so do responsibilities. In time, churches can become so focused on doing things right for God that they lose their romance with God. That is why God reminded the church of Ephesus and churches today of the reward awaiting them. When you remember, repent, and repeat the actions of your first love, you return to your life of romance with God, an experience beautifully described in verse 7:

> [7] "He who has an ear, let him hear what the Spirit says to the churches. To him who overcomes, I will give the right to eat from the tree of life, which is in the paradise of God."

---

7   David Jeremiah, *Escape the Coming Night* (Dallas: Word Publishing, 1990), 39.

God's promise in verse 7 is reminiscent of Jesus' promise in Luke 23:43. Jesus tells the repentant thief crucified beside Him, *"today you will be with me in paradise."* This word *paradise* is a word the Greeks actually borrowed from the Persians, and it means "walled garden." When a Persian king wanted to bestow a high honor upon an individual, he extended him an invitation to walk with him in his personal garden. There, they walked alone, giving the person the rare joy of an intimate conversation with the king.

The promise to the church in Ephesus is still God's promise to churches today. When you return to loving God first and living for Him second, your life with God becomes an intimate walk with your King. And once you reclaim your intimacy with God, you wonder, "Why did I ever put anything else first?"

MEMO #2
Let Suffering Make You Better, not Bitter

The second memo from God is one every church would love to have, but would hate to have to earn. In Revelation 2:8–11, God praises the church in Smyrna for allowing suffering to make it better, not bitter. Again, any church would love to receive such praise from God, but not at the price of suffering. Smyrna's memo reads,

> [8] "To the angel of the church in Smyrna write:

> These are the words of him who is the First and the Last, who died and came to life again. [9] I know your afflictions and your poverty — yet you are rich! I know the slander of those who say they are Jews and are not, but are a synagogue of Satan. [10] Do not be afraid of what you are about to suffer. I tell you, the devil will put some of you in prison to test you, and you will suffer

persecution for ten days. Be faithful, even to the point of death, and I will give you the crown of life.

[11] He who has an ear, let him hear what the Spirit says to the churches. He who overcomes will not be hurt at all by the second death."

Today, this memo would be sent to believers living in Izmir, a bustling Turkish city of 2.5 million. However, at the time of the original memo, the city's name was Smyrna. Though historians consider it one of the most exquisite cities the Greeks ever built, believers living there would have said the city lived up to its name, for Smyrna means "bitter."

God uses three words in verse 9 to describe the suffering that believers endured. God tells them, *"I know your afflictions."* The Greek word for "affliction" is translated in other verses as "tribulation." It's the word for the stone used to grind wheat into powder. The believers in Smyrna felt the constant crushing press of persecution. Furthermore, God says, *"I know . . . your poverty."* This word "poverty" is the same word used in Mark 12:42 to describe the widow who gave her last two coins to God. It literally means "beggary." Then, God also states, *"I know the slander,"* in other words, "I know all that is being said to belittle you."

What a painful contrast of experiences. In a city of exquisite beauty, the church was experiencing extreme suffering. It would have been so easy for them to say, "God, it's just not fair. We are being crushed for being faithful, and those doing the crushing have everything compared to our nothing. And when they are not grinding us physically or financially, they are doing it emotionally with their lies.

We've endured this for a season, but now you say the season is about to get longer and worse (v. 10). God, it's just not fair. We quit!"

You might think they would have become bitter with God and quit, but they didn't. Instead, they became better with God, and history records that when the church allows suffering to make them better and not bitter, God does some amazing things.

God sent this memo to Smyrna during the Roman persecution of the church. The church would endure 250 years of brutal treatment. Yet because believers allowed their suffering to make them better, the church actually grew. Historian Roland Baton wrote that the blood of the martyrs became the seeds of the faith: when one life was martyred, at least three who saw it surrendered to Christ. During this 250-year period of suffering, the church reached its greatest numbers in proportion to the population of the world, all because the church allowed their suffering to make them better, not bitter.

Today the persecution of the church is actually greater than when Smyrna received its memo from God. Some say more believers are being martyred today than at any time in history. And if you were to look at a map indicating where the most people are surrendering their lives to Jesus, it would be in the countries where most are suffering for Jesus. It's because they've allowed suffering to make them better, not bitter.

In America, believers aren't suffering and lives aren't being surrendered to Jesus as they are in other places of the world. I believe it's because Americans don't respond well to suffering. Our preachers preach that the rewards of faithfulness to God are wealth, health, success, and protection. So whenever we suffer, we feel that God has gone back on His promise, and we allow suffering to make us bitter with God. We prove Adrian Rogers right when he said, "Bitterness is like the acid that destroys its container." Our bitterness with God and life makes us weak, not strong.

If the believers in Smyrna had heard the health, wealth, and success messages Americans hear, they, too, would have been bitter with God. Instead, they heard a different message. God's memo promises the one reward that is worth the suffering—victory!

In verse 10, God promises a crown of life to those who suffer. There are two Greek words for crown used in the New Testament. One is the crown of royalty (*diadema*) and the other is the crown of victory (*stephanos*). The one used here is the crown of victory. Verse 11 explains that this crown is received when the second death is overcome. Jesus explains in Luke 12:4–5, that the first death is physical—the death of our body on earth. The second death is spiritual; it's the death of our soul in hell. In these two verses, God has given a vivid picture of suffering and rewards.

Smyrna held Olympic-style games that were famous throughout the Roman province of Asia Minor. When an athlete won an event, he received a laurel crown symbolic of his victory.

Today, Olympic champions receive medals instead, but the meaning is the same—victory! However, televising the Olympics has improved one aspect of the games: we know more of the drama behind the victory. We are told of the athlete's years of training, the sacrifices made, and the injuries endured. The camera lens captures his or her face straining in the event, agonizing to the very end. After breaking the tape or landing their dismount, the emotions take over as the athlete realizes: "I won!"

This is the image God gives to believers and churches who suffer. This is your time. This is your event with God. Training, sacrifice, and suffering are all a part of it. And when you allow the suffering to make you better instead of bitter, you won't endure life as a victim. You will end life with the crown of victory.

MEMO #3
Beware the Bite of Compromise

Not every church suffers as Smyrna did, yet every church faces a challenge that can weaken the strongest of churches. That's why God's memo to the church at Pergamum is to the point: "Beware the bite of compromise." In verses 12–13, God affirms them saying,

> [12] "To the angel of the church in Pergamum write:
>
> These are the words of him who has the sharp, double-edged sword. [13] I know where you live: where Satan has his throne. Yet you remain true to my name. You did not renounce your faith in me, even in the days of Antipas, my faithful witness, who was put to death in your city—where Satan lives."

Today, the Turkish city of Bergama would have received the letter. When the memo was first written, the city's name was Pergamum. It literally means "citadel." Not only did the name sound strong, but the city was strong. Built on the broad fertile plain atop a 1,000-foot-tall hill about 20 miles inland from the Aegean Sea, it served as the capital of Asia Minor for over 250 years. It embodied and enforced the Roman way of life—a way of life that conflicted with Christianity.

For example, Romans worshiped their emperors as though they were gods. They required everyone to cry "Caesar is Lord." Yet the early church would not do it, because of their surrender to Jesus alone as Lord. Antipas, who some believe to be the pastor of the church in Pergamum, refused to say "Caesar is Lord," and so was executed.

What a picture. In Pergamum you have a band of believers refusing to bow to ungodly ways of the Roman Empire. Without apology, they stood out in the face of opposition to uphold their convictions that Jesus alone is Lord.

There are some churches today, like the one in Pergamum, willing to stand up and stand out against an ungodly culture. When a culture says there is no absolute truth, some churches lift God's Word as absolute truth! When the culture says "Homosexuality is an orientation," some churches will stand up and say, "God calls it sin!" When a culture thinks life is so cheap that it can be aborted, there are still some churches that stand and say, "God creates life, and that makes it sacred!"

Yet be careful, dear church, when you think that standing strong against the culture makes you strong with God. Abraham Lincoln once said, "Character is like a tree and reputation like its shadow. The shadow is what we think of it; the tree is the real thing."[8] People inside and outside a church may think she has a strong reputation for standing against the culture. Yet that doesn't mean she is truly strong with God. In verses 14–16, God makes this clear in His memo to the believers in Pergamum,

> [14] "Nevertheless, I have a few things against you: You have people there who hold to the teaching of Balaam, who taught Balak to entice the Israelites to sin by eating food sacrificed to idols and by committing sexual immorality. [15] Likewise you also have those who hold to the teaching of the Nicolaitans. [16] Repent therefore!

---

8   Draper, *Quotations*, entry 1001.

Otherwise, I will soon come to you and will fight against them
with the sword of my mouth."

Horticulturalists will tell you that many great trees have fallen,
though not because of the attacks from the outside. They've been
toppled by the bite of beetles eating from within. This was happening
to the church at Pergamum as they were being eaten from within by
heresy and immorality.

God gives them two ugly examples of their condition. He reminds
them of what Balaam did to God's people in the Old Testament. He
told King Balak not to attack Israel, but to entice them with pagan
women and subtle sins (Num. 22–25; 31:16). They couldn't defeat
them directly, so they schemed to weaken them spiritually.

The Nicolaitans were a New Testament example. In Acts 6:5,
Nicolas was one of the respected seven selected by the church to meet
the needs of the widows. However, the second century theologian
and historian Irenaeus reports that Nicolas' teachings would later lead
some believers into the same immorality as Balaam did. Thus, they
were dishonorably labeled as Nicolaitans.

These two examples are rather personal, for Balaam was a prophet
in the Old Testament, and Nicolas was a church leader in the New
Testament. The beetles with the biggest bite of compromise were men
of God.

Each week, a church somewhere is dealing with the infidelity or
immorality of a minister or church leader. Each Sunday, there will
be pastors in pulpits using the Bible to espouse their personal opinion, because in their opinion the Bible is not entirely God's Word.
Every day churches grow weaker as the bites of such church leaders
go deeper into the life of the church.

Though such leaders are at fault, they should not receive the full blame. Someone has said, "A leader without followers is just taking a walk." Every member of a church is accountable to God for his or her life. There are strong churches taking strong stands that are made weaker by members living ungodly lives. When you cheat on a test, your taxes, or your spouse, you weaken the church from within. When you use your words to swear, lie, or belittle, you weaken the church from within. Each time you live like the world when you walk out the doors of a church, you weaken the church from within.

To be fair, it is hard to live a godly life. Temptation lurks at every turn. Yet when tempted to compromise your life with God, remember what Mark Twain said, "It is easier to stay out than get out."[9] I believe Twain is right. It seems that in verse 17 God provides what is needed to resist any temptation:

> [17] "He who has an ear, let him hear what the Spirit says to the churches. To him who overcomes, I will give some of the hidden manna. I will also give him a white stone with a new name written on it, known only to him who receives it."

You can grow weak from constantly resisting the temptation to compromise your life with God. Yet, God promises if you keep fighting, He'll keep feeding. He promises hidden manna to those who overcome the urges and opportunities to compromise.

You might remember that God fed Israel for forty years as they wandered in the wilderness. What God provided they had never seen before, so they called it "manna." "Manna" means, "What is it?" Though they didn't know what it was, they saw God supply enough to keep them

---

9   Ibid, entry 11073.

strong each day. What a great encouragement from God. No matter how often you are tempted, and no matter how strong the temptation might be, God promises to give you what you need each day to be strong enough to resist it.

There is another gift God gives to help you overcome temptation and compromise—His name. He says He'll give a white stone with a new name on it to those who overcome. In the first century, such a stone was called a *tesserae*, and it had several uses. It was used in houses of Rome as a credit card. Victorious athletes received it as a free pass to all public spectacles. Furthermore, it was given to gladiators who had fought a long time. On it was inscribed "SP," which stood for *spectactus*. *Spectactus* meant "a man whose valor has been proved beyond a doubt."

When God told the believers in Pergamum that He would give them a *tesserae* to help them overcome their temptations, I'm sure their eyes widened and so should ours. God was promising to give them— and us—His name on His credit card. Whatever you need to overcome your temptation, God provides. God was also providing a free pass to the grand celebration. Once your life on earth is over, you get to be with Him forever. And in His presence, you are seen as one worthy of the title *spectactus*. You fought hard. You resisted the temptation to compromise, and are seen by God as one "whose valor has been proved beyond a doubt."

Do you hear what God is saying to today's church? You may seem strong on the outside for the stands you have taken, but that doesn't mean you are strong on the inside. Each compromise by a leader or member eats away at the strength of the church. Therefore, to resist the temptations to compromise, God promises to supply you with the strength to overcome and the incentives to stay faithful. It's now up to you to do what is necessary to resist the bite of compromise.

You are now Responsible

Do you remember the quote from the Ford Motor Company that was used to open this chapter? It said,

> At Ford Motor Company, communication with employees is a priority. Communication lets them know both good news and bad. And by knowing, they become part of it for better or worse.[10]

Communicating His heart to the churches in Ephesus, Smyrna and Pergamum was a priority to God. That is why He sent the memos. Having the memos preserved in scripture means it is still a priority to God for churches today to hear them as well. Churches today need these messages from God because we are no different.

After forty-three years in the ministry, my dad had served seven churches in three states. Reflecting on his years as a pastor, Dad told me, "If God moves you from one church to serve another, remember this: though their faces and names change, the people will be the same."

Since people are the same, churches are the same. And since churches never change, neither do God's memos to the churches. We still need to hear God's memos, whether good or bad.

---

10   Griffith, Speaker's Library, 58

CHURCHES STILL NEED TO HEAR . . .

MEMO #1
God likes Responsibility, but not without Romance!

Don't let the responsibilities of a godly life
take all the romance out of your life with God.

MEMO #2
Let Suffering make you Better, not Bitter!

Don't endure life as a victim; live it as a victor,
for the day will come when you will break the tape of time victoriously.

MEMO #3
Beware the Bite of Compromise!

Let God strengthen you so that
your compromise will not weaken His church.

Ford believed that, once the message was communicated, each employee was responsible for what they heard and what they did. I doubt God would expect anything less from each believer in each church. We are now responsible unto God for what we've heard and what we now do.

CHAPTER 3

SEVEN URGENT MEMOS

(Part 2)

REVELATION 2:18–3:6

WHILE I WAS IN SEMINARY, Gibtown Baptist Church called me to be their pastor. Looking back, the process was fairly simple. After preaching Sunday's sermon, the three deacons of the church stopped me in the aisle and asked if I'd be the church's pastor. I told them I'd pray about it for a week, come back and preach, and let the church vote. The next Sunday I preached and the fifteen members in attendance voted for me to be their pastor.

There are times Loree and I reminisce about our days at Gibtown. While serving there, I often told Loree that I could do so much more if the church was larger. Then, Loree would tell me, "Mark, someday you will be in a church that's larger, and you will long for the simpler days at Gibtown." As usual, Loree was right.

One of the things I miss most from our days at Gibtown is how simple communication was. If the church needed to know anything, I could call one family and in a matter of minutes the other seven families or so were informed. Furthermore, because the message didn't have to be repeated again and again, it wasn't changed much when shared. In larger churches, it takes longer for a message to be heard, and many times it gets distorted in translation. That's why it's better if members can read a message instead of just hear it.

That's probably why God has placed His messages to the seven churches in print. Sure, He could have sent a messenger to each and communicated directly (much like the phone chain at Gibtown). However, God placed His messages in print because He knew that far more than seven churches would need to hear them. That's why we will look at memos four and five. God knows that today's churches need to read, understand, and heed them.

MEMO #4
Fear God and Hold On

God's fourth memo was sent to His church in Thyatira. The name of the city today is Akhisar. Just as it was then, the city remains one of the smallest of the seven, and yet God deemed it necessary to send them the longest memo. God knew that His message to that church, and future churches like them, was critical. He knew if churches didn't fear Him and hold on, more would become like the one in Thyatira. In verses 18–19, God says,

> [18] "To the angel of the church in Thyatira write:
>
> "These are the words of the Son of God, whose eyes are like blazing fire and whose feet are like burnished bronze. [19] I know your deeds, your love and faith, your service and perseverance, and that you are now doing more than you did at first."

Verse 18 reminds the believers of the way Jesus is seen in Revelation 1:12–16. He is the all-knowing Judge. His eyes burn away every lie. You bow at His feet as He sees and judges what is true. What Jesus sees in the church in Thyatira seems impressive, especially when compared to other churches.

Verse 19 states that like the church in Ephesus, the believers in Thyatira are responsible. God knows their deeds and service. The difference is Thyatira has not lost their romance with God. He tells them, "I know your love." Furthermore, like the church in Smyrna, Jesus' followers in Thyatira are suffering, yet they are remaining faithful to God. The greatest compliment comes at the end of verse 19. God tells them, *"You are now doing more than you did at first."* The church in Thyatira is growing.

The common statement among church growth consultants is: "growing churches are healthy churches." Though that is true some of the time, it is not true all of the time. Dr. Warren Hultgren, for over fifty years pastor and pastor emeritus of First Baptist Church in Tulsa, Oklahoma, once told me: "Mark, it's best to resolve problems while they're small. For when a church grows, the problem grows with them."

There was a problem in the church at Thyatira that needed to be resolved. As the church was growing, so was their problem. God addresses it in verses 20–21.

> [20] "Nevertheless, I have this against you: You tolerate that woman Jezebel, who calls herself a prophetess. By her teaching she misleads my servants into sexual immorality and the eating of food sacrificed to idols. [21] I have given her time to repent of her immorality, but she is unwilling."

The issue in Ephesus was that the believers emphasized responsibility over love. They lived truth without grace. In Thyatira, the church emphasized love over responsibility. They lived grace without truth.

History records, and scripture states, that churches who emphasize grace over truth will grow. In 2 Timothy 4:2–5, God says that people will abandon sound doctrine for a "feel good" message. Every generation has had preachers using God's name and God's Word to tell the people what they want to hear. Most of the time, they are able to gather a large crowd of followers. Therefore, be careful of a dangerous misconception: the growth of a church doesn't always mean there is godliness throughout the church.

The issue in Thyatira was with a woman God has labeled as Jezebel. Though this was not her real name, it was the true nature of her heart. Like Queen Jezebel of the Old Testament, this woman was influential in corrupting God's people and leading them into idolatry and immorality (1 Kings 16–21; 2 Kings 9). Like Queen Jezebel, she had no fear of God. Though God had given her time to repent, she refused.

Many, like this woman in Thyatira, misread God. In your heart, you know God is calling you to repent of a specific sin. Yet you keep on sinning. And because you receive no punishment from God, you think God has either forgotten about it, has decided to allow it, or actually approves of it. God has never responded to sin in any of these ways. However, scripture does cite occasions when God has been patient, even longsuffering, with our sin, hoping that we would repent.

When we don't repent, in time, God will act. When God acts, we will become His message to others that we need to fear God and hold on. You see this in verses 22–23:

²² "So I will cast her on a bed of suffering, and I will make those who commit adultery with her suffer intensely, unless they repent of her ways. ²³ I will strike her children dead. Then all the churches will know that I am he who searches hearts and minds, and I will repay each of you according to your deeds."

God's actions are strong. He first casts this Jezebel on a bed. The words "of suffering" are not in the original text, though it is fair to imply them. God didn't put her there for a nap. Furthermore, those that share this sin with her will also share the suffering. The suffering they will receive is the same intense suffering the believers in Smyrna received. It's the Greek word for tribulation. The difference is that the believers in Smyrna were feeling it from the hand of the godless; the believers in Thyatira were feeling it from the hand of God.

Finally, God knows illegitimate doctrines often give birth to illegitimate children. Some believe that the church in Thyatira was 40 years old when they received this letter. God has allowed this false teaching to go on long enough to allow those deceived by Jezebel to deceive others. Thus when false doctrines prevent full surrender, God refuses to render salvation. Unless those under Jezebel's teaching repent, God promises that they will never experience life with God.

Therefore, it is important to determine if the doctrines you are being taught are legitimate or illegitimate. When you receive biblical teaching from a church leader, pastor, or particular faith, ask the following.

First, "Is the Bible they hold the Bible God wrote?" Our study of Revelation 1 revealed that God inspired around 40 different authors over the span of 1500 years to write the Bible. The fulfillment of prophesies not only affirms God's authorship, but points to Jesus alone as Lord. However, there are some who will hold in their hand a book they call the Bible. It is one man's alterations of what God inspired the original authors to write. The premise of such a work implies that an all-knowing, all-powerful, perfect God couldn't get it right the first time. Furthermore, it also implies that though Hebrews 6:18 says it's impossible for God to lie, He did. God says in Matthew 5:18 and Revelation 22:19 that nothing is to be changed or taken away from what He has written. Thus when anyone says that God inspired another man to change what God originally wrote, either that person is a liar or God is—and I trust God.

Second, "How much of the Bible is in their message?" The difference between an inspiring speech and a message inspired by God is the Word of God. Those who deliver speeches will reference God's Word to endorse what they say. But those who deliver messages from God get what they say from God's Word. For them, the Bible is not a footnote to a speech. It is the message to be delivered. That is why God's charge to pastors in 2 Timothy 4:2 is not to *"Use the Word!"* It is to *"Preach the Word!"* Therefore, next time you listen to a preacher preach, ask yourself, "How much of the Bible is in his message?"

Third, "Does his message agree with all the Bible?" Be leery of the pastor who fits a lot of scripture in his sermon, but uses it in a way that doesn't fit the message of the Bible. Preachers are charged in 2 Timothy 2:15 to *"Do your best to present yourself to God as one approved, a workman who does not need to be ashamed and who correctly handles the word of truth."* The Greek word translated "correctly handles" was a seamstress's term for "cutting straight." A skilled seamstress knows that in preparing a dress each piece needs to be accurately cut from the material. A wrong cut produces a worthless dress. Therefore, when a passage is cut straight from the fabric of God's Word, it should fit what God has said within its chapter. It should fit what God has said within the book. It should fit what God has said throughout the Bible. And then, when you apply it to your life, you know it fits.

When God wrote His memo to the believers in Thyatira, He realized their problem would be a problem for other churches as well. He not only charged them to fear God, He also commanded them to "hold on." Look at verses 24–29:

> [24] "Now I say to the rest of you in Thyatira, to you who do not hold to her teaching and have not learned Satan's so-called deep secrets (I will not impose any other burden on you): [25] Only hold on to what you have until I come.

> [26] "To him who overcomes and does my will to the end, I will give authority over the nations—

> [27] 'He will rule them with an iron scepter;
> he will dash them to pieces like pottery'
> —just as I have received authority from my Father. [28] I will also give him the morning star. [29] He who has an ear, let him hear what the Spirit says to the churches."

The Greek word *krateo*, translated "hold on," is a strong word. It indicates that being faithful to God and His Word is not going to be easy. Therefore, God provides the following encouragement.

In verses 25–27, God tells those faithful to Him, "Hang on! I'm coming." He says in verse 25, *"Only hold on to what you have until I come."* Verses 26–27 describe what the faithful will experience when He comes. Those pressed down for Christ will be lifted up with Christ. This will not be a local or national deliverance, but a global one. Furthermore, you'll not only experience deliverance, but you will also be in the presence of your deliverer. The Bible confirms in verse 28 and in Revelation 22:16 that you will be with Jesus. These verses call Him your "morning star." In short, these verses encourage you to hang on, because it won't always be this way.

I never realized how powerful that assurance is until Loree and I went through a painful period of depression. Four surgeries, medical complications, and painful physical therapy had taken its toll on Loree. At the same time, I was serving a challenging church while working on my PhD. Shouldering these weights together, we both experienced the pain of depression. We talked to friends and family, looking for a message of hope. Hope finally came when a minister and counselor told us, "You won't always feel this way. It won't always be this way." His words gave us the strength to hang on and overcome.

In this memo to Thyatira, God says, "Fear me! When I convict you to repent, repent! Out of fear and reverence for me, distance yourself from the deceivers and stay faithful. It won't be easy to stay faithful, but hang on. It won't always be this way. You will overcome. And we will be together. So again, hang on."

MEMO #5
Wake Up! Your Reputation is Killing You!

As you read each memo, it seems that the condition of each church gets progressively worse.

> Ephesus had lost their romance with God.
>
> Smyrna was losing their strength in God.
>
> Pergamum was beginning to compromise with God.
>
> Thyatira had compromised their life with God.

Sardis was pronounced dead by God.

In case you missed it, here are the fatal steps that can lead to the death of a church.

When you lose your love, you'll lose your strength.

When you lose your strength, you'll lose your resolve.

When you lose your resolve, you'll lose your life.

You would think that a church could tell when its life with God was getting weaker. You would think that the believers in Sardis would have recognized that something was wrong and sought God's help. But they didn't. They didn't because they thought a healthy reputation meant a healthy life. In Revelation 3:1, God tells them otherwise.

> [1] "To the angel of the church in Sardis write:
>
> "These are the words of him who holds the seven spirits of God and the seven stars. I know your deeds; you have a reputation of being alive, but you are dead."

God's greeting to the church in Sardis is different than His greetings to Ephesus, Pergamum, and Thyatira. To these other churches, He uses the imagery in Revelation 1:12–20 that describes Jesus as the Supreme Judge. Sardis would eagerly welcome words from the Supreme Judge, because they feel they've done nothing wrong.

Instead, God tells them that the One speaking to them is the one who holds the seven spirits. Scholars attach this statement with Isaiah 11:2. Foretelling the attributes of the Holy Spirit seen in Jesus, it states,

² "The Spirit of the LORD will rest on him—
the Spirit of wisdom and of understanding,
the Spirit of counsel and of power,
the Spirit of knowledge and of the fear of the LORD."

God was telling Sardis that what they are about to hear doesn't come from the Supreme Judge, but from the all-knowing, sovereign God. God says, "You are dead!"

More specifically, God tells them, *"I know your deeds; you have a reputation of being alive, but you are dead."* Before they could cite the history of what they have done and list to God what they are doing, God says, "I know all about your deeds and your reputation. I'm all-knowing! Therefore, I KNOW you're dead."

Tragically, God knows when a church is dead long before the members do. A friend once told me of a bizarre experience. A church in Chicago asked for his help as a consultant. He was to preach the morning sermon and then meet with key leaders. The church had a prestigious name because of a great history. Stepping into the facilities, he noticed they were old, but well kept. As he addressed the congregation, his voice echoed in a sanctuary that once held well over a thousand, but on that day less than two dozen were in attendance. Confusing to him was the fact that though they worshipped together, they didn't sit together.

All in the service met with him afterwards. In the course of their discussion, he asked them, "Why don't you at least sit together when you worship?"

"Oh, we couldn't do that," they replied. Then they began to list all the names of those who had once sat there but had died. The church had died years ago, but the members didn't know it. Like a well-dressed corpse, their reputation made them look good, but they were still dead. Just as a lifeless body will physically deteriorate with time, in time the empty pews revealed to them what God had known—they were dead.

Surprisingly, there is hope for the church in Sardis, or God would not have sent them this memo. Therefore, there is hope for churches who are spiritually dead, if they recognize the signs soon enough. For the church in Sardis, and other churches like her, there are two signs.

SIGN #1: AN INCREASE IN SATISFACTION

The church in Sardis, like the city, became satisfied, and satisfaction led to its downfall. Sardis was built on a ridge jutting out from Mount Tmolus, 1500 feet up. Three sides of the ridge were smooth rock walls, which made residents feel safe from any attack. The city had been captured only twice in its history, when the sentries didn't do their job. The city's famed reputation for being impregnable increased the sentries' sense of satisfaction. All had been well for so long, they felt there was surely no need to stay alert on the job. The city's own reputation killed her.

What happened to this city happens to many churches—death by reputation. By length of years, a church develops a reputation for staying alive. Through various ministries, a church builds a reputation for being alive. Yet when the reputation of a church produces satisfaction within the church, that satisfaction can become fatal, if people begin to mistake lives and activities for life and vitality.

As the old farmer will tell you, "When you take the biggest hen in the hen house and cut off its head, it may still be the biggest hen, and for a while the most active hen. But make no mistake. It's still dead."

SIGN #2: A DECREASE IN
SATAN'S ATTENTION

When you look at God's memo to the believers in Sardis and com-pare it to His other memos, something is missing. There's no refer-ence to Satan. In verse 9, Smyrna was suffering from the slander of the Jews. Jesus said that Satan was the one behind the slander, as He said it was coming from the "synagogue of Satan." In verse 13, believers in Pergamum were resisting the Roman culture. Remember, Pergamum was the Roman capital for Asia Minor. So, Jesus says that the source of cultural attacks was coming from "Satan's throne." And in verse 24, Thyatira's theology was under attack by what Jesus calls, "the secret things of Satan." Yet Satan gives no attention to the believers in Sardis. Why should He? They're dead.

Corrie ten Boom said it well, "Satan wastes no ammunitions on those who are dead."[11] Therefore, if a church is not being slandered by the lost, pressured by the culture, or challenged by false teachers, she ought to check her pulse. She's probably dead.

Furthermore, if a church is dead, you can be certain that God will do something about it. His immediate actions are explained in verses 2–3. God tells the church in Thyatira,

> [2] "Wake up! Strengthen what remains and is about to die, for I have not found your deeds complete in the sight of my God. [3] Remember, therefore, what you have received and heard; obey it, and repent. But if you do not wake up, I will come like a thief, and you will not know at what time I will come to you."

---

11   Draper, *Quotations*, entry 9860.

God's first actions are to give the church in Thyatira a message and a massage. This is not to be confused with the gentle hand of your mother rubbing your back in the morning and sweetly saying, "Wake up." It's more the picture of a drill sergeant leaning over a soldier asleep at the post and yelling in his or her ear, "WAKE UP! WAKE UP! WAKE UP!" The sergeant keeps doing this until the troop is fully awake, energized, and where they need to be doing their job. That's the Greek imperative command for the word "Wake up!" Furthermore, it's not surprising that Jesus uses this same imperative command in Matthew 24:42 and Mark 13:35. In both accounts, Jesus is telling His followers to stay awake, active, and on the job, for they do not know when He will return.

Along with this strong message comes a life-saving massage. Thyatira is told, *"Strengthen what remains and is about to die, for I have not found your deeds complete in the sight of my God."*

On September 8, 1941, *Time Magazine* printed an article entitled, "How to Revive the Dead." Dr. Hamilton Bailey, of London's Royal Northern Hospital, said the normal practice of reviving a lifeless heart was to inject it with adrenalin. However, during his 22 years as a surgeon, he had employed the practice of opening the chest and massaging the heart. He had massaged forty hearts in his career, reviving four of them. Dr. Bailey was convinced that many more people could have been revived, if only the massaging had been started sooner. (It wasn't, because the technique was unusual and little known.)[12]

God refuses to let a church die without a fight. His initial command to "Wake up!" is like His shot of adrenalin. God's second imperative,

---

12   "How to Revive the Dead," *Time*, September 8, 1941, http://www.time.com/time/maga-zine/article/0,9171,849500,00.html.

"Strengthen what remains and is about to die," begins His act of massaging the heart of a dead church. Though by all indications the church is dead, God knows it's not too late to be revived. Furthermore, God says, *"I have not found your deeds complete."*

Here's the full picture. When God discovers a dead church, He pounds on the heart of the church yelling, "Wake up!" Then, He places the very heart of the church in His hands and begins to massage it. As He massages, He tells the church, *"I have not found your deeds complete—I'm not finished with you yet."*

God's massaging technique is explained in verse 3. He massages the heart of a church, trying to bring it back to life through remembrance, obedience, and repentance. When a church remembers what they've heard and received from God's Word, when they obey God completely and return to Him fully, a dead church comes back to life.

In my years as a pastor, I can recall moments in the churches I've served when it seemed we were fully alive with God. Those special moments had this in common—the church as a whole was fully open and obedient to God, and each member was awake and watchful. God was allowed to do what He wanted, whenever He wanted. What God did was amazing, and we were all in awe over how little effort it took on our part. All we needed to do was be open and obedient to God. All we needed was to be alive in His hands.

However, not every church wants to respond to God's message and massage. Therefore, in verses 4–6, God describes the consequences of churches that remain spiritually dead.

> 4 "Yet you have a few people in Sardis who have not soiled their clothes. They will walk with me, dressed in white, for they are

worthy. [5] He who overcomes will, like them, be dressed in white. I will never blot out his name from the book of life, but will acknowledge his name before my Father and his angels. [6] He who has an ear, let him hear what the Spirit says to the churches."

Verses 4–6 imply that God has already delivered His message and massage to the church in Sardis, and not all have responded. Those who did are those who have overcome. According to 1 John 5:1–4, they are the ones who have truly surrendered their lives to Jesus Christ. Verse 5 repeats what Jesus said in Matthew 10:32, *"Whoever acknowledges me before men, I will also acknowledge him before my Father in heaven."* Their name is written in and will forever stay in the book of life. And as Revelation 20:11–15 states, only those whose names are written in the book of life enter heaven.

It is frightening today to think that there are many churches today like the church in Sardis. They are spiritually dead. And after God's message and massage to the heart of the church, it's evident why they are dead, as most within the church have never truly surrendered their lives to Jesus Christ. One of the largest and most overlooked fields of lostness resides in our churches. Just because you attend church doesn't mean you are alive in Christ. Therefore, place a hand on the spiritual pulse of your life and see if you are spiritually dead or spiritually alive in Christ. Remember, your reputation as a Christian won't save you. Only if you have surrendered your life to Jesus Christ will you be spiritually alive.

SAYING A LOT WITH A LITTLE

There are people in life who say little, though they talk a lot. And then there are those who with very few words can say a lot. Unless you love time-consuming conversation, you usually like listening to those who can say a lot in a few words. The best at that, of course, is God.

He has written seven memos to seven churches. The longest memo was to the church in Thyatira. Its 286 words could be read in a few minutes. God's point could be made in one statement—"Fear God and hold fast."

God's memo to the church in Sardis was shorter. It contained only 186 words, and yet its message was probably stronger—"Wake up! Your reputation is killing you!"

In both cases God has said a lot with a little. The question remains, will today's churches do a little or a lot with what God has said?

CHAPTER 4

SEVEN URGENT MEMOS

(Part 3)

REVELATION 3:7-22

THOUGH HE WAS A STATESMAN and the President of France's Fifth Republic, the people of France endearingly refer to Charles de Gaulle as *Le General*, "The General." I was amused by The General's statement about church. He said that church is "the only place where someone speaks to me…and I do not have to answer back."[13]

It is surprising to hear such a statement from a general. Generals understand the importance of maintaining a chain of command. When a superior speaks, you respond. It could be that the speaker in de Gaulle's church delivered a speech, not a message; God's Word was merely a reference point and not the point of the message. Or, it could have been that the point of God's message was dulled by the crowd. When a message is addressed to the church, we think, "God is speaking to US" instead of "God is speaking to ME."

When Jesus addresses the church, He is speaking to believers representing the church. As we have seen in the first five memos to the churches in Asia Minor, Jesus reveals Himself as the Supreme Authority. Thus, these messages are meant for each member of the church. We need to hear them as though "Jesus is speaking to ME,"

---

13   Draper, *Quotations*, entry 1389.

not "Jesus is speaking to US." Since Jesus is the highest authority in the chain of command, when He speaks, He expects a response. The question at this point is, "What will your response be to memos six and seven from Jesus?"

MEMO #6
I'm Proud of You

Jesus's memo to His followers in Philadelphia is one every believer would love to receive. The heading would read, "I'm proud of you." You sense this when you read Revelation 3:7–8.

> [7] "To the angel of the church in Philadelphia write:
>
> These are the words of him who is holy and true, who holds the key of David. What he opens no one can shut, and what he shuts no one can open. [8] I know your deeds. See, I have placed before you an open door that no one can shut. I know that you have little strength, yet you have kept my word and have not denied my name."

Today, the city's name is Alasehir. Then, it was Philadelphia. Founded sometime after 189 BC by Attalus II, it was the youngest of the seven cities. Because of his deep love for his older brother King Eumenes of Pergamum, Attalus II's nickname was "Philadelphus," which means "brother lover." Thus, when the city was founded, it was given the name "Philadelphia."

The greeting to the believers in Philadelphia is different from many of the other memos. Previous memos refer to Revelation 1:12–20, depicting Jesus as the Supreme Judge. In His memo to the believers in Philadelphia, He is called the one who is "holy and true." The word "holy" in both the Old and New Testaments means to be "set apart." The Greek word for "true" (*alethinos*) means genuine, authentic, and real. In a culture smothered by false gods, false prophets, and false beliefs, the one who is set apart by His holiness is about to speak out. Jesus, the one real God in the midst of all the frauds, is about to say, "I know your deeds . . . and I'm so proud of you!"

I've always loved telling my boys that I'm proud of them. However, before he started kindergarten, my youngest son Lee once asked me, "Dad, what does 'proud' mean?" I had to stop and think, for it was hard to describe the depths of my emotions and to do it in a way that Lee would understand. Finally, I said, "Lee, when I say I'm proud of you, I'm telling you that you make my heart smile." As my boys will tell you, I usually can't stop with a short explanation, so I added the following:

> Lee, your Pawpaw used to always tell me that he was proud of me. I really didn't know what that meant until God gave me you and your brother. And you won't know what it truly means until you have children of your own. Yet, Lee, when I say I'm proud of you, I want you to know it's not just because of what you do. It's mainly because of who you are. I love the way God has made you. Then, when you act in a way that makes God smile, it makes my heart smile even more.

If you are a parent, you understand the depth of emotion behind the expression, "I'm proud of you." Can you imagine, then, Jesus' love for you when He tells you, "I'm proud of you . . . not just because of what you do, but because of who you are." Yet, when your actions with Christ reveal your closeness to Him, it makes His heart smile even more. That's the picture I get in verse 8. Here, Jesus says, "I know your deeds, and I'm so proud of your faithfulness."

In verse 8, Jesus tells them, *"I know your deeds. See, I have placed before you an open door that no one can shut."* Verse 7 points to Christ's authority to open or close doors of opportunity for ministry. That's the way the metaphor of an "open door" is used throughout the New Testament (Acts 14:27; 1 Corinthians 16:9; 2 Corinthians 2:12; Colossians 4:3). Jesus knew the open door He had provided His believers in Philadelphia, though the citizens of Philadelphia probably thought of it more as a gate.

Because it was located at the intersection of several trade routes, Philadelphia was called "the gateway to the east." That gate not only swung open for commerce, it swung wide for culture. When Attalus II founded Philadelphia, he did so with the intent of spreading Greek culture throughout the region. Thus, it was known by many as "Little Athens."

Though the citizens of Philadelphia saw themselves as the gateway to the east for commerce and culture, the believers in Philadelphia knew God had given them an open door to the east for another purpose. They were in a strategic position to make an impact for Christ.

I have always felt the same about serving God in Richmond, Virginia. When we moved here, Richmond had more Fortune 500 companies (per capita) than any other city in the United States. Even now, that means people from all over North America and the world are coming to and through Richmond.

Furthermore, within this congregation, we have people giving leadership and support to over 500 churches in Virginia, as well as individuals giving leadership and support to over 5,000 missionaries throughout the world. Within this congregation, we have civic leaders of various communities, and agency leaders supporting families

at the state capital, and marriages throughout Virginia. Through our
television ministry, we have the opportunity to be in millions of homes
each week all over the United States.

I'm confident there are other churches who also feel that Jesus has
given them an enormous door of opportunity. And like the believers in
Philadelphia, there are days you can feel weakened by the weight of the
door. Jesus realizes this and says in verse 8,

> ⁸ "I know your deeds. See, I have placed before you an open door
> that no one can shut. I know that you have little strength, yet you
> have kept my word and have not denied my name."

The Greek word for "strength" refers to one's ability. Jesus is
saying,

> I know your mental, physical, emotional, and financial abilities
> have been taxed to the max. I know that the size of your church is
> nowhere near the size of the opportunity I've given you. I know
> that, spiritually, you are drained. And yet, in the midst of your
> weakness you have remained strong. Unlike others who have bro-
> ken beneath theological pressures, you've kept My Word. Unlike
> others who have surrendered to cultural compromise, you have not
> denied My name.

As I told my boys, Jesus is telling His church, "I'm proud of you
simply because of who you are. However, I'm now even more proud
of you. Though you feel weak beneath the weight of the opportunity,
you've remained faithful. I'm so proud of you."

Verses 9–13 reveal that when you feel weak from the opportunity,
Jesus will support your faithfulness in three ways. He promises,

⁹ "I will make those who are of the synagogue of Satan, who claim to be Jews though they are not, but are liars—I will make them come and fall down at your feet and acknowledge that I have loved you. ¹⁰ Since you have kept my command to endure patiently, I will also keep you from the hour of trial that is going to come upon the whole world to test those who live on the earth.

¹¹ "I am coming soon. Hold on to what you have, so that no one will take your crown. ¹² Him who overcomes I will make a pillar in the temple of my God. Never again will he leave it. I will write on him the name of my God and the name of the city of my God, the new Jerusalem, which is coming down out of heaven from my God; and I will also write on him my new name. ¹³ He who has an ear, let him hear what the Spirit says to the churches."

Jesus' first promise to the faithful is, *"I'll make it right!"* Verse 9 says that the Jews in Philadelphia are like the ones in Smyrna. They know God by ritual but not by relationship (Rom. 2:28–29). They slandered Jesus' followers and caused them to suffer because of their faithfulness to Him. Therefore, Jesus says, "I'll make it right. The time will come when I will make them bow before you and declare that I love you."

When our boys were young, they would occasionally get into fights. Our first inclination as parents was to reprimand the one who had hurt the other. However, we learned it was far more effective to first love on the one who had been hurt. Not only did it secure him in our love, the expression of that love convicted the other of his actions. By the time we turned to him to address it, he was ready to listen and apologize.

Jesus says, "I know you feel the weight of your opportunity. I know you are trying to be faithful, and I see the way others are treating you.

Just stay faithful. In time I'll make it right, and they will have to bow before you and confess my I love for you."

Jesus' second promise to the faithful is, *"You'll be kept from my wrath."* Though His first step is to love the faithful, Jesus' second step is to release His wrath on the faithless. Jesus' wrath is vividly described in chapters 6–19 of Revelation. However, verse 10 indicates that those who have surrendered their lives to Christ will be kept from His wrath. It says that those who have faithfully kept God's command will be kept "from" the hour of trial, not kept "through" the hour of trial.

Furthermore, verse 10 explains that though the scope of Jesus' wrath is world-wide, the focus of His wrath is on unbelievers. The phrase *"to test those who live upon the earth"* is a recurring label for unbelievers throughout the book of Revelation (Rev. 6:10; 8:13; 11:10; 13:8, 12, 14; 14:6; 17:2, 8).

Finally, the fact that the word "church" or "churches" occurs nineteen times in the first three chapters, and not once during the chapters regarding the tribulation, leads me to believe that Jesus has physically kept the faithful from His wrath upon the faithless. This is more commonly known as the rapture of the church prior to the Great Tribulation. We will give specific attention to this after our study of Revelation 5.

Jesus' third promise to the faithful is *"I'll guarantee your security."* This was particularly valuable to those living in and around the city of Philadelphia. In 17 AD the city was devastated by an earthquake. Because Philadelphia was built near the epicenter of the quake, the people were traumatized for years by the recurring aftershocks. Some built huts outside the city. Those living in the city utilized various devices to help secure their homes. They lived under a cloud of despair that in any moment everything could be taken away from them.

Therefore, in verse 11, Jesus promises His faithful *"that no one will take your crown."* According to Revelation 2:10, this crown refers to "the crown of life," or one's salvation. Jesus reassures them, "No one can take your salvation from you."

Then in verses 12–13, Jesus gives them a picture of the security of their salvation. He tells them, "Because you are faithful, you are a pillar in heaven with three names inscribed." A pillar not only represented something set and immovable, it was also used at that time to honor great leaders. It's likely that those pillars had the names of the leaders chiseled on them. As a pillar in heaven, you will have three names upon you. First you will have the name of God. This indicates that you belong to Him. He owns you. Second, you will have the name of the city of God. This underscores that your citizenship in heaven cannot be revoked. Third, you will have a new name. According to Revelation 22:4, when all is fulfilled by God, He will write His name on those who are with Him forever. Thus, in these three names God tells His faithful that you belong to Him and heaven belongs to you, forever. What a great guarantee.

I played linebacker in high school. Mom and Dad went to every game, and before it was popular for parents to film their children's events, Dad was filming my games. In my mind, every play was an opportunity to do something great. When I didn't make as many plays as I thought I should, I'd come home discouraged about the game. Regardless of the hour I got home, Dad would get out of bed to tell me he was proud of me. During the week, I'd view the homemade game films to try and learn why I didn't make certain plays. Dad would sit and watch a while, and then say, "Son, you didn't do as bad as you thought. I'm proud of you."

Looking back, I truly believe my performances in the games would have been better if I had listened to Dad. He was at every game, seeing every play. He knew how hard I worked to make every tackle. Though I thought I could have done better, He was still proud of the effort I gave. Even if I had the worst game I thought I ever played, I always knew that when I got home Dad would be waiting to say, "I'm proud of you."

That's why this memo from Jesus is so important to me and should be important to you. Jesus, who sees every play of your life, who knows the sincere efforts you are giving, is saying, "I'm proud of you." Furthermore, He promises that when your game (your life) is over and you come home (to heaven), He'll be waiting to say, "Sure, you may not have fulfilled every opportunity the way you wanted, but you were always faithful. I'm so proud of you."

What a great memo from Jesus!

MEMO #7
Your Pride is Making Me Sick

The believers in Philadelphia loved their memo from Jesus, but the believers in Laodicea did not like theirs. Jesus was proud of the believers in Philadelphia, but the believers in Laodicea were proud of themselves. Thus, Jesus bluntly tells them, "Your pride is making me sick."

Pride has a way of blinding us to reality. Therefore, Jesus makes sure the believers in Laodicea knew that He had the real view of them. He opens His memo to them in verse 14 by saying,

¹⁴ "To the angel of the church in Laodicea write:

These are the words of the Amen, the faithful and true witness, the ruler of God's creation."

Today, ancient Laodicea is nothing more than an archeological site.[14] I am afraid the same will be true of churches who don't heed this memo. They talk about what they once did, but not about what they are doing with Christ.

That's why Jesus' greeting is so strong. He tells them that these are the words of "the Amen." This is the same title given to God twice in Isaiah 65:16, where He is called the God of truth. In Hebrew, it's the word for Amen. Jesus wants the believers to know that when He's talking, God's talking . . . and He's mad.

Jesus also calls Himself *the faithful and true witness."* This label occurs only one other time in Revelation. In Revelation 19:11, Jesus has mounted His white horse and is about to take His final action upon the godless of the earth. The name given to Him before He takes action is *"Faithful and True."*

Pride can blind us and give us a distorted picture of ourselves. It can also deafen. When someone tries to paint a real picture, our pride won't let us listen. That's why Jesus wants the believers in Laodicea to know that He is God. He sees them perfectly, and what He has seen has made Him mad. In verses 15–16, Jesus tells them,

> [15] "I know your deeds, that you are neither cold nor hot. I wish you were either one or the other! [16] So, because you are luke-warm—neither hot nor cold—I am about to spit you out of my mouth."

---

14   The archeological site is located near the city of Denizli. It's a city in Turkey with a population of around 200,000.

The Laodiceans enjoyed an aqueduct system that provided them with hot and cold running water from miles away. It's possible that they received their cold water from Colossae and their hot water from the hot springs of Hieropolis. So whenever they expected a refreshing drink of cold water, or a relaxing bath in hot water, and instead found it lukewarm, they knew that something had gone wrong between them and the source.

Do you understand that when you profess to be a follower of Jesus Christ, people expect you to be different? Believers and nonbelievers alike will hold you to a higher standard. Furthermore, Jesus will expect more of you than do others. Others expect you to be different; Jesus expects you to make a difference.

At least Jesus had something complimentary to say to the other six churches. However, there were no compliments for the believers in Laodicea. Apparently, others didn't see any difference within them, and God wasn't seeing any difference through them. Something had gone wrong between them and God. According to verses 17–18, the problem was pride.

> [17] "You say, 'I am rich; I have acquired wealth and do not need a thing.' But you do not realize that you are wretched, pitiful, poor, blind, and naked. [18] I counsel you to buy from me gold refined in the fire, so you can become rich; and white clothes to wear, so you can cover your shameful nakedness; and salve to put on your eyes, so you can see."

The believers in Laodicea had become proud of what they could do. Unknowingly, their self-reliant pride was causing them to live independent of God instead of dependent upon God.

Verse 17 calls them "rich." Laodicea was the strategic banking center of Asia Minor. When an earthquake leveled the city in AD 60, Rome offered financial aid to rebuild the city. The citizens said they didn't need it.

Laodicea was also famous for producing black wool for clothes and carpets. Furthermore, the city supported a medical school well known for creating a healing salve for eyes. There wasn't a need in Laodicea that could not be met.

The believers had taken on the same self-reliant pride as the citizens. They thought there wasn't a need they couldn't meet. They saw themselves one way, but Jesus saw them another. In verse 17, He calls them *"wretched, pitiful, poor, blind and naked."*

In their eyes, they were comfortable, but Jesus saw them as miserable and *wretched*. They were impressed with their lives, but Jesus thought they should be *pitied*. They thought they were rich, but Jesus knew they were *poor*. They saw themselves as visionaries, but Jesus knew they were *blind*. They thought they were wearing the spoils of a victorious life, but Jesus knew they were walking in the *naked* shame of defeat (Isa. 20).

Why were their views so different? It was because the believers in Laodicea were experiencing life based on what they could do, instead of living life according to what God can do. That's why Jesus tells them in verse 18 that if they want to experience the true riches of life, they need *"to buy from me gold refined in the fire."* Then they will reclaim the treasures of a life that comes from experiences that leave you completely dependent on God.

Two remarkable women underscore this truth—Corrie ten Boom and Joni Eareckson Tada. Corrie ten Boom experienced the riches of

God while enduring the atrocities of a Jewish concentration camp in WW II. Joni Eareckson Tada experienced those same riches after a diving accident at age 17 left her paralyzed from the neck down. Both women would probably say that their trials in life helped them realize how rich they were in God. Dependence on God does that.

It would be one more trial that would bring these two women together. In 1978, at the age of 86, Corrie ten Boom suffered a stroke that left her paralyzed for the remaining five years of her life. Joni Eareckson Tada went to see her and wrote about the experience.

> I relive each moment of my visit with Corrie ten Boom (paralyzed by a stroke). I recall how our eyes met as we were fed our cucumber sandwiches. Helpless and for the most part dependent, I felt our mutual weakness. Yet I am certain neither of us had ever felt stronger. It makes me think of the Cross of Christ—a symbol of weakness and humiliation, yet at the same time, a symbol of victory and strength.
>
> For a wheelchair may confine a body that is wasting away. But no wheelchair can confine the soul . . . the soul that is inwardly renewed day by day. For paralyzed people can walk with the Lord. Speechless people can talk with the Almighty. Sightless people can see Jesus. Deaf people can hear the Word of God. And those like Tante Corrie, their minds shadowy and obscure, can have the very mind of Christ.[15]

Believers who live life based on what *they* can do are the ones living life spiritually paralyzed. But believers who live life according

---

15   Joni Eareckson Tada, quoted in "My Heart Sings," *Christianity Today*, January 2004, vol. 33, no. 1, http://www.christianitytoday.com/ct/2004/january/3.46.html.

to what *God* can do are the ones who walk through life on the legs of God, see life with the eyes of God, and achieve impossible victories with the resources of God. When it appears that we are living spiritually paralyzed instead of spiritually powerful lives, Jesus loves us too much not to confront us. That is what He does with the believers of Laodicea in verses 19–20,

> [19] "Those whom I love I rebuke and discipline. So be earnest, and repent. [20] Here I am! I stand at the door and knock. If anyone hears my voice and opens the door, I will come in and eat with him, and he with me."

When you compare Jesus' statements to the churches of Philadelphia and Laodicea, you see the difference between living dependent upon God and living dependent upon yourself. The believers in Philiadephia lived dependent on God, and God opened a door of opportunities before them. The believers in Laodicea lived dependent upon themselves, and so they shut the door of their church to God.

Pride not only can blind us, it can make us stubborn. That's why the Greek grammar in verse 20 reveals that Jesus *continually* stands at the door of prideful, self-reliant churches and knocks. He does so waiting for anyone within the church to start living his or her life according to what God can do. If just one person will do that, they will give to God the open door of opportunity to come in and make a difference within their church.

When pride is replaced by humility, independence with dependence, you are reconnected to the source. You once again become a difference maker. The reward of a difference maker is described in verses 21–22.

[21] "To him who overcomes, I will give the right to sit with me on my throne, just as I overcame and sat down with my Father on his throne. [22] He who has an ear, let him hear what the Spirit says to the churches."

WHICH MEMO WOULD YOU RECEIVE?

Before taking his expedition to the South Pole, Sir Ernest Shackleton placed the following ad in a London newspaper:

> Men wanted for hazardous journey. Small wages, bitter cold, long months of complete darkness, constant danger, safe return doubtful.

When asked how the response had been to his ad, Shackleton said, "It seemed as though all the men in Great Britain were determined to accompany us."[16]

Apparently, they all wanted to be a part of an adventure that would challenge them, stretch them, and enable them to accomplish something they couldn't do alone.

When you look at the memo Jesus sent to the believers in Philadelphia, it sounds as though they are already on the adventure with Christ. They are being stretched and are seeing God do things through them they could have never done on their own. Thus, Jesus' memo is one of encouragement as He says, "I'm proud of you."

When you read the memo sent to the believers in Laodicea, it sounds as though Jesus is calling the believers to join Him in the adventure. They were proud of their lives and had become satisfied and soft. Thus, Jesus, says, "Your pride is making me sick, because I know you can experience and accomplish so much more. But you

16   Hewett, *Illustrations Unlimited*, 130.

will have to be willing to give up the comfortable life you have made, and depend on me for the adventure I have planned for you."

The question you have to ask yourself is, which memo would Jesus send you? Would He send you the one encouraging you because you are already being stretched on your adventure with God? Would your memo read, "I'm proud of you"?

Or would you receive the other memo? Would you receive the one that confronts you about living life according to what you can do, and calls you to living life relying on what God can do? Would your memo read, "Your pride is making me sick. So, swallow your pride, open the door, and let's go. You'll be surprised at the adventures you will experience when you depend on me."

CHAPTER 5

THE THRONE

REVELATION 4

THE SEVEN CHURCHES IN ASIA Minor, like churches today, struggled. They struggled from persecution by individuals outside the church, as well as by the compromise of members within the church. Any struggle, over time, will drain your strength. Jesus knew that if His followers' strength wasn't renewed, His cause would be lost. That's probably why Jesus deemed it important to give His followers a picture of heaven's throne: it alone would renew their strength.

In democratic societies today, thrones are not as esteemed as they were in historical times. Then they were seen as the seat of authority and power. The oldest surviving throne was built into the walls of the Minoan Palace of Knossos. This palace in Crete was first built around 2000 BC. After being destroyed and rebuilt 300 years later, it was destroyed a second time around 1350 BC, never to be built again. Today, it is nothing more than a tourist attraction at an excavation site.

One of the most magnificent thrones in history is the Peacock Throne. It was built during the reign of the Indian emperor Shah Jahan, who also built the Taj Mahal. His throne was six feet by four feet and made of pure gold, and was studded with diamonds, rubies, and emeralds. The diamonds were around 10–12 carats each, and the 100 or more rubies were between 100–200 carats. However, in 1739 the Persians invaded Delhi and stole the throne. The throne, now robbed of any authority or power, can be seen in a museum in Tehran, Iran.

The throne of heaven is mentioned ten times in Revelation 4, more than in any other chapter in the Bible. Jesus makes it clear that the throne of heaven is far older than the throne of Knossos and far more beautiful than the Peacock Throne of Delhi. Furthermore, its power and authority will never be destroyed or stolen. It will never become another impressive but impotent tourist attraction. The incomparable beauty, power, and authority of heaven's throne remain a source of strength for any believer drained by faithfulness to Jesus. John's description of heaven's throne in Revelation 4 explains why.

A THRONE
The Constant in a World of Change

One reason the throne of heaven strengthens believers is because it is our constant in a world of change. This is made clear in verses 1–2:

> [1] After this I looked, and there before me was a door standing open in heaven. And the voice I had first heard speaking to me like a trumpet said, "Come up here, and I will show you what must take place after this." [2] At once I was in the Spirit, and there before me was a throne in heaven with someone sitting on it.

In verse 1, you have the third and final time the word "door" is used in Revelation. Revelation 3:8 speaks of the open door of opportunity God has given the believers in Sardis. Revelation 3:20 cites how the pride of the Laodiceans has shut the door of their church to God. Now, Revelation 4:1 points to the open door of heaven. Once John peers through and sees the throne of heaven, what he writes humbles the proud and strengthens the weak.

John states in verse 1 that the same voice that spoke to him in Revelation 1:10 is speaking to him now. The trumpeting voice of Jesus bids him, *"Come up here, and I will show you what must take place after this."* With this call, Jesus does not transport John (rapture John), but He places John in a trance much like the one Paul describes in 2 Corinthians 12:1–4.

In this vision of heaven, John fixes his attention on a throne. Though the translation of the New International Version of verse 2 is compelling, it under-emphasizes a Greek verb that other translations underscore. The verb means "to set." As when entering a home with a dinner table set elegantly before you, John enters heaven with the throne set impressively before him. Looking upon it, John not only knows that the throne of heaven is set to be seen, but it is also set to stay.

In verse 1, he opens with *"After this I looked…"* and closes with Jesus' promise to John, *"…I will show you what must take place after this."* This phrase, "after this," or "after these things," appears throughout the book of Revelation to announce the beginning of a new vision (Rev. 7:9; 15:5; 18:1; 19:1). They mark the vision of another coming event or change. As John's vision changes from addressing seven churches to events of the end times, one constant remains unchanged—God's throne.

That is why John describes heaven's throne as a throne that is set to stay. In a world that constantly changes, believers need heaven's throne to be the constant that doesn't change.

For over 2000 years, mariners have used Polaris, better known as the North Star, to navigate in open waters. Located at the end of the Little Dipper, Polaris remains set in its location. Though other stars move as the earth rotates on its axis, the North Star remains fixed. Thus, regardless of the changing condition of the seas, if a mariner can find the North Star, he can chart a course for his journey.

As believers, the conditions around us, like the conditions in open water, can change. Governments can change and become either for or against Christianity. Economies can change. At one moment, you are looking for a new house and the next you are looking for a new job. Relationships can change. A divorce breaks your heart as well as your home. Your health can change from being strong and independent to being weak and dependent upon the care of others.

When your conditions change, you feel your course in life changes. Yet as a believer, Jesus says you will always have a constant you can use to chart your life— heaven's throne. It will always be the constant you can rely on to chart your life.

ON THE THRONE
One You can Trust

Another reason why heaven's throne strengthens believers is because you can trust the One who sits on it. Verses 2–3 explain:

> [2] At once I was in the Spirit, and there before me was a throne in heaven with someone sitting on it. [3] And the one who sat there had the appearance of jasper and carnelian. A rainbow, resembling an emerald, encircled the throne.

The One sitting on the throne has a different posture than is depicted in the book of Hebrews. Three times in the book of Hebrews it refers to Jesus completing His responsibility on earth and sitting at the right hand of the Father in heaven (Hebrews 1:3; 10:12; 12:2). Having sacrificed His life and fulfilled His task, Jesus now rests on the throne.

John's vision is different. With the throne of heaven spread out and set before him, John sees the One on the throne reigning, not resting. He has the strength of a lion, and yet the colors of a lamb.

John says the One on the throne appears in the colors of *"jasper and carnelian."* In the original Greek, the stones mentioned are jasper and sardine. Jasper appears clear as crystal, much like a diamond. The sardine stone is a fiery, blood-red ruby. It's the perfect combination of colors for the One who was our pure sacrifice and who shed His blood for our sins. The colors remind us of God's faithfulness to His promises.

Furthermore, these are two of the twelve stones identified on the breastplate of the priest in Exodus 28:17–20. Each of the twelve stones represents one of the twelve tribes of Israel. Sardine, the first stone, represents Reuben, the first born. Jasper, the last stone, stands for Benjamin, the last born. The colors of those two stones represent God's faithfulness to His people. Furthermore, the name Reuben means "behold a son" while Benjamin means "son of my right hand." The One on the throne has been faithful to keep God's promises, faithful to His people, and remains faithful to this day as He reigns.

In a world where people aren't always faithful, it's reassuring to know that God is still on His throne, and He is always faithful. I have a special friend who frequently reminds me of this.

Though she is one year younger than me, God made my friend so she will always have the sweet mind and innocence of a young girl. Her hugs are full of love and life: that's why they are so tight. Our special handshake took me a while to remember, but now I'll never forget it.

What makes our relationship so special is that both of us were reared in a pastor's home, and both of us loved our dads. Because her mind is sweet and innocent, when something happens in her life that's not so sweet or innocent, it can be unsettling for her. While telling me about an unsettling episode, she said, "Whenever I get upset, I just remember what my daddy taught me. He'd say, 'Remember, Honey, God is still on His throne.' When I remember that, I know that everything is going to be all right."

I believe that is why God has given us such a reassuring picture of the One on the throne. He's not resting because He's tired. He's reigning because He is Lord. Yet the reigning Lord was also the Faithful Lamb who fulfilled God's promises, remaining faithful to God's people. He is still on the throne, still faithful, and you can still trust Him.

SURROUNDING THE THRONE
Champions and Their Rewards

Not only does heaven's throne strengthen believers because of the One on it, it also strengthens us when we see those surrounding it. They are identified in verse 4:

> [4] Surrounding the throne were twenty-four other thrones, and seated on them were twenty-four elders. They were dressed in white and had crowns of gold on their heads.

Some believe the twenty-four elders represent the twelve tribes of Israel and the twelve apostles. Yet I agree with others who believe that the twenty-four elders have an even greater significance.

Since the book of Hebrews shows us that many Old Testament practices give us heavenly pictures, the same could be true of Revelation 4 and 1 Chronicles 24. In 1 Chronicles 24, King David appoints twenty-four elders to represent the Levitical order around his throne. Therefore it is likely that the twenty-four elders in Revelation 4 represent the entire heavenly priesthood, comprised of all who have placed their faith in Jesus Christ (1 Pet. 2:4–5, 9–10).

That these elders are wearing golden crowns and garments of white also supports this view. Jesus promised the believers in Sardis that those who overcome with Christ will walk with Christ, dressed in white (Rev. 3:4–5). Furthermore, the crowns worn by the elders confirm the crowns promised to believers throughout scripture. There are five crowns and they include:

1. *The Crown of Incorruption* – awarded to those who live a disciplined life, fulfilling God's aim for their life (1 Cor. 9:26).

2. *The Crown of Life* – awarded to those who patiently endure trials (James 1:12).

3. *The Crown of Rejoicing* – awarded to those who express their faith with joy (1 Thess. 2:19–20).

4. *The Crown of Glory* – awarded to those faithful in ministering the Word of God (1 Pet. 5:1–4).

5. *The Crown of Righteousness* – awarded to those who love Christ's appearing and eagerly await the return of Jesus (2 Tim. 4:8).[17]

---

17   Jeremiah, *Escape*, 87–88.

Though I don't know specifically who the twenty-four elders will be, I know what they represent for me. They represent a day when God, who knows all, will reward all who have faithfully overcome.

When you make sacrifices to fulfill God's aim for your life…

When you suffer through life for the cause of Christ…

When you share your faith with others and no one sees it…

When you faithfully handle and herald God's Word…

When you live today as though Jesus is coming tomorrow…

God, who sees all, will reward all who have been faithful.

FROM THE THRONE
Sounds of the Coming Judgment

For those who refuse to surrender to Jesus, there is a message for them from heaven's throne as well. Verse 5 reads,

> [5] From the throne came flashes of lightning, rumblings, and peals of thunder.

This same picture—of lightning, rumblings, and peals of thunder—is given on three occasions in the book of Revelation. All three times it refers to God's acts of judgment upon the godless (Rev. 8:5; 11:19; 16:18). Even Exodus 9:23 describes God's actions against Egypt in a similar fashion. Yet it is fitting that the warning is given here in chapter 4, for God's judgment begins in chapter 6, and it grows progressively worse through chapter 19.

I've never sat in a courtroom to view a case, but I have a mental picture of the procedures. A voice echoes saying, "All rise," and then announces the name of the judge and that court is in session. Periodically, the judge pounds his gavel with authority to get attention, and finally renders judgment.

In verse 5, the sights and sounds from heaven's throne should cause even the most jaded of hearts to realize they are before Almighty God. Throughout history God has pounded His gavel to get your attention. If you have yet to surrender your life to Christ, you had better make your plea now because God is about to render judgment and His judgment is final.

BEFORE THE THRONE
Reminders of God's Holiness

The image of heaven's throne in Revelation acts not only as a warning to the godless, but also as a reminder to the faithful. It reminds all of God's holiness. The images in verse 5 also occur in Exodus 19:16–25 at Mount Sinai. There, a cloud caps the mountain, and Israel becomes the audience to lightening, thunder, and trumpet blasts from the cloud. As Israel trembles, God tells Moses to warn the people not to come to the mountain, for He is holy. Boundaries are set to protect the people from the holiness of God.

John's vision of the holiness of heaven's throne is different. In verses 5b–6a, John is given reminders of the holiness of God—reminders that are both inviting and inspiring.

> Before the throne, seven lamps were blazing. These are the seven spirits of God. ⁶ Also before the throne there was what looked like a sea of glass, clear as crystal.

John sees seven lamps representing the seven spirits of God. Unlike the seven lamps referring to the seven churches in chapters 2–3, these seven lamps represent the endearing qualities of the Spirit of God mentioned in Isaiah 11:1–3. The number seven underscores the completeness of those qualities. Isaiah lists six of them: wisdom, understanding, counsel, power, knowledge, and delight in the fear of the Lord. Jesus also cites these qualities, in John 14–16.

Before heaven's throne, we are reminded of the relational character and capabilities of the Holy Spirit. We are reminded of His care and counsel, His encouragement and guidance, His understanding and knowledge, and His ability and longing to meet your needs. It's these remarkable endearing qualities that make the throne so inviting. Because of the character of the One on the throne, we want to draw near to it.

Furthermore, John is reminded that the conditions in heaven and of heaven's throne make drawing near the throne inspiring. Before heaven's throne, John sees a *"sea of glass."* A symbol of this sea is in Exodus 30:17–21, where God instructs Moses to tell Aaron and his sons to wash their hands and feet before entering the Tent of Meeting or offering a sacrifice at the altar. In Exodus 30:21, God tells Moses, *"This is to be a lasting ordinance for Aaron and his descendants for the generations to come."*

So when Solomon builds the Temple, he constructs a basin for washing so that God's requirements are kept. 1 Chronicles 4:1–6 and 1 Kings 7:23–26 record that a basin is built and placed outside the temple; Solomon calls the basin a "sea." There in a "sea" of water, the Priests wash their hands and feet before approaching the altar or entering the Holy Place. It was a reminder that they were about to approach a holy God, and they needed to be spiritually clean and holy before God.

In heaven, the sea is of glass, not water. It's of glass as pure as crystal, for those who approach God in heaven no longer have a need for washing. They can approach a holy God and worship Him, for they too are holy.

What an inspiring experience: greater than any experience one can have on earth! While on earth, we can talk with God. The conversations, however, are more casual than close. Close conversations come from close relationships. It's the heart-to-heart talk from two who know each other well and would die for each other. Without surrendering your life to Jesus Christ, your conversation with God will remain cordial, but not close. There will be an understood and uncrossed wall between you and God, because He is Holy and you are not.

When you surrender your life to Christ, John 14:17 says that the Holy Spirit of God comes to live within you. Your relationship is then no longer casual or cordial: it's close. Because of the Holy Spirit in you, you are seen as holy before God. This means you can approach Him and worship Him as He is worshipped in heaven. However, there is one problem. Though the Holy Spirit is in me, and I am seen as holy before God, I am not yet in heaven. While on earth, I still sin. My sins strain my relationship with God. That is why I still have to confess my sins, ask His forgiveness, and repent of them before I can approach Him intimately and meaningfully as in heaven.

Yet the day will come when believers will approach heaven's throne without the need for any confession or cleansing. There will be no guilt from our sin, no strain in our relationship with God. We will be holy as He is holy, and we will worship Him like never before.

AROUND THE THRONE

Worship!—Pure Worship!

As we worship God in Heaven, our worship will be prompted by those who have been with God and have known Him far longer than we have. They are the four living creatures mentioned in Revelation 4:6b–8a:

> In the center, around the throne, were four living creatures, and they were covered with eyes, in front and in back. [7] The first living creature was like a lion, the second was like an ox, the third had a face like a man, the fourth was like a flying eagle. [8] Each of the four living creatures had six wings and was covered with eyes all around, even under his wings.

If you read from the King James Version, these four are called "beasts." Some might confuse them as being similar to the beast that is mentioned later in Revelation. The Greek word for that creature is *therion*. It's commonly used in the Bible to describe a wild beast. The Greek word used to characterize these four creatures is *zoan*. It refers to something that has been created and has life.

Psalm 8 lists the hierarchy of God's creation. In that hierarchy, God created all and is over all. He created angels and they are superior to humans, and He created humans and they are superior to animals. When you compare the description of these four living creatures to the cherubim Ezekiel saw in Ezekiel chapters 1 and 10, and compare their actions to those of the seraphs in Isaiah 6, I believe that these four creatures are part of the angelic order of God.

Since they are depicted as being at the center of heaven's throne, you understand their closeness to God. The fact that they have eyes both in back and front reveals that they see everything in the past and future. And since they are close to God and have seen everything God has seen and everything God will see, it's no wonder that when they speak they can't help but herald God's eternal holiness and power. Verse 8b states,

> Day and night they never stop saying:
> "Holy, holy, holy
> is the Lord God Almighty,
> who was, and is, and is to come."

I've been in worship services where the worship leaders were musically gifted and in other services where they were not. I've heard preachers who were great orators and those who were not. Looking back, my greatest worship experiences in life were not because the worship leaders or speakers were gifted. It was because I knew that those leading the worship had truly been with God. Because they had been close to God, I wanted to be close to God. I wanted to know what they knew. I wanted to see what they had seen.

Because of their closeness to God, these angelic creatures announced what they knew about God. They cried, *"Holy, holy, holy is the Lord."* Being under God and yet superior to humans, they saw the great difference between the holiness of God and the sinfulness of man. No wonder the word "holy" in the Hebrew and Greek means "set apart." God is pure and perfect; there is none like Him.

Furthermore, these creatures announce, *"Holy, holy, holy is the Lord God Almighty."* The word "Almighty" is used to describe God over three hundred times in the New International Version of the Old Testament. That's because it translates both Hebrew words, *Sabaoth* and *Shadday* (shad-dah'-ee), as "Almighty." *Sabaoth* says God is mighty because of the size of His heavenly army. It literally means "the Lord of Hosts." *Shadday*, on the other hand, says God is mighty not because of the size of His army, but because of the strength of His abilities. Even without His army, God is still all-powerful. That's why I like the way the King James Version exclusively translates *Shadday* as "Almighty" and *Sabaoth* as "Lord of Hosts," for God would still be Almighty even if He didn't have an army.

Shadday as "Almighty" appears in the King James Version of the Old Testament forty-eight times. Remarkably, thirty-one of these occur in the book of Job. You might remember that Job was a man who was hurting. All his children were killed by a storm. He was the wealthiest man in his region, yet he lost all his wealth to thieves. His friends told him everything was his fault, and his wife nagged him to curse God and die. In his misery, Job was more interested in the strength of God's abilities than in the size of His army. Job wasn't looking for a general who could rule, but an almighty God who was real and who could help. He longed to see God Almighty.

The Greek word for "Almighty" has at its root the awe of God's ability, but also with the awareness of His army. It appears only nine times in the New Testament, and all but one are in the book of Revelation. Here's why. The book of Revelation gives us clearer pictures of how God is seen in heaven than any other book of the Bible. Furthermore, Revelation 1–3 addresses believers and churches struggling in life as they faithfully serve God. They need a picture of an Almighty God who will always be more than they need. In Revelation 4, God gives them that picture.

Believers and churches today, like those in Revelation 4, still need the picture of a holy and almighty God Who will always be more than we need. It still amazes me how so often, when we stop to see and worship God the way He is seen and worshipped in heaven, we are restored. Worshipping God not only restores us, but it inspires others as well. Pastor and author Chuck Swindoll writes of a time when he was moved by someone else's need to see and worship God. He writes,

> When I was overseas, I was working with a man who was under great stress and great pressure. He was a maverick sort of missionary. He didn't fit the pattern or the mold of what you think of as a missionary. His ministry was in great part to the soldiers, who happened to be on the island of Okinawa by the thousands — in fact, it might be safe to say tens of thousands.

> I went to his home one evening to visit with him, and his wife said he wasn't there, but was probably down at the office. The office was downtown in a little alley area off the streets of Naha. It was a rainy night. And I decided that I would get on the bus and travel down to be with Bob. She'd mentioned his stress and pressure, so I expected to find the man folded up in despondency, discouragement, and depression, and just ready to finish it off.

> I got off that little bus and I walked down the alley about a block and a half and I turned right, down a little smaller alley, to a little hut with a tatami mat inside. As I got away from the street noise, I heard singing, "Come, Thou fount of every blessing, / Tune my heart to sing Thy grace." And then that next stanza, "Prone to wander, Lord, I feel it, / Prone to leave the God I love."

Quietly I eavesdropped on his private praise service. As I stood in the rain and looked through the walls of that little cheap hut, I saw a man on his knees with his hands toward heaven giving God praise, with his Bible on one side and an InterVarsity Christian hymnal on the other side, his little spiral notebook, worn from use. And I saw him turn from page to page, where he would read it to God, then he would find a hymn and he would sing it to God.

And the remarkable thing is that that pressure that he was under did not leave for perhaps another two weeks, it seems. But that praise service alone before God absolutely revolutionized his life.[18]

Obviously, seeing and worshiping God as He is seen and worshipped in heaven revolutionized this missionary's life. Furthermore, the missionary's genuine worship experience left a lasting impression on Chuck Swindoll as well.

And why shouldn't it? That is why God, in Revelation 4, gave us a vivid picture of heaven's throne. Heaven's throne is set and here to stay. It will be our constant in a world of change. It will constantly remind the godly that God is still on His throne, and it will constantly warn the godless that God's judgment is not far away. It will constantly encourage you to be faithful, as God sees and rewards the faithfulness that others overlook. And it will constantly restore you when you stop to see and worship God as He is seen and worshipped in heaven. When you do, remember that it will not only benefit you, but it will also benefit those around you.

---

18   Charles R. Swindoll, *The Tale of the Tardy Oxcart* (Nashville: Word Publishing, 1998), 627–628.

That's the way it happens—even in heaven. Verses 9–11 show that once the angels began to worship, everyone else was moved to do the same.

> [9] Whenever the living creatures give glory, honor and thanks to him who sits on the throne and who lives forever and ever, [10] the twenty-four elders fall down before him who sits on the throne, and worship him who lives forever and ever. They lay their crowns before the throne and say:

> [11] "You are worthy, our Lord and God,
> to receive glory and honor and power,
> for you created all things,
> and by your will they were created
> and have their being."

What a great experience, and all it takes is a glimpse of heaven's throne.

CHAPTER 6

THREE PHOTOGRAPHS

REVELATION 5

FOR SOME, PHOTOGRAPHY HAS BECOME quite lucrative. Annual auctions set records each year for the highest-priced photograph. Prior to the 21st century, auction crowds gasped when a single photograph was purchased for over $800,000. Now it is common for the record-setting photos to be worth millions.

The old adage is that beauty is in the eye of the beholder. A photograph must be meaningful for someone to pay millions for it. Yet in photography, I believe it's also true that beauty is in the eye of the photographer. Before a snapshot can become meaningful to me, a photographer had to have the eye to see it and capture it in a meaningful way.

Revelation 5 can be seen as a series of photographs taken by the Apostle John. Verses 1, 2, 6, and 11 all begin with the same Greek words *kai eidon*, which mean "I saw." From these verses and this chapter, John gives us three photographs from heaven. The way he captures them lets you know each was meaningful to John, the photographer. After we look at each of them, you will have to determine how valuable they are to you.

Before we look at them, however, it's important to recognize how they have been framed and matted. Revelation 4 gave us a detailed description of heaven's throne.

It is the constant in a word of change (vv. 1–2).

The One on it can be trusted (vv. 2–3).

He rewards and judges for He is holy (vv. 4–6).

When all of heaven sees the greatness of God through His throne,

they can't help but worship Him (vv. 6–11).

Undoubtedly the value of a photograph is enhanced by the frame. Each of the photographs in Revelation 5 is enhanced by the greatness of God displayed by His throne in Chapter 4.

Furthermore, many of the valuable photographs in history were given titles. I believe John could have done the same with his three photographs in Revelation 5. The first photograph could be labeled "A Scroll" with the subtitle "The Great Problem."

A SCROLL
The Great Problem

A description of John's first photograph is provided in verses 1–4.

> [1] Then I saw in the right hand of him who sat on the throne a scroll with writing on both sides and sealed with seven seals. [2] And I saw a mighty angel proclaiming in a loud voice, "Who is worthy to break the seals and open the scroll?" [3] But no one in heaven or on earth or under the earth could open the scroll or even look inside it. [4] I wept and wept because no one was found who was worthy to open the scroll or look inside.

The focal point of John's first photograph is a scroll. Because bound books have replaced rolled scrolls, a little history is necessary.

Dr. Robert L. Thomas explains that from the time of Nero on, rolled scrolls were used for contracts throughout the Middle East and by the Romans. The full contract was written on the inside of a scroll.

Upon being rolled up, a summary of the contract was penned on the outside. The scroll was then sealed with seven seals. Among the Hebrews, the document most resembling this form was usually a title deed.[19]

If the scroll in the hand of the one on the throne represents a title deed, a good question to ask is, "A title deed to what?" I believe it's a title deed to the world. Here's why. Genesis 1–2 describes the world as God created it. After each of the six days of creation, God looked at all He created, including man and woman, and said "It is good." Then, in Genesis 3, Adam and Eve are tempted by Satan and sin against God. At that point, God's creation was changed physically and spiritually. Physically, the world was marred, making it painful to give birth and live. Spiritually, the world was marred, as now everyone was born separated from God by sin.

Our world today is not the world that God created. It is a world altered by sin: a sin initiated by Satan. Furthermore, the Bible says this is a world ruled by sin, with Satan in charge. 2 Corinthians 4:4 calls Satan, *"the god of this age."* Ephesians 2:1–3 explain that the ways of this world are influenced by Satan. Before John was exiled to the Isle of Patmos and wrote the book of Revelation, he wrote 1 John to the churches of Asia Minor. Even then, God allowed him to see and write in 1 John 2:16, *"For everything in the world—the cravings of sinful man, the lust of his eyes and the boasting of what he has and does—comes not from the Father but from the world."* And in 1 John 5:19, John tells the believers in the churches, *"We know that we are children of God, and that the whole world is under the control of the evil one."*

---

19   John MacArthur, *The MacArthur New Testament Commentary: Revelation 1–11* (Chicago: Moody Press, 1999), 163.

This explains a lot. No wonder we have such problems in the world. Governments run without God are godless governments. They create and enforce godless laws that support godless living. In such a society, individual values are formed without God, and these godless values lead to godless priorities. If God is not in our priorities, He'll not be in our decisions. If God does not govern our decisions, you will see it in our actions. Therefore, read a daily paper or watch the evening news and ask yourself, "Is this what God wanted when He created the world?" Look back to Genesis 1–2 and you will see that the answer is "No!"

But according to Revelation 5:2–3, the altered condition of the world is only part of the problem. John writes,

> ² And I saw a mighty angel proclaiming in a loud voice, "Who is worthy to break the seals and open the scroll?" ³ But no one in heaven or on earth or under the earth could open the scroll or even look inside it.

Though Satan has altered the world and rules its ways, he still doesn't own it. The title deed remains in God's hand. Like a landowner allowing an unscrupulous sharecropper to work the land for a season, the day will come when God will say to Satan, "That's enough! I want you and all your workers off my land."

According to verse 2, that day will come when God finds someone who is worthy to take His title deed, open the seals, and reclaim the world. Yet verse 3 states that God has looked throughout heaven, earth, and hell, yet has found no one worthy. When John hears this, he confesses in verse 4, *"I wept and wept because no one was found who was worthy to open the scroll or look inside."* In John 20:11, John uses the same Greek word to describe the weeping of Mary Magdalene outside Jesus' tomb. That word meant "the sob of a woman without hope." Now John sobs the same way—without hope.

Here now is the great problem seen in John's photograph of the scroll. The scroll in verses 1–4 represents what was, what is, and what may never change. The scroll represents God's title deed to the world He once created, a world created so we could know Him in a meaningful way. But now the scroll represents what is. Our world is a world that Satan has altered to keep us from experiencing God on earth and to keep us from spending eternity with Him in heaven. We are deceived, diseased, and physically and spiritually dying, which is not the life God planned for us when He created the world. All this can change, however, because God still holds the title deed to the world. He still owns His creation and can reclaim control. But while the scroll is still in God's hand, it represents what might never change. God has looked in heaven, earth, and hell and has found no one worthy to take the title deed from His hand and act upon it. That's the great problem, and that's why John sobs.

Whether you realize it or not, God's great problem and John's great problem is your great problem. Think about it. How would you feel if your life in this world was as good as it gets for you? You may have been healthy, successful, and had a wonderful family. You may have struggled financially, been abused, or never been healthy. Whether your conditions in life have been good or bad, what if this was as good as it gets for you, and in this life you never experienced life with the One who created you, knows you, and loves you? Furthermore, in death, what if you were deprived of life with God in heaven and spend eternity away from God in hell? There, in hell, you finally realize how it was all a scam and how Satan had set up a world designed to keep you from the life that God always wanted you to have.

If you thought that there was no hope of that ever changing, no hope of you ever experiencing the life God always wanted you to have on earth and in heaven, then like John, you too should sob. However, you should know that this life is not as good as it gets. In verses 5–10, John's eye is directed away from "A Scroll: The Great Problem" and he takes a photograph that could be labeled "A Lamb" with the subtitle "The Great Answer."

A LAMB
The Great Answer

To be fair, John didn't see the Lamb on his own. It's possible that his head was in his hands as he wept. One of the elders mentioned in chapter 4 came to him and told him to stop weeping or he would miss seeing someone important. When you read Revelation 5:5–6, you will find that though John and this elder are looking at the same person, each gives a different description.

> [5] Then one of the elders said to me, "Do not weep! See, the Lion of the tribe of Judah, the Root of David, has triumphed. He is able to open the scroll and its seven seals."

> [6] Then I saw a Lamb, looking as if it had been slain, standing in the center of the throne, encircled by the four living creatures and the elders. He had seven horns and seven eyes, which are the seven spirits of God sent out into all the earth.

Both the elder and John are looking at Jesus, and yet both describe him differently. It's a matter of perspective, and both perspectives provide a complete picture. The elder's view is eternal, while John's view is personal.

The elder looks at Jesus and sees Him as the *Lion of the tribe of Judah*. This refers to the prophesy given in Genesis 49:8–10. It states that the line of kings will come from the tribe of Judah until the greatest king, the Messiah, holds the scepter. David was from the tribe of Judah, as was Jesus. In heaven, Jesus stands as the last and greatest king in that line of kings. However, the elder also calls Jesus the *Root of David*. It's not only that Jesus marks the end of the line of great kings, He also marks the beginning. The One reigning at the last was also reigning at the first. Jesus has been, is, and always will be the King of Kings and Lord of Lords. Spend any time in heaven, like this elder has, and I'm sure that this picture will become even more clear.

There is much in the elder's description that encourages me. As was described in chapter 4, it's likely that the elders are representative of all who have surrendered their lives to Christ. That means when you die, if you have surrendered your life to Jesus on earth, you will be with Him in heaven. Furthermore, you will recognize Him and see Him as He truly is. No matter how hard we try to picture the greatness of Jesus, we still see Him through the lenses of earth's limitations. We are only so strong and can only live so long, therefore it's hard to picture someone who is all powerful, all knowing, and has always been and always will be. On earth we accept this by faith. In heaven, we will see it and understand when seeing Him face to face.

John, however, sees Jesus differently. He hasn't had the same time in heaven as the elder has. But I also think the elder didn't have the time on earth with Jesus that John did. That's why John's description isn't so much eternal as it is personal.

In verse 6, John says, *"I saw a Lamb."* This was the way John was introduced to Jesus. In John 1:36, John records how John the Baptist points to Jesus and says, *"Behold the Lamb of God!"* John remembers this well because he was there that day. He heard John the Baptist say this, and so he began following Jesus. His relationship with Jesus was so close that five times in his gospel John labels himself as Jesus' "beloved" (John 13:23; 19:26; 20:2; 21:7, 20). John was the only disciple at the cross (John 19:25–27). He was the first disciple to reach the empty tomb (John 20:1–9). He saw Jesus resurrected and alive (John 21:20–25). And he was there when Jesus ascended into heaven (Acts 1:1–14).

With all this in mind, try to picture John's emotion when he says, *"I saw a Lamb, looking as if it had been slain, standing."* John was at the cross, and the scars from the cross are still evident on Jesus in heaven. Revelation 21 talks of how, in heaven, the lame walk, the blind see, the deaf hear, and the broken are made whole. Apparently, this will apply to Jesus' followers but not to Jesus. Though He is alive and healthy, Jesus still bears His scars. This leads Dr. Ed Hindson to ponder that the only manmade things to enter heaven are the wounds of Jesus.[20]

Yet the One who John saw sacrificed is now standing. Furthermore, look where He is standing. John sees Him *"…standing in the center of the throne, encircled by the four living creatures and the elders."* The One who John saw resurrected is now reigning. He's reigning in the full glory John only had glimpses of while on earth (Matt. 17:1–9). In heaven, John sees Jesus with *"seven horns"* referring to His perfect

---

20   Edward Hindson, *The Book of Revelation: Unlocking the Future* (Chattanooga, TN: AMG Publishers, 2002), 63.

power, *"seven eyes"* referring to His perfect wisdom, and *"seven spirits"* referring to the fullness of the Holy Spirit of God. Though John saw Jesus transfigured on earth, it cannot compare to how He is truly seen in heaven. Now the One who ascended out of sight stands before John in full view. And in heaven, John sees the fullness of Jesus' divine power, wisdom, and character.

It's no wonder that John's weeping is about to turn to cheering and singing. But before we look at the next several verses, an important point needs to be made. The elders' view and John's view of Jesus are not two separate views of the same person. Jesus wasn't one way to satisfy the elders and another way to satisfy John. He is who He has always been, and will always be the person He is. Therefore, you had better have the true picture of Jesus, for your salvation depends on it.

Throughout history, Jesus has been viewed differently by many. You have the Jewish Jesus, Islamic Jesus, Catholic Jesus, Protestant Jesus, Evangelical Jesus, Mormon Jesus, Jehovah's Witness Jesus, and the New Age Jesus. Oh, and don't forget the Agnostic's Jesus and the Atheist's Jesus. In a cordial conversation, each would say that their view of Jesus satisfies them. However, the real question is not if your view of Jesus satisfies you, but rather, "Does your view of Jesus satisfy God?"[21]   For God fully knows who Jesus is, what He has done, and that He alone is the great answer to our great problem.

Thus, your view of Jesus had better be the same as God's, for God and all heaven know that only Jesus can take the scroll from God's hand. Look at verses 7–8.

---

21   Dr. Hindson writes, "The symbol of the lamb appears twenty-eight times in the Revelation. His death is the only atonement for sins that God the Father will accept. The issue is not whether your religion satisfies you, but whether it satisfies God!" Ibid, 65.

> [7] He came and took the scroll from the right hand of him who sat on the throne. [8] And when he had taken it, the four living creatures and the twenty-four elders fell down before the Lamb. Each one had a harp and they were holding golden bowls full of incense, which are the prayers of the saints.

When you read Revelation 4, you say to yourself, "The worship in heaven can't get any better than that!" Yet when Jesus takes the title deed of the world from the hand of God in verse 7, the worship in heaven rises to a new level. Here's why.

Verse 8 says that the four living creatures and the twenty-four elders resume the same position of worship they had in chapter 4. This time it adds that the elders were holding harps and golden bowls. In the Old Testament, harps were associated with acts of worship and prophesy.[22] The golden bowls were used to burn incense in the tabernacle and temple as the priests prayed for the people (Luke 1:8–10). At other times, the people used them to offer their own prayers to God (Psalm 141:2).

Truly, only heaven knows the significance of all this. But it is moving to consider that when Jesus takes the scroll from God, the harps and bowls are offered to God in celebration. Prayers for this day have now been answered. Prophesy has been fulfilled. The Lion of heaven became our sacrificial Lamb. But now our sacrificial Lamb is alive in heaven and is worthy to reclaim the world as Lord of all. It's no wonder that with this act, verses 9–10 record that the elders break into song.

---

22   MacArthur, *Commentary*, 170–171.

[9] And they sang a new song:

"You are worthy to take the scroll and

to open its seals,

because you were slain,

and with your blood you purchased men for God

from every tribe and language and people and nation.

[10] You have made them to be a kingdom and priests to serve our

God,

and they will reign on the earth."

Verse 9 says, *"And they sang a new song."* I believe "they" refers to the elders alone and not to the four living creatures who are angelic beings. Here's why. There are fourteen songs recorded in Revelation.[23] This song is the song of redemption. The lyrics speak of the Lamb who was slain, whose blood purchased mankind for God from every tribe, language, and nation, and who made them a kingdom of priests.

Angels have never been separated from God, so they don't know what it's like to be lost. They've always known Jesus as Lord and never needed Him as a Lamb. But we have. Therefore, we relate to the elders. And the thrust of our song should be the same three words that opens their song—"You are worthy."

This was the great problem before Jesus came to earth and it's now the great answer because He did. Before He came, no one in heaven, earth, or hell was worthy to reclaim the world for God. Yet because Jesus came, lived a sinless life, sacrificed Himself for our sins, rose from the dead, and has ascended to heaven, no one but Jesus is now worthy to reclaim the world for God.

---

23   Hindson, 61.

Before his murder, Russian Orthodox priest Aleksandr Menn said, "Every religion is an attempt to reach God. But Jesus is the only answer."[24] In a radio interview two months before his death, Menn was asked why he saw Jesus as the only answer. He said it wasn't because of scripture (though I believe scripture validates it.) Other beliefs have writings they deem sacred. Menn also said it wasn't because of Jesus' morality (though I believe no one ever lived as Jesus lived). Other beliefs promote moral values. For Menn, what makes Jesus the only answer for reaching God was Jesus himself. Jesus is unique.[25] Menn is right.

ONLY JESUS...

- claimed to be God, while others merely claim to be His messenger.
- gave His life that we might surrender to God, while other beliefs will take your life if you don't.
- promised life after death and proved it. His empty tomb is the exclamation point that He is unique. The occupied graves of all the others make the point that they are not.

Our great problem has one great answer. It's Jesus Christ. The Lion of heaven became our sacrificial Lamb. That's why the saved sing, and why their celebration is about to get bigger.

---

24   Slain Russian Orthodox priest Aleksandr Menn, cited by Larry Woiwode in Books & Culture 2, no 2, http://www.preachingtoday.com/illustrations/1998/april/1933.html.

25   Larry Woiwode, "The Life and Death of Aleksandr Menn," http://www.opc.org/nh.html?article_id=297.

A CHOIR
The Great Response

When still photographs are placed side by side, they can tell a story. That seems to be what is happening in Revelation 5. The first photograph is in verses 1–4 when John sees a scroll that represents our great problem. This is not the world God wanted. Satan's lies and our sins have altered it. Though with the scroll God still owns the title deed to the world, He hadn't found anyone worthy to take the scroll, open it, and reclaim the world. That's why the second photograph is important.

The second photograph is of a Lamb. This is taken in verses 5–10. He is God's great answer to our great problem. He takes the title deed because He alone is worthy. The moment He does, the saved in heaven begin to sing. They sing of what Jesus has done. But once the saved start singing, it's as though all of creation wants to join them. This leads to John's third photograph.

In verses 11–14, John takes a photograph of an ever growing choir singing "Worthy is the Lamb." The saved were the first to sing, and they sang their praises to Jesus for being the only one worthy to reach for the scroll. Now the rest of creation becomes a mass choir, and they sing of what Jesus will receive because He did.

Like a choir singing in sections, the saved began in verses 5–10. In verses 11–12, they are joined by the angels.

> [11] Then I looked and heard the voice of many angels, numbering thousands upon thousands, and ten thousand times ten thousand. They encircled the throne and the living creatures and the elders.
> [12] In a loud voice they sang:

"Worthy is the Lamb, who was slain,

to receive power and wealth and wisdom and strength

and honor and glory and praise!"

For those who like numbers, verse 11 will frustrate you. You can't simply multiply 10,000 times 10,000 to come up with the exact size of the angelic choir. The Greek word for ten thousand used here is *murios*. From it we get our word "myriad." Ten thousand was the highest number used in everyday Greek language.

John confesses that the angelic choir was far too big to count. If you asked him if they numbered in the millions, he'd probably say, "No doubt, but I was more interested in hearing them than counting them. Besides, it wasn't long before the rest of creation added their voices to the song." John records this in verses 13–14.

[13] Then I heard every creature in heaven and on earth and under the earth and on the sea, and all that is in them, singing:

"To him who sits on the throne and to the Lamb

be praise and honor and glory and power,

forever and ever!"

[14] The four living creatures said, "Amen," and the elders fell down and worshiped.

By this point, everything created by God joins in on the celebration! All creation acknowledges that Jesus was worthy to do what He did, and is worthy to receive all He has received, which is power, riches, wisdom, might, honor, glory, and blessing. And as all creation sings this to Jesus, the four living creatures have their own part. In the Greek, the grammar makes it clear that they are saying "Amen" repeatedly throughout creation's song, as in Handel's *Messiah*, with one section singing and another section responding.

When Creation Sings	The Four Living Creatures
Jesus is Worthy to Receive . . .	Respond . . .
power!	Amen!
riches!	Amen!
wisdom!	Amen!
might!	Amen!
honor!	Amen!
glory!	Amen!
blessing!	Amen!

Why would all creation celebrate when Jesus grabs the title deed of the world? It's not just because He can because He is worthy, it's because all creation knows that the world as it is now is not the world God intended it to be—and Jesus will now make it right.

Making the Photographs Personal

Earlier I mentioned that some photographs are auctioned and sold for millions of dollars. Furthermore, I said that each of us would have to determine how valuable the photographs John took in Revelation 5 are to us.

How valuable to you is John's photograph of "A Scroll"? I hope it's valuable in opening your eyes that this is not the world God intended. It's been altered by Satan's lies and our sins. This world is not God's fault, so stop blaming Him, and instead surrender your life to Him. If you will allow this photograph to open your eyes to your need for God, it will become priceless to you.

How valuable to you is John's photograph of "A Lamb"? It should be valuable at helping you realize who Jesus is. Many times, we create the Jesus we want in order to do and believe what we want. John's photograph of "A Lamb" reminds you that Jesus is who He is, not who you make Him to be. He alone is the great answer to the world's great problem. He alone was born of a virgin, lived a sinless life, foretold His death and resurrection, and then accomplished it. Others throughout history said they knew the way to God; Jesus not only said, "I am the way," but He made the way. If John's photograph of Jesus enabled you to see Him for who He truly is and fully surrender your life to Him, that photograph would be priceless.

How valuable to you is John's photograph of "A Choir"? If you have surrendered your life to Jesus Christ, it should be priceless. In hard times you are reminded of the great times to come. When weary in serving God and in sharing your faith, this should strengthen and inspire you to stay faithful.

In my office, I have several photographs. You'll not find any photographs of places I haven't been or people I don't know. The photos that are valuable to me are the ones that are personal. Usually I'm in them with people I love, and so they are valuable to me. I truly believe if you place yourself within John's photographs of "A Scroll," "A Lamb," and "A Choir" in Revelation 5, it will not only change the way you view these photographs, but the photographs will change the way you see your life. They will make a difference in you that is priceless.

CHAPTER 7

THE UNAVOIDABLE TALK

"The Second Coming of Jesus"

EVERYONE HAS FELT THE TENSION of having an unavoidable talk. The subject matter makes the conversation uncomfortable. A doctor informs a friend they have cancer. A boss tells a long time employee they've reorganized the company, and their job is not in the picture. A sixteen-year-old with their new license tells Mom and Dad they just put a dent in the family car. You get the picture.

Most of these conversations begin with warm generalities. "How are you?" "How's the family?" "Dad, Mom, you've never really liked the family car, have you?" Like an airplane circling the airport, you keep your conversation in the air. But just as every airplane has to land, at some point you have to have the unavoidable talk.

For some people, the subject of the second coming of Jesus can be uncomfortable. The young don't want to talk about it because they're afraid Jesus will come before they can start their families or fulfill their dreams. The middle-aged don't want to talk about it because they're consumed with their families and dreams. The old don't want to talk about it because it reminds them of their mortality. Though this is more the case for nonbelievers, it is also true of many believers—even pastors.

Many believers avoid learning about the second coming of Jesus because of a lack of maturity. Hebrews 6:1–3 states,

> [1] Therefore let us leave the elementary teachings about Christ and go on to maturity, not laying again the foundation of repentance from acts that lead to death, and of faith in God, [2] instruction about baptisms, the laying on of hands, the resurrection of the dead, and eternal judgment. [3] And God permitting, we will do so.

The resurrection of the dead and eternal judgment are aspects of the second coming of Jesus. These verses also consider them as elementary teachings about Christ. Here, the Bible says we can't move on and mature until we have made these lessons our own, yet our love-hate relationship with any form of maturity makes it hard.

Physically, we want all the benefits of the next phase in life without changing who we are or what we do. Spiritually, we do the same. We want to grow as Christians without having to change who we are or what we do. But God knows and we know that it's not possible. That means, in order for us to mature as believers, we have to have the unavoidable talk about the second coming of Jesus. We each need to learn these truths and make them our own.

Again, such a talk is not easy or we would have already had it. However, talking about the second coming of Jesus may not be as bad as you think. It actually helps us eliminate some of the unknown about the future and live a life of hope and purpose now. So let's talk about the second coming of Jesus.

GOD HAS A PLAN
"Don't be Ignorant"

Though Revelation chapters 1–5 have been exhilarating, they can be seen as the circling before the hard talk. Chapter 1 gives us a vision of Jesus' authority in heaven. In chapters 2–3, He addresses the condition and needs of seven churches. Chapter 4 describes the greatness of heaven's throne, while chapter 5 states that the One on the throne still owns the title deed of earth, and that Jesus is the only one worthy to reclaim the earth for God. Then, chapters 6–21 unfold how Jesus will do it.

Part of what makes the second coming of Jesus an uncomfortable conversation is the unknown—not on God's part, but on ours. Yet the book of Revelation reveals that God has a plan, and 1 Thessalonians 4:13–18 makes it clear that God doesn't want us ignorant about it.

> [13] Brothers, we do not want you to be ignorant about those who fall asleep, or to grieve like the rest of men, who have no hope. [14] We believe that Jesus died and rose again and so we believe that God will bring with Jesus those who have fallen asleep in him. [15] According to the Lord's own word, we tell you that we who are still alive, who are left until the coming of the Lord, will certainly not precede those who have fallen asleep. [16] For the Lord himself will come down from heaven, with a loud command, with the voice of the archangel and with the trumpet call of God, and the dead in Christ will rise first. [17] After that, we who are still alive and are left will be caught up together with them in the clouds to meet the Lord in the air. And so we will be with the Lord forever. [18] Therefore encourage each other with these words.

Generally speaking, God's plan for the second coming of Jesus Christ can be seen in four phases. The first phase involves the rapture of the church.

Phase #1: The Rapture of the Church

I understand that there is military protocol describing how officers enter and leave a vehicle. The junior officers enter first with the highest ranking officers entering last. According to these verses, there seems to be a protocol describing how Jesus' followers will join Him in heaven. At a loud command and trumpet blast, the believers who are dead rise first. Then, the believers who are still alive rise second. If this heavenly protocol were given a name it would be the protocol of the rapture.

There has been much debate over what I have described as the protocol of the rapture. Respected biblical scholars for centuries have discussed this. Some believe there will be no rapture, while others debate whether it will happen before, during or after the Great Tribulation. Let me share with you why I believe there will be a rapture and why I believe it will happen prior to the events beginning in Revelation 6—the events of the Great Tribulation.

I Believe in the Rapture Because...
1 Thessalonians 4:17 Describes It

1 Thessalonians 4:17 describes that believers who are still alive "will be caught up in the air." The Greek word for being caught up is *harpazo*. It's the same Greek word used to describe the way God transported Philip from a roadside baptismal pool outside Gaza to Azotus in Acts 8:39. However, in the rapture, believers are not transported to Azotus but up in the air to meet with Christ.

I remember hearing a Christian comedian once say, "At the rapture I hope to be standing beside two nonbelievers. As I'm being raptured, I'd like to grab both of them by the collar. At about 30,000 feet I'd like to say to them, 'Believe...or I'll drop you.'" It's a great thought, but the rapture will happen so quickly you won't have time to grab anyone. Besides, it's only for those who have fully surrendered their lives to Jesus.

Being caught up in the air highlights why I believe 1 Thessalonians 4:17 speaks of the rapture instead of the second coming of Jesus. The verse indicates that the believers meet Jesus *"in the air."* According to Revelation 19:15–21, the second coming of Jesus occurs when Jesus comes back to reclaim the earth.

I Believe in the Rapture Because...

Revelation 3:10 Points to It

I also believe in the rapture because it fulfills Jesus' promise to the church. In Revelation 3:10, Jesus tells the church in Philadelphia,

> [10] "Since you have kept my command to endure patiently, I will also keep you from the hour of trial that is going to come upon the whole world to test those who live on the earth."

Here, Jesus promises to keep His believers from the hour of trial. I believe that *"the hour of trial"* refers to the Great Tribulation period that is described in Revelation 6–18. It's important to see that Jesus promises to keep us "from" the hour of trial, not "through" the hour of trial. This points to the rapture occurring before, not after, the Great Tribulation.

Furthermore, verse 10 explains that the focus of this hour of trial is upon unbelievers. The phrase *"to test those who live upon the earth"* appears as a reoccurring label for unbelievers throughout Revelation (Rev. 6:10; 8:13; 11:10; 13:8, 12, 14; 14:6; 17:2, 8). This is corroborated by the fact that the word "church," or "churches," occurs nineteen times in the first three chapters, and not once during the chapters of the Great Tribulation. That's because Jesus has fulfilled His promise and has raptured His church from the hour of trial (1 Thessalonians 1:10).

Phase #2: The Preparation of the Bride

Jesus not only raptures us to rescue us from the hour of trial, but He also does so to prepare us as His bride. On two occasions, Jesus refers to Himself as the bridegroom (Matt. 9:14–15; 25:1–13), and four times the church is called His bride. All four of those metaphors appear in Revelation 19–22—regarding His second coming. Before He returns, Jesus prepares His bride. According to Romans 14:9–12, the process of preparation takes place at the judgment seat of Christ.

> [9] For this very reason, Christ died and returned to life so that he might be the Lord of both the dead and the living. [10] You, then, why do you judge your brother? Or why do you look down on your brother? For we will all stand before God's judgment seat. [11] It is written:

> "'As surely as I live,' says the Lord,
> 'every knee will bow before me;
> every tongue will confess to God.'"

> [12] So then, each of us will give an account of himself to God.

The word "judgment seat" in the Greek is *bema*. *Bema* was a platform where Roman officials rendered judgment and where judges at the annual Olympic games issued their rewards.

When believers stand at the judgment seat of Christ, we will not be judged for our sin—what we did against Jesus. Romans 8:1 promises that *"therefore, there is now no condemnation for those who are in Christ Jesus."* However, we will be held accountable for the accomplishments of our lives—what we did for Jesus.

Three passages of scripture describe what Jesus is looking for when He judges believers. 1 Corinthians 3:10–15 says that as a believer you will be *judged for the quality of your work*. Though in your life you were involved in a lot of projects, only the projects of God are the ones that will last. 1 Corinthians 4:1–5 adds that you will also be *judged for the character of your heart*. You may have been involved in a lot of projects with God, but if you did it to build your reputation instead of God's kingdom, it won't last. If you did God's work your way for your benefit, it won't pass His judgment. Finally, 2 Corinthians 5:10 explains that at the judgment seat of Christ you will be *compensated for work that lasts*. The verse explains,

> [10] For we must all appear before the judgment seat of Christ, that each one may receive what is due him for the things done while in the body, whether good or bad.

The Greek word for "appear" literally means all believers must "be revealed" before the judgment seat of Christ. The things done in your life will be judged whether they are good (acceptable) or bad (flawed, worthless, and unacceptable). You will only be rewarded for works that pass Jesus' inspection.

I see it much like the process of passing through security at the airport. I have my ticket and all I want to take with me on the flight. Yet before I board, everything I've packed has to be checked—everything, even the things in my pockets. No matter how many times I've gone through airport security, I still have a twinge of fear that I've forgotten to take something out of my pocket or have packed something that won't be allowed on the flight. At the judgment seat of Christ only the right work, done with the right heart, will pass Jesus' inspection. Only the approved works will be allowed and rewarded in heaven.

Furthermore, Romans 14:10 reminds you not to waste your time trying to inspect or judge the luggage of others. That is Jesus' job, not yours. Besides, in Matthew 25:14–30 Jesus says that God gives different talents to different people. You will not be held accountable for what God has given others, but you will be accountable for the life, gifts, and opportunities God has given you. Therefore it's best if you focus on what you are or are not doing, and stop judging what others are or are not doing.

Once you have passed through the judgment seat of Christ, the worthless is removed and only what is righteous remains. That's why Revelation 19:7–8 explains,

> [7] "Let us rejoice and be glad
> and give him glory!
> For the wedding of the Lamb has come,
> and his bride has made herself ready.
> [8] Fine linen, bright and clean,
> was given her to wear."

John's great challenge was trying to explain these heavenly images in earthly terms. "Fine linen" stands for the righteous acts of the saints. Thus, the fine linen he describes was like the expensive, beautiful material worn by Joseph (Gen. 41:42), David (1 Chron. 15:27), and Mordecai (Esther 8:15). It was bright and clean. A more accurate picture from the Greek would say that the bride looked radiant and pure. It was truly the picture of a bride beaming with righteousness.

To this day, I can still remember when I first saw Loree in her wedding dress. Loree and I kept the tradition that I would not see her that day until the wedding. When the doors opened for her to enter, the people stood. Since Loree is not very tall, all I could see was the crown of her head and her flowing veil. But when she stepped past the people so I could see all of her, I was, and to this day remain, in awe. She was beautiful. I soaked in everything. Her golden hair, glistening blue eyes, the softness of her make-up were all accented by the beauty of her dress. To this day, I know that her dad walked her down the aisle of the church, but I don't remember seeing him. As a song was played, I took Loree by the hand. So moved by the moment, I could not help but express my heart to her. I told her I had waited my whole life for her and that she was more than I had prayed for. That's when Loree spoke, and in her soft voice whispered, "Mark, shut up! Just shut up!" With all my talking, she couldn't think what was coming next in the ceremony.

In some way, I believe that's the way Jesus will feel when He sees us after the judgment seat. Anything and everything unrighteous about our lives will have been removed. We will stand radiant and pure before Him, and He won't be able to withhold His heart. 1 Corinthians 4:5 states, *"At that time each will receive his praise from God."* Think of it. Hearing Jesus lovingly praise you will probably be the greatest reward of all.

Phase #3: The Great Tribulation and Revival

Don't assume that one phase waits for the previous one to end. While Jesus is preparing His bride in heaven, He is also at work on earth. He initiates the Great Tribulation and revival. It will be a time when God's wrath and grace work together.

The late Bible teacher Dr. David L. Cooper described this third phase as a fireworks display. Professional fireworks displays are well-timed. Just as the effects of one explosion ends, another begins; sometimes one rocket goes off in the midst of another. That aptly describes the period of the Great Tribulation and revival.[26]

The Great Tribulation pierces the dark with three explosions of God's wrath. The first explosion surfaces in Revelation 6–8—the opening of the seven seals. The opening of the last seal ignites the second explosion of God's wrath in Revelation 8–15—the seven trumpets. The sound of the last trumpet will set off the final explosion of God's wrath in Revelation 16–17—the seven bowls.

From within these explosions of God's wrath emerge the explosion of His grace. In chapter 7, God will seal and set aside 144,000 Jews—12,000 from each tribe of Israel. Those who once denied Jesus as the Messiah will proclaim Him to the world. As a result, people from every tribe, nation, and tongue will surrender to Christ. Then in

---

26   Tim LaHaye, *Revelation Illustrated and Made Plain* (Grand Rapids, MI: Zondervan, 1975), 94.

chapter 14, God sends two witnesses. They will proclaim and display the power of God to an unbelieving world.

Tragically, I know that upon hearing that there will be a great revival in the midst of the Great Tribulation, some will see this as a reason to put off surrendering to Jesus. Listen. You should want nothing to do with the Great Tribulation. You need to hear and heed Jesus' warning to those living through the Great Tribulation. In Matthew 24:16–21, He says,

> [16] "then let those who are in Judea flee to the mountains. [17] Let no one on the roof of his house go down to take anything out of the house. [18] Let no one in the field go back to get his cloak. [19] How dreadful it will be in those days for pregnant women and nursing mothers! [20] Pray that your flight will not take place in winter or on the Sabbath. [21] For then there will be great distress, unequaled from the beginning of the world until now—and never to be equaled again."

Revelation 14:20 gives a gruesome picture of the Great Tribulation. It reports that persecution and wars will be so great that a river of blood will be four feet deep and flow for 200 miles.

Yet a wide-angle view of phase three gives a clear picture of God's nature and human nature. God's nature is seen in His ability to offer full grace in the midst of His full wrath. This is nothing new for God. When He came to earth as Jesus, John 1:14 states, *"We have seen his glory, the glory of the One and Only, who came from the Father, full of grace and truth."*

Phase three also gives us a clear picture of human nature. Our nature is to question until proven and to postpone until pressed. That's why many will be left behind to endure the Great Tribulation. They had every opportunity to surrender to Christ earlier but didn't.

That's why it is important to hear this message, "DON'T TAKE GOD'S GRACE LIGHTLY!" Though by His nature God still offers His grace during the Great Tribulation, He offers it under the heavy hand of His wrath. That's one of the reasons why God doesn't want you ignorant of His plan. He wants you to experience His grace today without having to endure His wrath tomorrow.

Phase #4: The Second Coming of Christ

Earlier I mentioned the military protocol for entering a vehicle— junior officers first and senior officers last. The protocol for leaving a vehicle is senior officers first, with junior officers last. The protocol for the rapture (entering heaven) involves the dead rising first, with those alive in Christ rising next. Then, all meet Christ in the air as He prepares His bride at the judgment seat. The protocol for Jesus' return (leaving heaven) is simple. Revelation 19 describes Jesus stepping out first with His bride not far behind.

I also said at the outset that many avoid this conversation because it's uncomfortable. The unknown factor makes it uncomfortable for many. That's why God has revealed His plans regarding the second coming of Jesus Christ. However, many are still uncomfortable with the subject because you don't like God's plans.

Many believers don't like it because we don't like the thought of being accountable for our lives—standing before Jesus at the judgment seat. It makes us have to evaluate our efforts. We have to ask, "Am I truly doing what God wants, the way God wants and with His heart?" If so, we are to be encouraged and continue. If not, we have to make changes.

Of course, unbelievers don't like God's plan at all. It's uncomfortable to think that God raptures only believers before the Great Tribulation. And even though God will still offer His grace, it will be with the heavy hand of His wrath. Furthermore, God's plan doesn't allow for any options or alternatives. It's God's heaven, God's earth, and God's plan. You can either take the hand of His grace and surrender to Jesus, or experience the hand of His wrath. God leaves the choice up to you.

GOD MADE A PROMISE
"Don't Live Hopeless"

A closer look at the second coming of Jesus reveals something important. God hasn't shared His plan in order to strong-arm you into heaven. He has revealed His plan so that you won't have to live a hopeless life while on earth. Look once more at 1 Thessalonians 4:13. It says,

> [13] Brothers, we do not want you to be ignorant about those who
> fall asleep, or to grieve like the rest of men, who have no hope.

When God inspired the Apostle Paul to write this, it was evident that people were living and dying every day without hope. A typical inscription on a grave in Paul's day read,

> I was not; I became; I am not; I care not.[27]

---

27   Warren W. Wiersbe, *The Bible Exposition Commentary Volume* 2 (Wheaton, IL: Victor Books, 1989), 178.

That's why God has made His plan clear, especially the phase regarding Jesus' second coming. He didn't create us to live hopeless lives, but hope-filled lives.

Revelation 5 reminds us that though God created the world, this is not the world God planned. Satan's deception and our sins separated us from a holy God. The only one worthy to reunite us with God and reclaim this world for God was Jesus. He was born of a virgin and lived a sinless life. He died on the cross to pay the price for our sins and rose from the grave to render forgiveness. Before He ascended into heaven, He promised to send His Holy Spirit to help us (John 14–16), and He promised to return, giving us hope (John 14:1–6).

When our oldest son John Mark was three, Loree took him one day a week to a Mother's Day Out program at a nearby church. Loree thought the time with other children would be good for him, and a day to run errands would be good for her. Since this was new to John Mark, Loree explained everything to him and assured him that she was coming back to get him. At lunchtime, Loree picked up John Mark and on the way home she asked him what they did. He briefly mentioned the projects he worked on and went straight to talking about his naptime. He wanted to be sure Loree heard him say, "Mommie, at naptime I put my towel right beside the window. I kept looking outside hoping you would come for me."

Though we wouldn't admit it out loud, many of us as adults have felt like John Mark. Change makes us uncomfortable. Still busy with the various projects of life, it's when we are still that we truly long for Jesus to return. Well, just as Loree promised John Mark that she would return for him, God has promised repeatedly in scripture that Jesus will return for and with those who belong to Him.

The New Testament mentions Jesus' return 318 times. That's impressive, when you realize there are only 216 chapters in the New Testament. That means one out of every thirty verses speaks about the return of Jesus. All but five books of the New Testament address His return. Three of those books are the single-chapter books of Philemon, 2 John, and 3 John.

Furthermore, if you think that Jesus' promise to return only occurs in the New Testament, think again. Though Jude is a New Testament book, it makes an amazing Old Testament reference. Verses 14–16 state,

> [14] Enoch, the seventh from Adam, prophesied about these men: "See, the Lord is coming with thousands upon thousands of his holy ones [15] to judge everyone, and to convict all the ungodly of all the ungodly acts they have done in the ungodly way, and of all the harsh words ungodly sinners have spoken against him." [16] These men are grumblers and faultfinders; they follow their own evil desires; they boast about themselves and flatter others for their own advantage.

Enoch was just seven generations removed from Adam. He lived thousands of years before Jesus was born. And yet, God divinely informed him of Jesus' return.

God has made countless promises for thousands of years and has yet to break one. He's been promising Jesus' return since Enoch, and He reiterated it 318 times in the New Testament. No matter how many changes you may go through in life, one thing will never change—

Jesus' promise to return. What a blessed hope for broken hearts. What a daily hope for daily hurts. Jesus is coming!

GOD IS NOT FINISHED
"Don't Stop Now"

Hopefully, talking about the second coming of Jesus has eliminated some of your fears of the unknown regarding the future. Furthermore, I pray that in a constantly changing world you have been reminded of this changeless hope—Jesus is coming! Yet I particularly pray that this talk about the second coming of Jesus has also encouraged you to serve Jesus faithfully until He comes. Since Jesus hasn't returned yet, that means God is not finished with His plan for reaching others. Therefore, neither should you be.

It was inspiring to learn that God has informed us of His plan and reminded us of Jesus' return not only to calm us, but to also encourage us. Two of the passages explaining the rapture of the church emphasize this. After explaining the protocol of the rapture, 1 Thessalonians 4:13–18 ends with the charge, *"Therefore encourage each other with these words."* After 1 Corinthians 15:50–58 explains how the rapture will occur in the twinkling of an eye, it ends by exhorting us, *"Therefore, my dear brothers, stand firm. Let nothing move you. Always give yourselves fully to the work of the Lord, because you know that your labor in the Lord is not in vain."* And when you have grown tired serving Jesus while waiting for His return, James 5:7–8 implores you,

> [7] Be patient, then, brothers, until the Lord's coming. See how the farmer waits for the land to yield its valuable crop and how patient he is for the autumn and spring rains. [8] You too, be patient and stand firm, because the Lord's coming is near.

I was amused to read of a tourist in northern Italy visiting the Villa Asconati. The castle grounds were immaculate. When the tourist learned that the owner of the castle hadn't stepped foot on the grounds in over twelve years, they were even more impressed with the gardener's work. Before leaving, the tourist approached the gardener and said, "You keep this garden in such fine condition, just as though you expected your master to come tomorrow." The gardener quickly replied, "Today, Sir, I work as though he were coming today."[28]

No longer ignorant of God's plan, no longer hopeless of Jesus' return, let's each work as though Jesus were coming today.

---

28   Raymond McHenry, *McHenry's Stories for the Soul* (Peabody, MA: Hendrickson, 2001), 257–258.

CHAPTER 8

GOD'S TOUGH LOVE

REVELATION 6

LISTENING TO A POPULAR COMEDIAN being interviewed, I was happily surprised. Many comedians earn a living by being crude. This man was talking about putting God first, family second, and his career third. He spoke of the importance of a day of rest, and how he had learned so much more about the way God loved him by comparing it to the way he loved his daughters.

I couldn't believe how much our convictions were alike. But then, the interviewer asked him, "You don't believe that God is a God of vengeance, do you?" He answered, "No," elaborating more how God is all about love.

As his comments soaked in, it was evident that he was speaking the theology of the day. Believers and nonbelievers alike agree God is all about love. Yet many who say God is all about love don't know all about God or His love. To explain God and His love, they quickly quote 1 Corinthians 13: 4–5, *"Love is patient, love is kind. It does not envy, it does not boast, it is not proud. It is not rude, it is not self-seeking, it is not easily angered, it keeps no record of wrongs."* Though this is all true, many forget that verse 6 says, *"Love does not delight in evil but rejoices with the truth."* That's why it will be hard for them to understand what Numbers 14:18 or Deuteronomy 7:9–11 say about God's love:

[18] "The LORD is slow to anger, abounding in love, and forgiving sin and rebellion. Yet he does not leave the guilty unpunished; he punishes the children for the sin of the fathers to the third and fourth generation."

— Numbers 14:18

[9] Know therefore that the LORD your God is God; he is the faithful God, keeping his covenant of love to a thousand generations of those who love him and keep his commands. [10] But those who hate him he will repay to their face by destruction; he will not be slow to repay to their face those who hate him.

— Deuteronomy 7:9–10

Many want God's love to be a caring hug but not a correcting hand. Yet God's love is both. Most want God's love to stand up for you when you've *been* wronged, but not stand against you when you *are* wrong. Face it, the God of love that many want today is all smiles, but no substance; he's nothing more than the grandparent who knows nothing of your life between visits, but never forgets to give you a smile and a hug whenever you drop by. This may be the God many want, but it's not the way God is.

As we look at Revelation 6, we will explore a side of God's love many don't want to see. It's the love of God that emerges in consequences allowed, justice rendered, and a wrath that is right. It's God's tough love.

LOVE THAT ALLOWS FOR CONSEQUENCES

A brief review is important to appreciate what takes place in verses 1–8. Revelation 4 provides a magnificent vision of heaven's throne. Through

John's eyes and pen, we are a part of a grand worship experience. Then in Revelation 5, the worship stops because of a dilemma. God holds a scroll sealed with seven seals. It's His title deed to earth. God has looked throughout heaven, earth, and hell, but has found no one worthy to open the seals and enforce the deed. Then in Revelation 5:6–7, Jesus steps forward as the Lamb of God, and takes the scroll from God's hand. Once again, heaven erupts in worship.

Now, in Revelation 6:1–8, Jesus opens the first four seals unleashing what has been called the Four Horsemen of the Apocalypse. It describes some unthinkable consequences allowed by God.

The Consequences of Deception

Revelation 6:1–2 points to a consequence that was foretold by Daniel 600 years before John's experience and vision. God inspires John to write,

> [1] I watched as the Lamb opened the first of the seven seals. Then I heard one of the four living creatures say in a voice like thunder, "Come!" [2] I looked, and there before me was a white horse! Its rider held a bow, and he was given a crown, and he rode out as a conqueror bent on conquest.

As He did with the Apostle John, God gave Daniel a vision of the end times. Daniel 9:27 records that the Tribulation period will last for seven years. It begins with the Antichrist coming to assume power. Many believe the rider on the white horse in John's vision is the Antichrist, for he rides out *"as a conqueror bent on conquest."* Yet this causes some confusion.

Because John describes Jesus riding a white horse and wearing many crowns in Revelation 19:11–12, some see the rider on the white horse in Revelation 6 as Jesus. I believe it's the Antichrist. Here's why. Both are on a white horse, because a white horse was associated with conquest and triumph. The difference, however, is seen in their crowns. The crown of the Antichrist in Revelation 6:2 is the Greek word *stephanos,* which was the crown given to those who had won an event. The many crowns worn by Jesus in Revelation 19:12 are not *stephanos* but *diademas.* They are the crowns worn by royalty. See the distinction? Though the Antichrist may be victorious for a season, Jesus is forever victorious.

The Antichrist will not assume power by force. Revelation 6:2 explains that though the rider carries *"a bow,"* there are no arrows. Make no mistake, though; he will assume power and he will do so through deception.

Consider the setting of his coming. The church has been raptured. The world stumbles in disarray. As you will see when the other seals are opened, wars and famines will plague the world. In the midst of all this, the Antichrist stands in the spotlight promising peace. According to Daniel 9:27, he makes a seven-year agreement with Israel and others. However, halfway into that agreement he breaks it, showing his true colors. As a result, those who remain during the Tribulation endure the consequences of life under a great deceiver (2 Thessalonians 2:8–12).

The Consequences of War

With the title deed of the world in His hand, Jesus opens the second seal in Revelation 6:3–4.

> [3] When the Lamb opened the second seal, I heard the second living creature say, "Come!" [4] Then another horse came out, a

fiery red one. Its rider was given power to take peace from the earth and to make men slay each other. To him was given a large sword.

Like the color of the dragon in Revelation 12:3 and the beast in Revelation 17:3, a red horse emerges. Red is the color of terror, death, and bloodshed. The bow has been replaced with a sword, and peace with war. It's a violent time to be alive, and with a deceiver in power.

The Consequences of Famine

With the deceiver in power, a third seal is opened. Revelation 6:5–6 describes a time when you would want your leader to rule with compassion, not deception, for a great famine blankets the world.

> ⁵ When the Lamb opened the third seal, I heard the third living creature say, "Come!" I looked, and there before me was a black horse! Its rider was holding a pair of scales in his hand. ⁶ Then I heard what sounded like a voice among the four living creatures, saying, "A quart of wheat for a day's wages, and three quarts of barley for a day's wages, and do not damage the oil and the wine!"

War and famine go hand in hand. Farmers can't tend to the fields and the fields are devastated by war. Consequently, the rider sits astride a black horse. Twice the King James Version uses black to describe a time of famine (Jeremiah 14:1–2; Lamentations 5:10). The rider carries scales to show that during the famine a laborer's daily wages may buy enough food for him but not his family. Therefore, to care for his family, he buys barley instead of wheat. Barley had far less nutritional value; that's why it was given to livestock. But now he buys it to feed his family, just so they can survive.

The Consequences of Death

The outcome of deception, war, and famine are understood as Jesus opens the fourth seal and summons the last horseman. Revelation 6:7–8 states,

> [7] When the Lamb opened the fourth seal, I heard the voice of the fourth living creature say, "Come!" [8] I looked, and there before me was a pale horse! Its rider was named Death, and Hades was following close behind him. They were given power over a fourth of the earth to kill by sword, famine, and plague, and by the wild beasts of the earth.

The Greek language literally depicts the pale horse in a greenish-yellow color. It's the same word used by Homer to describe the ashen color of a face drained of blood by fear. It's fitting that the horse resembles the color of a corpse, for its rider is Death and it's being followed closely by Hades. The years of deception, war, and famine take their toll, as one-fourth of the world's inhabitants are destroyed, body and soul.

As people today read these consequences, many do so skeptically, saying: "A loving God would never allow this to happen." But they forget the times in history when He already has.

In Exodus 7–11, God allowed Egypt to endure ten plagues, the last of which was the death of every firstborn male. God allowed it so that Egypt would know that Israel belonged to God. In 1 Kings 18, God allowed Israel to experience a three-year drought. Israel's heart was spiritually dry, so God caused the land to become dry until they acknowledged their sin and turned their hearts back to God. In Luke 15, Jesus tells the story of a loving father with a prodigal son. The son leaves home to live his own way, not his father's. When the son wastes all his money and a famine dries the land, he finds himself longing to eat the food given to livestock. (This sounds like the famine described in Revelation 6:5–6.) Broken, he returns home to ask his father's forgiveness and surrender to his father's ways. He made this dramatic turn because his father allowed him to experience the consequences of his stubbornness.

Please try to understand, by rapturing only the church and allowing unbelievers to endure the consequence of the tribulation, God sends a telling message to those left behind. Through the rapture He says, "Those who are no longer here truly did belong to me." And by allowing those who remain to endure the famine in the land, God hopes they see themselves as spiritually dry and surrender their lives to Him. Revelation 7 explains that during the tribulation, God appoints 144,000 Jews to be worldwide evangelists. God still offers His grace in the midst of His wrath. By allowing the stubborn to endure the consequences of their own actions, some might actually be saved.

For the father of the prodigal son, it took amazing love to let his son go and experience his consequences—for there was no guarantee he would come around and come home. For God the Father, it takes amazing love for Him to allow those left behind to endure the consequences of the tribulation. But it's worth it for the hope that some will come around and come home.

LOVE THAT IS JUST

God's love is not only seen in the consequences He allows, it's also evident in the action He takes. Benjamin Disraeli, Great Britain's first and only Jewish Prime Minister, said it well, "Justice is truth in action." It's clear in Revelation 6:9–11 that God's love compels Him to put His truth into action.

> [9] When he opened the fifth seal, I saw under the altar the souls of those who had been slain because of the word of God and the testimony they had maintained. [10] They called out in a loud voice, "How long, Sovereign Lord, holy and true, until you judge the inhabitants of the earth and avenge our blood?" [11] Then each of them was given a white robe, and they were told to wait a little longer, until the number of their fellow servants and brothers who were to be killed as they had been was completed.

An old African proverb states, "Corn can't expect justice from a court composed of chickens." As was made clear in our study of Revelation 5, though God still owns the title deed of earth, this is not the world God hoped it would be. Satan's deception and our sins have skewed the world's sense of justice. Since the birth of the church, believers have been persecuted and, during the Tribulation period, that persecution elevates to an unimaginable extreme.

Until Jesus returns, believers have been and will continue to be the corn in the courtroom of chickens. Yet when Jesus opens the fifth seal, God's love takes action. And God will have justice for His martyrs and His Son.

Justice for God's Martyrs

Verse 9 reports that John *"saw under the altar the souls of those who had been slain because of the word of God and the testimony they had maintained."* Leviticus 4 explains that when an animal was sacrificed in the Old Testament, its blood was poured out at the base of the brazen altar.

During the years of tribulation, many who surrender to Jesus are martyred (Rev. 1:2, 9; 11:7; 12:11, 17; 14:13; 20:4). Like the animals' blood at the base of the Old Testament altar, John sees the souls of those martyred for Jesus' sake.

What is so moving is that not one of them asks, "Why?" None of them ask God, "Why did you allow me to be martyred?" I'm afraid that many believers today are asking God "Why?" for far less. "Why did you allow my illness? Why did you allow me to be fired? Why did you allow the accident to take place?" Don't get me wrong. I don't believe it's wrong to ask God, when you're trying to understand how best to honor Him in an unwanted situation that He has allowed. However, many believers are asking God "Why?" because we think it's God's job to protect us from those situations. Actually, as a believer it's our job to give our life to Him. It's our job to live for Him and honor Him regardless of what He allows. It seems that martyrs understand this.

Still, they did ask one question. In verse 10 the martyred souls asked God, *"How long...until you judge the inhabitants of the earth and avenge our blood?"* Though the question comes from those martyred during the tribulation, it could be asked by others persecuted for God throughout history. Others in scripture have asked God how long until He deals justly with the actions of the ungodly (Psalm 74:9–10; 94:3–7; 119:84–88; Habakkuk 1:2–4).

God renders His justice during the Tribulation by making life in those days feel unbearable. God promises martyrs that His justice will be made complete; until then, He cares for them by placing a robe of glory upon them and asks them to wait. Out of His love for them, God will make it right. He will render His justice.

Justice for God's Son

If God's love for His martyrs causes Him to render justice, then His love for His Son demands it. John makes this clear when in 1 John 4:9–10 he wrote,

> [9] This is how God showed his love among us: He sent his one and only Son into the world that we might live through him. [10] This is love: not that we loved God, but that he loved us and sent his Son as an atoning sacrifice for our sins.

Around 500 BC, the government of the Locians flourished because of the strict but benevolent leadership of Zaleusus. One of his strict laws said that the eyes of an adulterer must be put out. When his own son became guilty of adultery, Zaleusus didn't amend his law, but neither did he hide his love for his son. He had one of his own eyes put out along with one of his son's.

Romans 6:23 underscores the law and the love of our heavenly Father when stating, *"For the wages of sin is death, but the gift of God is eternal life in Christ Jesus our Lord."* God didn't amend His law for us, but neither did He withhold His love from us. He sent His own Son to die for our sins. And if God doesn't render justice to those who have rejected His love, then He will have to apologize to His Son for sending Him to die.

God's love for His martyrs and His Son is too strong not to render justice. I saw such love displayed recently by Loree's mom. Ganny, as we affectionately call her, has the privilege of keeping her great-grandsons a few days each week while their parents work. Mason is three years old and his younger brother Luke is almost one. Mason's routine once he enters Ganny and Papa's house is to head for his toy spot. There, he puts on an old towel as a cape, reaches for a weathered stick that has become his sword, and is immediately transformed into Captain Hook. I guess one day he saw his little brother Luke as Peter Pan and pushed him over as he walked by. Ganny quickly picked up a crying Luke and exclaimed to Mason, "Mason, you apologize to your brother." Slowly Mason turned to his Ganny, lifted his sword to her nose and said, "Captain Hook doesn't apologize." With that statement, Captain Hook promptly found himself without his sword, sitting in the timeout chair. There Ganny told him, "You can get down once you have apologized to Luke." It seemed that Captain Hook wasn't ever going to apologize. Then easily he slid from his chair, walked over to his brother and said, "Sorry, Lukie." At that moment all was well again in Ganny's Neverland.

I love what Ganny did because it mirrors God's love. Because Ganny loved Luke, she wasn't going to let his mistreatment go without justice. And because Ganny loved Mason, she wasn't going to let Mason get by thinking she would change her ways so he could do whatever he wanted. In time, when Mason realized Ganny wasn't going to budge, he changed his ways to live in her house.

I see God's love that way. God's love for His martyrs and His Son will not allow their sacrifice to go without justice. And I believe that one of the reasons God makes it clear that His love will have justice is so that those who think that God will change His ways for them will in time surrender their will, their ways, and their lives for Him.

LOVE THAT PROMISES WRATH

To send a strong message of His unchanging ways, God promises that a day will come that His love will be seen in His wrath. You hear this in Revelation 6:12–17.

> [12] I watched as he opened the sixth seal. There was a great earthquake. The sun turned black like sackcloth made of goat hair, the whole moon turned blood red, [13] and the stars in the sky fell to earth, as late figs drop from a fig tree when shaken by a strong wind. [14] The sky receded like a scroll, rolling up, and every mountain and island was removed from its place.

> [15] Then the kings of the earth, the princes, the generals, the rich, the mighty, and every slave and every free man hid in caves and among the rocks of the mountains. [16] They called to the mountains and the rocks, "Fall on us and hide us from the face of him who sits on the throne and from the wrath of the Lamb! [17] For the great day of their wrath has come, and who can stand?"

As we come to the end of chapter 6, there are two aspects of this chapter that often go unrecognized. One is that in the original manuscripts, every verse except verse 17 begins with the Greek word *kai*; *kai* is our word for "and." Thus the chapter doesn't read as a sequential checklist of end-time events. Chapter 6 reads more as one dramatic vision that is continually unfolding before John's eyes.

When we read chapter 6 with that understanding, we discover an amazing similarity to what John saw and what Jesus said in Matthew 24. In Matthew 24:3, Jesus' disciples ask Him, *"Tell us…when will this happen, and what will be the sign of your coming and of the end of the age?"* In his book, *Because the Time is Near*, pastor and author John

MacArthur places what Jesus said and what John saw side-by-side. The comparison is gripping.

JESUS SAID	JOHN SAW	THE CONTENTS
Matthew 24:4–5	1st Seal	False Peace
Matthew 24:6–7	2nd Seal	Worldwide War
Matthew 24:7	3rd Seal	Famine
Matthew 24:7	4th Seal	Earthquakes – death
Matthew 24:9	5th Seal	Divine Judgment
Matthew 24:29	6th Seal	Cosmic Darkness – physical destruction
Matthew 24:37ff	7th Seal	Cataclysmic Events (seven trumpets)[29]

From Daniel's visions (Daniel 9) 530 years before Jesus' birth, to Jesus' statements in Matthew 24, to John's vision over 60 years after Jesus' death (Rev. 6), to our reading it today, for over 2500 years God has made it clear what will happen to those who are left behind. He makes it known what the consequences will be and what His wrath will look like. What type of parent would God be if He only gave threats? What kind of children would we be if God never took action?

I remember James Dobson telling the story of a family sitting at a restaurant. The son was acting horribly, so his dad asked him to stop. When the son didn't mind, the dad said, "Son, if you don't mind, I'll have to spank you." Well, the son continued misbehaving, so the dad walked him outside and spanked him. Apparently, a woman in the restaurant heard the conversation—especially the word "spank"—and

---

29   John MacArthur, *Because the Time is Near* (Chicago: Moody, 2007), 126.

followed them outside. When the dad finished spanking his son, the appalled woman berated the dad for his mistreatment of his son and stomped away. As she was walking away, the son looked up to his dad and said, "Dad, what's her problem?"

For the son, there was no problem. His dad had told him in advance what the consequences would be if he didn't mind. I'm sure his dad had fulfilled his promise before when his son misbehaved. For this boy, his dad's actions were consistent with his love. However, it would have been abusive if the dad spanked without any warning or without any explanation of the inappropriate behavior and promised consequences.

God has made it clear that He loves you. He has also made it clear that living your life outside His will and ways is unacceptable. Through Daniel's visions, Jesus' statements, and John's vision, God makes it clear. If you don't surrender your life to Him you will experience His wrath. That's not a statement of abuse but one of love, particularly when God has given you foreknowledge of what He will do and what you need to do to avoid it. That's actually love.

A TRAGIC RESPONSE

There are still many today, like the comedian I mentioned earlier, who think that God is all about love, not wrath. Yet, I like what A.W. Tozer said. Tozer surrendered his life to Jesus at age seventeen and became a pastor at twenty-two. In his forty-four years of ministry, Tozer published over forty works. Surprisingly, most of his books were published after he died. According to his biographer, James Snyder, what made Tozer's works so appealing was that "His preaching as well as his writings were but extensions of his prayer life." For Tozer, life was all about his sincere desire to know God more. Knowing God more,

Tozer believed we weaken God's love if we take away His wrath. God's compassion requires both goodness and justice. Tozer wrote,

> God's compassion flows out of his goodness, and goodness without justice is not goodness. God spares us because he is good, but he could not be good if he were not just.[30]

God is good and He is just. That's why His love will allow for consequences, justice, and wrath. If there were no justice in God, we would take advantage of His goodness. We'd do and live as we pleased and assume that God would understand because He is good. Yet because God is just and good, because His love has wrath, we know we can't get away with doing what we want. That's why it's best to run to Him now because of His love, instead of running from Him later because of His wrath.

In case you missed it, that is the great tragedy recorded in Revelation 6:15–17:

> [15] Then the kings of the earth, the princes, the generals, the rich, the mighty, and every slave and every free man hid in caves and among the rocks of the mountains. [16] They called to the mountains and the rocks, "Fall on us and hide us from the face of him who sits on the throne and from the wrath of the Lamb! [17] For the great day of their wrath has come, and who can stand?"

The first tragedy was that they waited too long to surrender their lives to Jesus, so they now face God's wrath. But the greatest tragedy of all was that, in the midst of God's wrath, they broke and ran to hide from God instead of running humbled and broken before God.

---

30   Draper, *Quotations*, entry 4724.

No matter how much you want to, you can't change the way God is, nor can you change the promises He has made. His love is strong, not soft. He is good and just. He allows for consequences to get our attention and has promised wrath when we fail to heed. You can't change Him to fit your ways, but a loving God is giving us time to change our life to fit His. When we do, we will be so grateful for God's tough love.

CHAPTER 9

GOD'S ABSURD GRACE
REVELATION 7

THE JOURNEY THROUGH REVELATION 7 was personally convicting. At the first reading, I was amazed at God's grace. God withheld His wrath for such a long time, and it appears in chapter 7 that He's doing it again. My first thought was that God's grace is truly amazing, but when I looked back at all the times God's grace was abused, I became upset.

I remembered how by God's grace He delivered Israel from Egypt, to establish a relationship with Israel. But Israel was repeatedly unfaithful to God, making the love relationship one-sided on God's part. Yet God continued to show His grace by coming to the world as Jesus. As Jesus, God would show His love by sacrificing Himself to restore the broken relationship with Israel. When Israel as a whole rejected Jesus, God offered His grace to the world. Yet, like Israel, the world as a whole has rejected Jesus. Thus for thousands of years God has said, "A day is coming when I will remove my followers and reveal my wrath." By Revelation 7, that has occurred. Yet in chapter 7, it appears that God offers His grace again.

In my mind, God's grace has now moved from amazing to absurd. God has every right to say,

141

Enough is enough! What else can I do? How many times can I say to you and show you that I love you? I came and died for you. I've given you thousands of years of warnings and time to repent. Still, either you snub Me with your arrogance, ignore Me with your business, or tease Me with your goodness and occasional interest. Even then, you refuse to surrender to Me the way I have surrendered to you. Well, I've had enough. For years you have rejected My grace, so now you will face My wrath.

In my mind, God has every right to show His wrath without grace. Yet because He is God, it's only right that He reveals His wrath with grace. For God to do anything less would make Him less of God. But I didn't see that at first.

I thought God's grace was absurd because those living after the rapture had their chance. Before the rapture God sent messengers and they were rejected. Now God sends messengers again offering His grace. That to me seemed absurd.

Then I realized that what God was doing for those living in the Tribulation was the same thing He did for me prior to the Tribulation. I deserved God's wrath, yet He withheld it. He sent messengers so I could hear of His grace. And because I surrendered my life to Jesus, I was promised all the benefits of heaven—benefits I could never earn or deserve.

I guess the difference between seeing God's grace as amazing or absurd is the same difference between major and minor surgery. If you haven't heard it before, "Minor surgery is when it's performed on someone else; major surgery is when it's performed on you!" Sadly, believers often see God's grace as amazing when it's offered to us, but absurd when offered to others. Yet God does offer it, even in the midst of His wrath, even when it might seem absurd. As we look at Revelation 7, see if it challenges you as it did me.

ABSURD GRACE!
When God Withholds His Wrath

In Revelation 6, six of the seven seals have been opened. God unleashes His wrath. Those experiencing it call for the mountains and rocks to fall on them and hide them from Jesus' wrath. Still, Revelation 7:1–4 explains God's efforts to give those who have rejected Him another opportunity to stand with Him.

> [1] After this I saw four angels standing at the four corners of the earth, holding back the four winds of the earth to prevent any wind from blowing on the land or on the sea or on any tree. [2] Then I saw another angel coming up from the east, having the seal of the living God. He called out in a loud voice to the four angels who had been given power to harm the land and the sea: [3] "Do not harm the land or the sea or the trees, until we put a seal on the foreheads of the servants of our God."

Revelation 7 puts the reader in the eye of a hurricane. The winds of God's wrath have blown in chapter 6 and will resume in chapter 8. But for this chapter, for this moment, God holds them back.

The ones used to hold back God's wrath are His angels. In seven of Revelation's remaining chapters, you will find them as instruments of His wrath (Rev. 8, 9, 11, 14, 16, 18, 19). Here, however, they are positioned at the four corners of the earth and God instructs them to hold back the wind. The four corners represent the four corners of the compass—North, South, East, and West. In Jeremiah 49:36, Daniel 7:2 and Hosea 13:15, the four winds are associated with God's judgment. The Greek word for "holding back" is *krateo*. It conveys that the winds of God's wrath are strong and the angels are struggling to hold them back.

A fifth angel appears in verses 2–3 charging them to stay strong, because they won't have to hold back the winds of God's wrath forever. Some have assumed that this fifth angel is Jesus, but it's not. The Greek word for another (*allos*) means another of the same kind in numerical order. Yet, the angel's charge reveals that the winds won't be held back for long. Verse 3 states that they will be able to release God's wrath once He has placed His seal on the foreheads of His servants.

In his book, *What's So Amazing About Grace?*, Philip Yancey tells of the conversation overheard between two people on a bus. Yancey writes,

> A friend of mine riding a bus to work overheard a conversation between the young woman sitting next to him and her neighbor across the aisle. The woman was reading Scott Peck's *The Road Less Traveled,* the book that has stayed (at that time) on *The New York Times* Best-Sellers list longer than any other.
>
> "What are you reading?" asked the neighbor.
>
> "A book a friend gave me. She said it changed her life."
>
> "Oh, yeah? What's it about?"
>
> "I'm not sure. Some sort of guide to life. I haven't got very far yet." She began flipping through the book. "Here are the chapter titles: 'Discipline, Love, Grace,...'"
>
> The man stopped her. "What's grace?"

"I don't know. I haven't got to Grace yet."[31]

Her statement remains tragically true of many today and will be tragically true of many in the future. During the future tribulation, there will be a season when God withholds His wrath, while He seals His messengers. He will do this with the hope that, even during the Tribulation, people will see their sin, turn and surrender to Him, and experience the full benefits of His grace.

This not only depicts God's desire for the Tribulation period of tomorrow, it also expresses His heart today. God is withholding His wrath right now. At any moment, He could rapture His church, allowing Jesus to open six of the seven seals of His wrath upon the earth. The only thing keeping Him from doing so is His hope that many will see their sin, surrender to Him, and experience His grace right now. To withhold the wrath we deserve, in order to offer us the grace we don't, makes God's grace seem truly absurd.

ABSURD GRACE!
When God Sends Out Messengers

What also seems absurd about God's grace during the Tribulation is God's use of messengers. In the Old Testament, God sent leaders like Moses and Joshua, judges like Samuel, and prophets like Elijah and others to inform the people of God and His ways. In the New Testament, God came Himself as Jesus. Then after His resurrection and ascension, He charged His followers to be witnesses in Jerusalem, Judea, Samaria, and to the ends of the earth. As He did before the tribulation, God, during the tribulation, sends messengers to inform the world of His grace. This is explained in Revelation 7: 2–8.

---

31   Philip Yancey, *What's So Amazing About Grace?* (Grand Rapids, MI: Zondervan, 1997) 29.

² Then I saw another angel coming up from the east, having the seal of the living God. He called out in a loud voice to the four angels who had been given power to harm the land and the sea: ³ "Do not harm the land or the sea or the trees until we put a seal on the foreheads of the servants of our God." ⁴ Then I heard the number of those who were sealed: 144,000 from all the tribes of Israel.

⁵ From the tribe of Judah 12,000 were sealed,
from the tribe of Reuben 12,000,
from the tribe of Gad 12,000,
⁶ from the tribe of Asher 12,000,
from the tribe of Naphtali 12,000,
from the tribe of Manasseh 12,000,
⁷ from the tribe of Simeon 12,000,
from the tribe of Levi 12,000,
from the tribe of Issachar 12,000,
⁸ from the tribe of Zebulun 12,000,
from the tribe of Joseph 12,000,
from the tribe of Benjamin 12,000.

Grace for Israel

Opinions have abounded for years regarding the 144,000. Some believe they represent Seventh-Day Adventists because they have observed the Jewish Sabbath. Others think they will come from the Jehovah's Witnesses. Years ago, Jehovah's Witnesses claimed they were the 144,000 until their membership exceeded 144,000. A man once told preacher and author Warren Wiersbe that he was one of the

144,000. To the man's surprise, Wiersbe asked him, "To which tribe do you belong, and can you prove it?"[32]

Even a surface reading of the text makes it clear that the 144,000 will come from the Jews. Verses 5–8 specify that 12,000 will be sealed and sent from each of the twelve tribes of Israel. There are nineteen different listings of the twelve tribes in Scripture. In this particular list, Dan has been replaced by Joseph, and of Joseph's two sons, Manasseh is mentioned but not Ephraim. When you look at the history of the tribes of Dan and Ephraim you see their unfaithfulness to God (Dan – Judges18:14–31; Ephraim – Isaiah 7:17 and Hosea 4:17). Thus, God makes a strong point: He wants messengers who are reliable.

This answers a question asked by many believers today: "How come some believers are better than others at helping people surrender to Christ?" In my opinion, it has little to do with being an introvert or extravert, persuasive or passive. It has everything to do with being open and obedient to God. I truly believe that God opens opportunities to those open to God.

The tribes of Dan and Ephraim will still be recognized in heaven. However, God will not include them in the evangelistic force of the future because they were not faithful to God in the past. God's work is too important to entrust to people He can't count on. When souls are at risk, God will not take a risk on followers who are unreliable. That's why the tribes of Dan and Ephraim will be excluded from this great campaign with God. That's also why many believers miss out on the great experiences with God.

---

32   Warren W. Wiersbe, *Be Victorious* (USA: Victor Books, 1987), 70.

Not only do I believe the 144,000 will be from Israel because the Bible says it, I also believe it because God promised it. Listen to Romans 11:25–27.

> [25] I do not want you to be ignorant of this mystery, brothers, so that you may not be conceited: Israel has experienced a hardening in part until the full number of the Gentiles has come in. [26] And so all Israel will be saved, as it is written:

> "The deliverer will come from Zion;
>   he will turn godlessness away from Jacob.
>   [27] And this is my covenant with them
>   when I take away their sins."

Furthermore, Zechariah 12:1–14 foretells the day when all the clans of Israel will look upon the pierced hands of Jesus and weep with repentance. The Jews will experience a national revival and 144,000 will be sealed and sent by God.

What a picture of God's absurd grace toward Israel. They have always been and always will be His chosen people. (Romans 11 represents God's exclamation point to that truth.) Yet, since the birth, death and resurrection of Jesus, Israel as a whole has not chosen to see Him as the Messiah. But by God's absurd grace, He will keep His promise to Israel. They will see and surrender to Jesus. They will experience a great revival and 144,000 of them will be sealed by God to spread His grace to the world.

Grace for the World

Verse 3 states that God will put His seal on the foreheads of the 144,000. Revelation 13:16–17 records that the mark of the beast will be placed on the right hand and forehead of earth's inhabitants. Only those with this mark will be able to transact business, including buying food. Because of this, many believe that the seal of God will also be a visible mark on the foreheads of the 144,000. Yet the Greek words for "seal" and "mark" are different. Though both the seal of God and mark of the beast will be seen, I believe the mark of the beast will be tangible, while the seal of God will be intangible. Here's why.

The Greek word used for "seal" in this verse is the same one used in Ephesians 1:13. There it says that at salvation we receive the seal of God, which is the promised Holy Spirit. This word for seal refers to a signet that verifies authenticity, authority, and security.

Even today, as believers, it should be evident that we belong to God. If we have surrendered our lives to Jesus, we should live a life that verifies the authenticity and authority of Jesus to forgive sins and transform lives. So when God seals the 144,000, the evidence of their lives will give authentic and authoritative proof of God's ability to forgive sins and transform lives. According to Revelation 7:9–10, they will be the most effective evangelists and missionaries the world has ever seen.

> [9] After this I looked and there before me was a great multitude that no one could count, from every nation, tribe, people and language, standing before the throne and in front of the Lamb. They were wearing white robes and were holding palm branches in their hands. [10] And they cried out in a loud voice:

> "Salvation belongs to our God,
> who sits on the throne,
> and to the Lamb."

Verse 9 begins with the words *"After this"*. Those two words appear seven times in Revelation, and each time they mark the movement from one vision to another. Revelation 7:1–8 captures John's vision of God withholding His wrath in order to seal and send His messengers. Verses 9–17 describe John's vision of the results of the messengers' work.

As was true of Revelation 4 & 5, John is once again caught up in a moving worship experience. Those who surrendered to Christ and died during the Tribulation are now assembled in heaven and are worshipping God. In verse 9, John says that they have come from every nation (*ethnos*, or "ethnic group"), tribe (*phule*, or "family group"), people (*laos*, or "people group"), and language (*glossa*, or "language group"). John witnesses the heavenly celebration of a worldwide revival!

In the history of great revivals, nothing compares to the revival during the Great Tribulation. You may ask, "What made the Tribulation revival greater than all the others?" I believe it's because the Jews are the messengers. When 120 Jews left the upper room and entered the streets of Jerusalem (Acts 2), within six months (Acts 6) the believers grew from 120 to 8,000. Now you have 144,000 Jews released on the world. No wonder John says the number celebrating in heaven was too great to count!

Something else to note is that every ethnic, family, people, and language group will hear the gospel during the Great Tribulation—not before. Here's why that's important. Because there are hundreds of people groups who have yet to hear of Christ, believers think, "I still have time. I still have time to ask my mom, dad, or child whether or not they have truly surrendered to Jesus. I still have time to talk with my friend at school or work. I still have time to come back to their question about Jesus, or go overseas and present Jesus to a people group that's never heard of Him." If you are waiting for every people group to hear of Jesus before you get your urgency to share Jesus, understand this: All groups will one day hear of Jesus, but according to Revelation 7, only after the church is gone. That means Jesus could come for the church at any moment. Therefore as believers, we had better take advantage of every opportunity to share Jesus before He calls us home. Right now, we are the messenger of God's absurd grace.

ABSURD GRACE!
When God Offers the Benefits of Heaven

In Matthew 20:1–16, Jesus tells the story of a landowner who hires laborers to work for him. Some are hired in the morning, others during the day, and a last group is hired right before the day's work is finished. As all the laborers assemble to be paid, the landowner says that those who were hired last should be paid first. Furthermore, they are to receive the same pay and benefits promised to those who were hired first. As you might think, those hired first complained, because they expected to be paid first and to be paid more. Yet in verses 15–16, the landowner tells them, *"'Don't I have the right to do what I want with my own money? Or are you envious because I am generous?'* [16] *So the last will be first, and the first will be last."*

When some believers read Revelation 7:9–17, they may get upset. They may not like hearing that these who rejected God prior to the rapture are now offered God's grace during the tribulation. They won't like it that those people will also receive all the benefits of heaven. However, like the landowner, God can say, "It's my grace! Whether you think it unfair or absurd, I have the right to do what I want with my grace."

Because it is God's grace, God can do with it want He wants. And what God wants is to offer all the benefits of heaven to those who surrender to Him—even if it's during the Tribulation. Look at some of the benefits they will receive.

Praise

The first benefit of heaven described in Revelation 7:9–12 is praise, pure heavenly praise.

> [9] After this I looked and there before me was a great multitude that no one could count, from every nation, tribe, people, and language, standing before the throne and in front of the Lamb. They were wearing white robes and were holding palm branches in their hands. [10] And they cried out in a loud voice:
>
> "Salvation belongs to our God,
> who sits on the throne,
> and to the Lamb."
>
> [11] All the angels were standing around the throne and around the elders and the four living creatures. They fell down on their faces before the throne and worshiped God, [12] saying:
>
> "Amen!
> Praise and glory
> and wisdom and thanks and honor
> and power and strength
> be to our God forever and ever.
> Amen!"

Verse 9 describes the Tribulation believers in heaven wearing white robes—*they are clean before God*, holding palm branches—*symbols of victory*, and they are continually crying in a loud voice—*God saved me!*

How wonderful to hear redeemed martyrs worship in heaven! Nine times in Revelation it describes them constantly crying out with a loud voice (Rev. 5:12; 6:10; 11:12, 15; 12:10; 14:7; 16:1; 19:1; 21:3) Though such worship would shock many in our churches today, Psalm 66:1 and Psalm 100:1 say that God desires it.

Furthermore, the angels are moved by the praise. Consider this: the martyrs in heaven are singing a song the angels will never know—"I'm Saved! Saved! Saved!" When the angels hear it, they are moved to sing of the greatness of God which they have always known. Bracketed between two "Amens" (which loosely means "I'm telling you the truth"), the angels add their voices and sing *"Praise and glory and wisdom and thanks, and honor and power and strength be to our God forever and ever."* And if you think that the worship in heaven is all about volume, look at the position of the martyrs and the angels in verse 11. They are on their faces before God's throne as they worship Him.

What an experience! What a benefit of God's grace! What a series of lessons to be learned about heavenly worship! Here they are in rapid succession, from Revelation 7:9–17.

- Unless you are an angel, you can't truly worship God until you've been saved.
- When the saved worship, there should be some volume to our praise.
- When the saved sincerely praise God, it prompts others to do the same.
- Volume without reverence is a concert. Reverence with volume is sincere praise.

To be offered that experience with God shows His absurd grace. To experience some degree of that while on earth is an indescribable blessing.

Protection

Another benefit from God's absurd grace is God's protection. In Revelation 7:13–17, you hear what the Tribulation believers receive while in heaven.

> [13] Then one of the elders asked me, "These in white robes—who are they, and where did they come from?"
>
> [14] I answered, "Sir, you know."
>
> And he said, "These are they who have come out of the Great Tribulation; they have washed their robes and made them white in the blood of the Lamb. [15] Therefore,
>
> "they are before the throne of God
>
> and serve him day and night in his temple;
>
> and he who sits on the throne will spread his tent over them.
>
> [16] Never again will they hunger;
>
> never again will they thirst.
>
> The sun will not beat upon them,
>
> nor any scorching heat.
>
> [17] For the Lamb at the center of the throne will be their shepherd;
>
> he will lead them to springs of living water.
>
> And God will wipe away every tear from their eyes."

Revelation frequently describes the gruesome treatment of Tribulation believers. Yet in these verses we get an idea of what they endured on earth, by how God treats them in heaven. Specifically, verse 16 says they never suffer hunger (13:17), thirst (16:4), or lack of shelter again (16:8–9). In fact, verse 15 states that the One on the throne spreads His tent over them. What a great description. The Greek word for tent means "dwelling." For some reason, John's description of the believer's experience in Revelation 7 points to Jesus' longing for Jerusalem in Luke 13:34. Looking upon the city, Jesus says, *"O Jerusalem, Jerusalem, you who kill the prophets and stone those sent to you, how often I have longed to gather your children together, as a hen gathers her chicks under her wings , but you were not willing!"* What Jesus longed for Jerusalem then, He experiences with the Tribulation believers in heaven. They are under His protection. They are under His care. And all because of God's absurd grace.

OTHER ABSURDITIES OF GOD'S GRACE

It seems absurd to think that God would withhold His wrath in order to seal and send messengers, so that those living during the Tribulation could still experience all the benefits of God's grace. Surprisingly, there are two other absurdities to mention—not on God's part, but on ours.

The Selfishness of Those who Experience It

First, on the part of believers, I think it's absurd when you consider the selfishness of us who have experienced God's grace. How selfish of us to think that those in the Tribulation don't deserve God's grace. What did we ever do to deserve God's grace? Nothing! We received His gift of grace by surrendering to Him. It had nothing to do with us, and everything to do with Him.

Furthermore, how selfish of those of us in the spiritual concentration camp who have found the way out for everyone, and yet we keep silent. We are the ones in the spiritual cancer ward who have found the cure, yet keep it to ourselves.

If our Heavenly Father offers His grace to those in the tribulation, we should never stop sharing His grace before the tribulation. It's absurd for us to live selfishly with God's grace.

The Stupidity of Those who Reject It

The last absurdity comes from unbelievers. For God to show His grace by coming as Jesus to sacrifice Himself for your sins, and for God to share His grace by sending messengers now and even during the tribulation makes it absurd stupidity for anyone to reject God's grace. You cannot say, "I didn't know." If you are reading this book, you know. You can't say, "I didn't have time." God has withheld the wrath you deserve to offer you the grace you don't. Besides, you have this moment right now.

How far God will go to offer you His grace can seem absurd. However, it's even more absurd if you reject it. Don't reject Him. Surrender your life to Jesus, and experience His grace today.

CHAPTER 10

THE EARTH IS THE LORD'S ... PHYSICALLY!

REVELATION 8

¹ The earth is the LORD's, and everything in it,

the world, and all who live in it;

² for he founded it upon the seas

and established it upon the waters.

— PSALM 24:1–2

SOME PEOPLE TAKE EXCEPTION TO the statement, "The earth is the LORD's, and everything in it." They would rather see the earth as its own entity: that's why they call the earth "Mother Earth" or "Mother Nature." They'd rather see the earth that way than see it as being owned by God. For if the earth is owned by God, everyone on earth will be accountable to God. So to avoid any acknowledgement or accountability to God, it's easier to say that the earth somehow came together on its own, instead of saying it is owned by the God who created it.

Even if a painting doesn't bear the name Rembrandt, the brush strokes and colors point to the artist. The more that science uncovers the intelligent design of the earth, the more the facts point to God as the creator. In fact, several years ago a scientist published an article entitled, "Seven Reasons Why I Believe in God." Here are some of them.

- Consider the rotation of the earth. Our globe spins on its axis at the rate of one thousand miles an hour. If it were just a hundred miles an hour, our days and nights would be ten times as long. The vegetation would freeze in the long night or it would burn in the long day, and there could be no life.

- Consider the heat of the sun. Twelve thousand degrees at surface temperature, and we're just far enough away to be blessed by that terrific heat. If the sun gave off half its radiation, we would freeze to death. If it gave off one half more, we would all be crispy critters.

- Consider the slant of the earth. (I think he said twenty-three degrees.) If it were different than that, the vapors from the oceans would ice over the continents. There could be no life.

- Consider the moon. If the moon were fifty thousand miles away rather than its present distance, twice each day giant tides would inundate every bit of land mass on this earth.

- Think of the crust of the earth. Just a little bit thicker and there could be no life because there would be no oxygen.

- Think of the thinness of the atmosphere. If our atmosphere was just a little thinner, the millions of meteors now burning themselves out in space would [pummel] this earth into oblivion.[33]

Now I am told there are several hundred facts revealing the miraculous order and design of earth.

---

33   Frank Pollard, "Our Greatest Victory," *Preaching Today*, tape no. 175.

One reason why many reject God as earth's creator and owner is because the world no longer looks like something God would have created. Ignoring the landscape, they point to the disease, death, and disorder that pervade it. Many forget, though, that the world God created has been altered by Satan's lies and our sins. Revelation 8 aptly reminds us that though the world God created may have been altered, God still owns it. He makes that clear in His efforts to restore it.

OPENING THE SEVENTH SEAL

In Revelation 5, we learned that God holds in His hand the title deed to the earth. It's been sealed with seven seals and Jesus alone can open it. Jesus opens six of the seven seals in Revelation 6 releasing the initial wave of God's wrath. Before opening the seventh seal, Jesus appoints 144,000 Jews as evangelists in Revelation 7. They announce to the world, "You can still experience God's grace in the midst of His wrath." Now in Revelation 8 Jesus opens the last seal, announcing God's ownership of the earth. Verses 1–6 describe what takes place in heaven with the opening of the last seal.

> ¹ When he opened the seventh seal, there was silence in heaven for about half an hour.

> ² And I saw the seven angels who stand before God, and to them were given seven trumpets.

> ³ Another angel, who had a golden censer, came and stood at the altar. He was given much incense to offer, with the prayers of all the saints, on the golden altar before the throne. ⁴ The smoke of the incense, together with the prayers of the saints, went up before God from the angel's hand. ⁵ Then the angel took the censer,

filled it with fire from the altar, and hurled it on the earth; and there came peals of thunder, rumblings, flashes of lightning and an earthquake.

[6] Then the seven angels who had the seven trumpets prepared to sound them.

Prior to verse 1, heaven has been filled with the majestic sounds of power and praise. John hears a voice that sounds like a trumpet in Revelation 1 and 4. In chapter 4 the living creatures praise God saying *"Holy, holy, holy is the Lord Almighty."* The twenty-four elders cry out *"Worthy is the Lamb who was slain"* in chapter 5. In chapter 6, martyred saints call out to God, *"How long, Sovereign Lord, holy and true, until you judge the inhabitants of the earth and avenge our blood?"* In chapter 7, the saved in heaven shout *"Salvation belongs to our God"* and the angels join in saying *"Amen!"* With the title deed of earth in His hand, Jesus now opens the last seal...and there is silence in heaven for thirty minutes.

A dramatic pause is a powerful tool in public speaking. It can either cause the listener to absorb what has been said, or to anticipate what he's about to hear. The thirty minutes of silence in heaven does both. It causes all in heaven to absorb all that God has promised. God promised a Messiah, and Jesus came. God promised salvation, and Jesus died and rose again. God promised a day when He would rapture His believers, release His tribulation, Jesus would return, and the earth would be restored. With the opening of the seventh seal, heaven knows—THIS IS IT!

Heaven also knows what's about to come. Earth will soon be restored, but until then, the labor pains will get worse. As shared earlier,

Jesus' statements regarding the end times in Matthew 24 describe the events that transpire with the opening of the seven seals. In Matthew 24:8, Jesus calls these tribulation experiences "the beginning of birth pains" leading up to His return.

In order for our son John Mark to be born, Loree's labor had to be induced. In some way, it was nice. A date was set so that we could make sure family was informed, his room was ready, and we could get excited about having him. We drove to the hospital early, and they started Loree on the pitocin to induce labor. By mid-morning, Loree was getting bored and frustrated. She told me, "I can't believe I'm not hurting." Then before noon, Loree gasped. Her eyes filled with excitement as her first labor pain hit and she said, "It's starting." There seemed to be silence as we waited for a second labor pain. When it came, Loree said, "Yes...it's starting." But this time her tone was more nervous than excited as she realized how the pains would have to grow before John Mark could come.

It's possible to see the silence in heaven as the excited anticipation of Christ's coming. But it's also possible that the silence of heaven could be the hush of reality, as they realize the pains that earth is about to go through before Jesus comes.

Before continuing, it's important to ask, "Where will you be when heaven is silent?" Will you be in heaven experiencing the silence with all the saints, or will you be on earth about to experience what has made them silent? Where you stand and what you experience when heaven is silent depends on whether or not you surrender your life to Jesus while living on earth. As you will see, the best place to be at that time is in heaven.

During the thirty minutes of silence, the saints see movement around God's throne. Verse 2 reads, *"And I saw the seven angels who stand before God, and to them were given seven trumpets."* Scripture identifies various ranks of angels (cherubim—Genesis 3:24; seraphim—Isaiah 6:2; archangels—1 Thessalonians 4:16, Jude 9). The Greek word for "the" classifies these seven angels as a special order of angels. Their close proximity to God makes them special. The Greek word for "stand" indicates that they have been in the presence of God for some time. It's believed that the angel Gabriel is one of the seven. When introducing himself to Zechariah in Luke 1:19, he says, *"I am Gabriel. I stand in the presence of God."* Each of the seven angels possesses a trumpet. According to Numbers 10:1–10, Israel used the trumpets to summon the people and announce times of war or special occasions. Blowing these trumpets, the angels announce both the coming of war and a special occasion.

Before one trumpet sounds, though, something else occurs. Verses 3–5 explain that another angel holds a golden censor. Exodus 30:1–10 teaches that in the tabernacle and temple the golden altar stood before the Holy of Holies—the presence of God. Incense burned there morning and night as an act of reverence to God, as well as on the Day of Atonement. At that time, priests offer prayers on behalf of the people. Here in Revelation 8, the golden censor in the hand of the angel represents the prayers of the people to God. The angel will hurl those prayers toward earth, indicating that God will soon answer them.

Some may wonder which prayers are about to be answered. For me, two come to mind. One is the prayer of the martyrs. In Revelation 6:10, their prayers rise to God from beneath the altar:

"How long, Sovereign Lord, holy and true, until you judge the inhabitants of the earth and avenge our blood?" God will soon answer their prayers and avenge their blood. Furthermore, in Matthew 6:10 we are taught to pray, *"your kingdom come, your will be done on earth as it is in heaven."* The New Testament teaches that the Kingdom of God comes to earth three ways. First, it comes within you as the spirit of God claims more sovereignty of your life (Luke 17:20–21). Second, it comes through you as you help others surrender their lives to Jesus (Luke 13:18–21). Third, it comes in time (1 Cor. 15:23–24). This is when Jesus returns and restores the earth. For all who have prayed *"your kingdom come, your will be done on earth as it is in heaven"* and have longed for Jesus' return and for the earth to be restored, those prayers are about to be answered.

Furthermore, don't miss the significance of God hurling these prayers to earth. Martyrs have prayed for God to act on their behalf for thousands of years. Believers have prayed for Christ's return for just as long. When you think God is not listening, or when you wonder if God has said "No," think again. God has neither ignored nor forgotten our prayers. If we pray according to God's will, He will answer it, and He will do so when the time is right. So don't stop praying.

When Jesus opens the seventh seal and God answers the countless prayers, those living on earth will see that the earth belongs to God. It will be evident in what He does. With each trumpet blast, God will do something to prove that the earth is His.

THE FIRST TRUMPET
The Land is Mine!

In verse 7, the first angel blows his trumpet. When he does, God proves that the land is His.

> [7] The first angel sounded his trumpet, and there came hail and fire mixed with blood, and it was hurled down upon the earth. A third of the earth was burned up, a third of the trees were burned up, and all the green grass was burned up.

Though Satan's lies and our sins have altered the order and ways of the world, God's actions reveal that the earth belongs to Him. In fact it always has, for many of the acts God performs in Revelation 8 He also did in the book of Exodus.

The first trumpet blast sounds like the seventh plague on Egypt in Exodus 9:18–26. At that time, Egypt was devastated by hail. In Revelation 8:7, the whole earth suffers the effects of hail and fire mixed with blood. As a result, a third of the earth's trees and all the green grass will be burned.

Consider the following effects from this. First, a third of the trees are gone. The Greek word for trees in this verse usually refers to "fruit trees." That means a third of the earth's produce and vegetation are gone. Also gone are all of the earth's grasses. That means livestock won't be able to graze, making less meat to eat and milk to drink. And basic science teaches that people breathe air and produce carbon dioxide. Plants consume the carbon dioxide to put oxygen in the air. Fewer plants dramatically reduces the quality of the air breathed.

This is something God can do and verse 7 says He will do it, because the land is His.

THE SECOND TRUMPET
The Seas are Mine!

Some might say, "If that happens, then earth's inhabitants will turn to the seas. Since land covers around 30% of the earth's surface and water covers around 70%, there will be plenty of food to survive." Yet, God says in verses 8–9, "The seas are mine, too!"

> [8] The second angel sounded his trumpet, and something like a huge mountain, all ablaze, was thrown into the sea. A third of the sea turned into blood, [9] a third of the living creatures in the sea died, and a third of the ships were destroyed.

Some might see this mountain ablaze as a great volcanic eruption. John was likely familiar with one. When Mount Vesuvius erupted in AD 79, it buried the city of Pompeii beneath molten lava, destroying some of the ships in the Gulf of Naples.[34]

Others assume it refers to a great meteorite striking an ocean. An article in *Time* magazine once gave a scientist's assessment of what would happen if an asteroid one mile in diameter hit the middle of the Atlantic Ocean. The impact would be equivalent to a 500 megaton blast, creating a crater on the ocean floor fifteen miles across. One thousand cubic miles of sea water would be displaced, producing waves up to 100 feet high. Earthquakes 100 times worse than ever recorded would ripple across the earth.[35]

We can only assume what this mountain ablaze might be. However, we do have a good idea of what it will do. Just as when God turned the Nile River into blood in Exodus 7:14–25, a third of the seawater will turn to blood. Furthermore, a third of the creatures living in seawater will die. Finally, a third of all ships will be destroyed.

Seafood will be reduced a third. Imagine the stench of carcasses floating in bays and washing ashore. The shipping industry will be

---

34   Hindson, *Revelation*, 102.
35   Draper, *The Unveiling*, 142. Draper credits Dr. Paul Sandorf of the Massachusetts Institute of Technology for the information.

decimated. Currently there are over 33,000 merchant ships registered; 11,000 of them would be destroyed, as would a third of all military vessels.

What a reminder that we fish, travel, and defend ourselves at the mercy of God's seas. . . for the seas are God's.

THE THIRD TRUMPET
The Rivers and Springs are Mine!

Having been raised in Oklahoma and Texas, I could hear some who live there saying, "I could still survive. As long as I have a well, stock tank, or pond, I can raise my own crops, catch my own fish, and hunt on my land." You can try, but in verses 10–11, God will remind you that the rivers and springs are His as well.

> [10] The third angel sounded his trumpet, and a great star, blazing like a torch, fell from the sky on a third of the rivers and on the springs of water- [11] the name of the star is Wormwood. A third of the waters turned bitter, and many people died from the waters that had become bitter.

Since the Greek word for "star" can refer to any celestial body other than the sun or moon, and since meteors and comets were often described as torches in Greek literature, it's likely this is a meteor or comet.

The impact of this meteor or comet will make a third of the fresh water from rivers and streams undrinkable. Thus, it's given the name "Wormwood", which means bitter. The water not only became bitter, it was deadly. Many died from drinking it.

To those thinking you can still live off the land, you might. But you will have to be careful. One-third of your fishing spots will be poisoned. It's likely that much of the game you once hunted died from drinking the water. Oh, and be careful watering your crops. Remember, a third of your irrigation water is lethal.

And, when you think it couldn't get any worse, an angel blows the fourth trumpet. Now you see that the sun, moon, and stars belong to God, too.

THE FOURTH TRUMPET
The Sun, Moon, and Stars are Mine!

I love what Albert Einstein once said: "One thing I have learned in a long life—that all our science, measured against reality, is primitive and childlike."[36] Einstein admitted that all he knew about the universe was primitive compared to what truly was. God agrees, in verse 12. God makes it clear that everything created is His.

> [12] The fourth angel sounded his trumpet, and a third of the sun was struck, a third of the moon, and a third of the stars, so that a third of them turned dark. A third of the day was without light, and also a third of the night.

Again, God did something similar to Egypt. Exodus 10:21–23 records the ninth plague. Here, God darkens the sun over Egypt for three days. Yet God's action in verse 12 is worse. The effect is not just upon Egypt, but the world. It's not just the sun, but God darkens one-third of the sun, moon and stars. And, it's not just for three days. It's believed this will last for three and a half years.

Consider the consequences of this trumpet blast. With the sun, a third of our warmth, energy, and light are gone. You could deal with it if Miami were cooler, but you wouldn't want Minnesota any colder.

---

36   Draper, *Quotations*, entry 9867.

However, Minnesota might be better than Miami. With the moon affected, the tides could be dangerously unpredictable. No matter where you live the nights will be colder and darker. Days and nights will be reversed, as there will be only eight hours of daylight and sixteen hours of darkness. You can imagine the emotional effects of living under such conditions.

If anything, the four trumpet blasts show all that we take for granted. We assume that, since the land has always been there, it will always be there. We assume since we paid someone for our land, placed a fence around it, and take care of it, that it belongs to us. But it actually belongs to God, and He can take it away at any time.

We also assume that, since the seas have always had their currents, tides, and are teeming with life, they are ours for food, travel, and business. Yet, they don't belong to us. They belong to God, and He can do with them what He likes, when He likes.

We are such an industrious generation. We feel we can plant our own crops, hunt our own game, and take a drink of water whenever we like. We forget that all these opportunities are gifts from God.

We even plan what to wear, as if we invented the seasons. We schedule when to swim and when not to swim, as if we control the tides. We schedule our lives as though we have the upper hand on the sun, moon and stars. But we don't.

We live our lives as though the earth belongs to us, but it never has. It's fair to say that by Satan's lies and our sins we have altered the ways of the world, but we have never taken ownership of it. It still belongs to God. When the four trumpets blow, all will see that the earth is His and that He is beginning to restore it.

KEY CHANGE

I once read of the Mountain Valley Cathedral, located in a remote Swiss village. Though its architecture and stained glass were striking, what truly stirred the hearts of the people were the beautiful sounds from its pipe organ. The music filled the valley, and people would travel from distant lands just to hear it.

But then something went wrong. The organ's sweet tones became sour, so no one wanted to play it or hear it. Musicians and experts from around the world did their best to fix the organ. Everyone near the village listened, pained by their efforts. But no one could fix it, so the organ sat silent.

One day, an old man came unannounced to the church and asked the sexton if he could work on the organ. After much persuasion, the sexton timidly agreed. For the next two days, the man worked on the organ, but never played it. Then, at noon on the third day, he sat at the organ and began to play. Farmers stopped in their fields and merchants closed their shops, as people were drawn to the church. The sour tones had once again become sweet.

When the man finished playing, someone asked how he was able to fix it, when all the other experts could not. The old man's eyes smiled as he said, "I'm the one who built this organ fifty years ago. I built it, and now I've restored it."[37]

God seems to be making the same statement in Revelation chapters 8 and 9. By His actions on earth, all will know that He is the one who created it, and He is now in the process of restoring it.

I wonder if, when the old man played the organ, his music called for any key changes. When you hear them, you know they are a part

---

37   Hewett, *Illustrations Unlimited*, 244–245.

of the same song, it's just that the key has changed. In Revelation chapters 8 and 9, God is playing the same song. It's entitled "The Earth Is Mine!" Yet there seems to be a clear key change in verse 13. John writes,

> [13] As I watched, I heard an eagle that was flying in midair call out in a loud voice: "Woe! Woe! Woe to the inhabitants of the earth, because of the trumpet blasts about to be sounded by the other three angels!"

The three woes are the reminder of the three trumpet blasts yet to come. It's hard to think that God can do anything more to prove that the earth is His. Yet the four trumpet blasts that have sounded have only proved that the earth is the Lord's physically—the land, seas, rivers, springs, sun, moon, and stars. The three blasts to come will now prove that the earth is the Lord's spiritually. When we read Revelation 9, we will be shocked at what God releases spiritually.

CHAPTER 11

THE EARTH IS THE LORD'S ... SPIRITUALLY!

REVELATION 9

¹ The earth is the LORD's, and everything in it,

the world, and all who live in it;

² for he founded it upon the seas

and established it upon the waters.

— Psalm 24:1–2

READING *"THE EARTH IS THE LORD'S, and everything in it,"* we naturally think of everything we see. In fact, Revelation 8 does a good job of itemizing everything seen. As we learned, the land, seas, rivers, streams, sun, moon, stars, and everything that lives on, within, or under them are God's. In short, *EVERYTHING SEEN* belongs to God.

Absorbing Revelation 9, we learn that *EVERYTHING UNSEEN* belongs to God as well. Not only does the earth belong to the Lord physically, it belongs to Him spiritually. And spiritually, unseen war wages on earth. Verse 1 refers to it.

> ¹ The fifth angel sounded his trumpet, and I saw a star that had fallen from the sky to the earth. The star was given the key to the shaft of the Abyss.

THE UNSEEN WAR

A high school student surprised me with the following question. Sincerely, she offered, "I've always been taught that there's no sin in heaven. How can we be sure? Didn't Satan sin while in heaven?" I had never been asked that before. However, I responded with a quick and confident, "Uh . . . let me get back to you."

Obviously, I never forgot the question and was confident that God's Word would reveal an answer. And it does. We can be certain there is no sin in heaven because God resolved that problem long ago.

Revelation 9:1 talks about *"a star that had fallen from the sky to earth."* In the Greek, the word "fallen" here communicates a past action with ongoing implications. The word "star" in Hebrew is Satan's name before rebelling against God. He was called Lucifer, which in Hebrew means "Morning Star." It appears only once in scripture, in Isaiah 14:12–13:

> [12] How you have fallen from heaven,
> O morning star, son of the dawn!
> You have been cast down to the earth,
> you who once laid low the nations!
>
> [13] You said in your heart,
> "I will ascend to heaven;
> I will raise my throne
> above the stars of God;
> I will sit enthroned on the mount of assembly,
> on the utmost heights of the sacred mountain."

Revelation 12 will show how Lucifer's arrogant pride made him scheme to unseat God in heaven. When his efforts were foiled, God cast him out of heaven along with a third of the angels, who had joined Lucifer's rebellion.

Having lost their fight for heaven's throne, they continue to wage an unseen war against God on earth. They fight against God for what is dearest to God—you and me! If they can't have what they want (heaven's throne), they will try to keep God from having what He wants—a meaningful relationship with us. The Apostle Paul alludes to this unseen war in Ephesians 6:11–12.

> [11] Put on the full armor of God so that you can take your stand against the devil's schemes. [12] For our struggle is not against flesh and blood, but against the rulers, against the authorities, against the powers of this dark world and against the spiritual forces of evil in the heavenly realms.

After his defeat in heaven, Lucifer's name changes to reflect his true nature. He is now called "Satan," meaning "adversary," and "Devil," which means "accuser." In this unseen war, he strives to either keep relationships from being established with God, or to keep established relationships with God from becoming meaningful. He does this by either slandering God to us (Genesis 3) or us to God (Job 1).

Ephesians 6:11–12 reminds us that Satan is good at what he does and that he doesn't do it alone. Verse 11 warns us of the *"devil's schemes."* "Schemes" is the Greek word *methodeia*, and in it you hear the English word for "method." Satan has always been a cunning, diabolical strategist, and his strategies employ the efforts of his angels. Like Satan, however, their names have been changed. No longer worthy to be called angels, they are more frequently called demons (Luke 8:26–39).

When Plato looked at the etymology of the Greek word for "demon" (*daimon*), he saw it came from an adjective meaning "knowing" or "intelligent."[38] Therefore, Satan's demons are not dumb thugs, but crafty schemers like their leader.

Furthermore, verse 12 indicates that they are organized and influential. Just as we've seen that the angels in heaven have a sense of rank and order, we see the demons do as well. It's possible that verse 12 uncovers that demonic order.

First, Paul makes it clear that he's not talking about "flesh and blood." These are unseen spiritual entities at work. Among the demons you have "rulers" (*achas*). These are the demon chiefs, the ones in charge. Then you have the "authorities" (*exousias*), the demonic doers. They have the ability to fulfill the schemes of the "rulers" and the "powers." The "powers" (*kosmokratoras*) are demons given responsibility to rule the affairs of the world. No wonder Jesus says in Matthew 24:6 that before He comes to restore the earth, *"You will hear of wars and rumors of wars."* The demon "powers" constantly stir strife among nations, people groups, and individuals. Finally, you have the all-inclusive *"spiritual forces of evil in the heavenly realms."* This either identifies a fourth order of demons, or it classifies all demons as unseen and evil.

Considering this unseen war on earth, it is natural to ask, "What is the objective of each side?" You don't go to war without an objective. John, who pens the final scenes of this war in Revelation, tells why it's taking place in John 10:10. Quoting Jesus, John writes,

> [10] "The thief comes only to steal and kill and destroy; I have come that they may have life, and have it to the full."

---

38   Merrill F. Unger, *Demons in the World Today* (Wheaton, IL: Tyndale , 1971), 25

Satan and his demons want to steal, kill, and destroy every opportunity we have for a meaningful relationship with God. God fights for us to have that opportunity and enjoy it.

It's important to hear that though Satan and his demons are organized, shrewd and strong, they are not God. Though 1 Peter 5:8 describes Satan as a roaring lion, compared to God he's still nothing more than a squeaking rabbit. The following poem says it well.

> A tiger met a lion as they sat beside a pool.
> Said the tiger to the lion, "Why are you roaring like a fool?"
>
> "That's not foolish," said the lion, with a twinkle in his eyes.
> "They call me the king of the beasts because I advertise."
>
> A rabbit heard them talking, ran on like a streak.
> He thought he would try the lion's plan, but his roar was just a squeak.
>
> A fox came to investigate and had lunch in the woods,
> And so my friend, when you advertise, you be sure you've got the goods.[39]

Though Satan and his demons are well organized and deceptive, compared to God, they just don't have the goods. Therefore, remember this. At salvation, the Bible says that the Spirit of God comes to live within you (John 14:17). Regardless of the attacks, deception, and temptations that Satan and his demons may use against you, remem-

---

39   Adrian Rogers, *The Incredible Power of Kingdom Authority* (Nashville, TN: Broadman & Holman Publishers, 2002), 115–116.

ber 1 John 4:4, *"You, dear children, are from God and have overcome them, because the one who is in you is greater than the one who is in the world."*

What if you've not surrendered your life to Jesus? God promises to help you as well. In John 16:8–11, He promises to keep on convicting you of your need for Him, in the hope that you will see your need and surrender your life to Him. Once you do that, you will find His help and strength coming from within you.

God promises to help you in one other way. He promises to limit the amount of demonic activity on earth for a while. However, He warns you not to wait too long to surrender to Him. The day will come when He will rapture His believers and release the demons He has been holding back. This happens with the fifth trumpet.

THE FIFTH TRUMPET
The Demons are Mine!

The fifth trumpet blast is unveiling the unseen war and one other truth. In Revelation 9:1–12, God says, "The demons are mine!"

> [1] The fifth angel sounded his trumpet, and I saw a star that had fallen from the sky to the earth. The star was given the key to the shaft of the Abyss. [2] When he opened the Abyss, smoke rose from it like the smoke from a gigantic furnace. The sun and sky were darkened by the smoke from the Abyss. [3] And out of the smoke locusts came down upon the earth and were given power like that of scorpions of the earth. [4] They were told not to harm the grass of the earth or any plant or tree, but only those people who did not have the seal of God on their foreheads. [5] They were not given power to kill them, but only to torture them for five months. And the agony they suffered was like that of the sting of

a scorpion when it strikes a man. ⁶ During those days men will seek death, but will not find it; they will long to die, but death will elude them.

⁷ The locusts looked like horses prepared for battle. On their heads they wore something like crowns of gold, and their faces resembled human faces. ⁸ Their hair was like women's hair, and their teeth were like lions' teeth. ⁹ They had breastplates like breastplates of iron, and the sound of their wings was like the thundering of many horses and chariots rushing into battle. ¹⁰ They had tails and stings like scorpions, and in their tails they had power to torment people for five months. ¹¹ They had as king over them the angel of the Abyss, whose name in Hebrew is Abaddon, and in Greek, Apollyon.

¹² The first woe is past; two other woes are yet to come.

As was seen in chapter 8, this experience in chapter 9 resembles one of the eight plagues in Egypt (Exodus 10:1–20), only worse. This time the whole world is affected, not just Egypt. Furthermore, the locusts attack humans, not crops. Finally, they are not insects. They are demons that John describes as locusts.

John has never seen anything like them. That is why in verses 5–10 he uses the word *"like"* eight times. He can only describe them through comparisons. But one thing stands out in his description: nothing can be done, humanly, to stop them. Only God can stop them, for the earth is His, spiritually.

These verses repeatedly remind us that everything spiritual resides under God's control. In verse 1, Satan could not release these demons without asking Jesus for the key (Rev. 1:18). Upon their release, their activity was limited by God. Verses 3–5 explain that God wouldn't allow them to hurt the foliage, only humans, and only the humans who didn't have the seal of God (Rev. 7:3–4). Furthermore, they could only sting them, not kill them, and they could only sting them for five months.

Revelation chapters 8 and 9 further assert that nothing happens on earth, physically or spiritually, without God's permission. The earth is His and everything in it.

Though God has limited the activity of these demons, what He has allowed is still hard to grasp. When the abyss opens, smoke dims the sun, a sun whose light was already darkened a third by God (Rev. 8:12). As the demon-locusts fly, the sound of their wings grinds out a constant feeling of anxiety and fear. When you read William Barclay's description of a plague of locusts invading Algiers in 1866, you get a feel for the experience.

> The noise of the millions of their wings is variously de-scribed as the dashing of waters in a mill-wheel, or the sound of a great cataract. When the millions of them settle on the ground, the sound of their eating has been described as the crackling of a prairie fire. The sound of their march is like the heavy rain falling on a distant forest.[40]

Those living in Revelation 9 will hear the demon-locusts fly and march. Though they will not hear them eat, they will feel the sting and hear the screams of those being stung. Verse 5 says they will sting like scorpions. Though not often fatal, the sting of a scorpion is listed among the most painful. Its venom causes one's veins and nervous

---

40   William Barclay, *The Revelation of John: Vol. 2* (Philadelphia: Westminster Press, 1976), 50.

system to feel as if they were on fire, and the effects last for several days.[41]

Without being stung, 200,000 people died from the 1866 Algiers invasion of locusts, Barclay said. Yet, no one will die from their stings in Revelation 9. Countless will want to die, but God won't allow their stings to bring death, *"For the earth is the LORD'S and everything in it"*—everything, physically and spiritually.

The fifth trumpet's blast announces that nothing physically or spiritually happens on earth without God's approval. Even before the fifth trumpet sounds, we need to remember that.

Our spiritual pantry may be full enough to handle one tragedy. But what if tragedies enter like unexpected guests for dinner? Do you have enough stored away to meet the need? This happened to one couple. Though they were both strong believers, one of them finally said it: "I'd just like to ask God, 'Why us!'" In an unexpected moment of strength, the other said, "Why not us?" With that simple statement, their rage became strength. Their strength became resolve, and soon their resolve became an unforgettable experience with God.

Because everything physically and spiritually belongs to God, every experience you face only comes with God's permission. Some hard experiences are of our own making, while others are allowed by God to make us what He wants us to be. Here are some wonderful lessons we would never learn if God had not allowed a temptation or hardship to take place in the lives of others.

We would have never learned from . . .

---

41   LaHaye, *Revelation*, 137.

- Paul – *"The greater my thorns, the greater God's grace."*
- Daniel – *"When God shuts the mouths of lions, He opens the heart of a nation."*
- Peter – *"Satan wants to sift you when he knows God wants to use you."*
- David – *"When hungry, hurting, confused, or scared, the Shepherd's there."*
- Job – *Stay faithful. It makes Satan mad.*
- Jesus – *There's a reason for the cup!*

As the fifth trumpet blows in Revelation 9, the people see that the demons are under God's control. And though their activity will be harsher than today, the rule remains the same: the demons can do nothing without God's permission. When the fifth trumpet blasts, all will be reminded, "The demons are mine."

THE SIXTH TRUMPET
The Conditions are Mine!

With the fifth trumpet God shows everyone that "The demons are mine." And now with the sixth trumpet, He reminds everyone that "The conditions of the earth are mine as well." You see this when reading Revelation 9:13–19.

> [13] The sixth angel sounded his trumpet, and I heard a voice coming from the horns of the golden altar that is before God. [14] It said to the sixth angel who had the trumpet, "Release the four angels who are bound at the great river Euphrates." [15] And the four angels who had been kept ready for this very hour and day and month and year were released to kill a third of mankind. [16]

The number of the mounted troops was two hundred million. I heard their number.

[17] The horses and riders I saw in my vision looked like this: Their breastplates were fiery red, dark blue, and yellow as sulfur. The heads of the horses resembled the heads of lions, and out of their mouths came fire, smoke, and sulfur. [18] A third of mankind was killed by the three plagues of fire, smoke, and sulfur that came out of their mouths. [19] The power of the horses was in their mouths and in their tails; for their tails were like snakes, having heads with which they inflict injury.

With its lips still buzzing from the blast, the sixth angel releases the four angels bound at the river Euphrates. Since the four angels are bound, they too are demons. I don't know why they were bound at this river. It could be that the Euphrates River was the cradle of all civilization (Genesis 2:14). This was where the creation, deception, and fall of humanity took place. Or they could have been bound at the Euphrates River because it borders Israel (Rev. 15:18), and God knows that's where it will all be restored.

The article "the" sets these demons aside as a select group. Verses 15–16 explain that they will lead a demon force of 200,000,000. The word translated "troops" in verse 16 is a Greek word better translated as "armies," plural. Possibly, each of these four demons will lead these armies. Unlike the demon-locusts that could only sting, these demon armies will kill one-third of mankind. Since a fourth of mankind was already killed in Revelation 6:8, this brings the Tribulation death toll to around half of the earth's population. The number of deaths is staggering, yet when you look at the conditions in which they died, the clearest way to describe it is "hell on earth."

Listen to John's description of the riders in verse 17. Their breast-plates were red like fire. They bore the color hyacinth (a dark blue or black, smoke-like color), and a sulfurous yellow, like brimstone. These are the colors and features of hell described elsewhere in Revelation (14:10; 19:20; 20:10; 21:8). Furthermore, in verses 18–19, John writes how death will come from these demons and their horses. It will come via incineration by fire, and asphyxiation by smoke and the gases given off by the sulfurous brimstone. Again, it's a taste of hell on earth.

Until this moment, any picture of hell was verbal. Jesus often called hell Gehenna. The valley of Gehenna was south of Jerusalem. There Jerusalem's trash and the bodies of criminals and others were burned. Its fires and smoke never stopped. However now, in Revelation 9:13–19, those alive during the Tribulation experience a form of hell on earth.

Occasionally, Loree and I will drive a back road and see an abandoned farmhouse. Looking at the gray weathered boards of the leaning house, I've said, "Loree, I would like to have been there the day the farmer and his family walked into that house for the first time. The smell of new paint, the sight of fresh drapes, and the excitement of children running in and out made it a great experience, I'm sure."

Going back beyond the farmhouse, wouldn't you like to have been with Adam and Eve when God's creation was new? No roads or buildings, just walking with God under a clear blue sky. With each step, seeing something so grand you would find yourself amazed at

God's work. Oh, God's work is still all around us; it's just that we sometimes take it all for granted.

I read of two friends standing at the edge of the Grand Canyon. One leaned back, sighed, and said, "I can't believe that God did all this." His friend, however, only leaned forward to spit over the edge and then said, "I can't believe I spit a mile just now." One takes it all in, while the other takes it for granted. Sadly, these two friends speak for many today. Some see all that God has created and are in awe of Him. They see each day as a gift. Others see the earth as a self-managing globe, nothing more than a cosmic accident. Yet, Revelation 9:13–19 reminds us that God says, "The conditions are mine. Everything you see, touch, and enjoy is there by my permission. And, by my permission, the day will come when all that will change."

STILL NO REPENTANCE

The last two verses of Revelation 9 explain a great deal, and yet, I'm still baffled. Look at verses 20–21:

> [20] The rest of mankind that were not killed by these plagues still did not repent of the work of their hands; they did not stop worshiping demons, and idols of gold, silver, bronze, stone and wood-idols that cannot see or hear or walk. [21] Nor did they repent of their murders, their magic arts, their sexual immorality, or their thefts.

These verses explain that though they experienced the sting of the demon-locusts and wished they had died, and though half of the earth's inhabitants ultimately did die from a hell-like experience, as a whole they still refused to repent and turn to God. It seems as if this was hard for John to believe as well, for he lists several reasons why they failed to repent.

In verse 20, they refused to repent of *the work of their hands*. John lists the demons and inanimate idols they chose to worship instead of God. They made God the way they wanted and were living their lives the way they wanted. In spite of all they were experiencing, they saw no need to change.

In verse 21, they refused to repent of their *murders and magic arts*. The Greek word for *magic arts* is translated elsewhere as "sorcery." In English it becomes our words for "pharmacy" and "pharmaceuticals." They refused to run from their drugs and run to God. However, it's fair to add any other addiction you like. Though it must have been painful to watch, they still chose their addictions over God.

Finally, they wouldn't repent of their *sexual immorality* or *thefts,* either.

Here's a sobering thought. The same reasons the masses fail to turn to God during the Tribulation are the same reasons the masses refuse to surrender to God today. Are these your reasons? Do you refuse to turn to God because you are

> ...satisfied with the god you have created and the life you have made?
>
> ...addicted to something or someone else?
>
> ...consumed with ungodly sexual passions and practices?
>
> ...unwilling to give up what you want, for what God wants for you?

Here's another sobering thought. What is described in Revelation 9 is not something that might happen: it's something that will happen. The numbers are exact. John was given the number of 200,000,000 for the demon armies. One-third of the earth will die. The times are precise. In Revelation 9:15, God tells John that He knows the exact year, month, day, and hour this will take place.

I said that John explains a great deal in verses 20–21, and yet there's something I still don't understand. Having heard what you've heard, and now knowing what you know, I still don't understand why you refuse to surrender your life to God. This is not something about which you can say, "I'll do it later." Later may only make your heart harder. The time to turn is now!

CHAPTER 12

SOMETHING EXTRA FOR THE EXTRA-STUBBORN

REVELATION 10

MOST EVERYONE HAS HAD THE embarrassing experience of pushing on the front door of a store, only to realize it won't open unless you pull it. But it shouldn't take long to figure out the problem—unless you're stubborn. An extremely stubborn person might even think they can change the way the door swings, if they just keep pushing.

That's the way I picture those mentioned in Revelation 9:20–21. Stubbornly, they refuse to surrender their lives to Jesus. Therefore when God raptures the church, they are left behind to face God's wrath. In Revelation 6, six of the seven seals of God's wrath are opened and the people endure deception, war, famine, and death. Yet instead of turning to God, they run to hide from Him (Rev. 6:15–17). In chapters 8 and 9, the seventh seal is opened and God's wrath grows, as seven angels blow seven trumpets. With each trumpet blast, those left behind experience the physical and spiritual wrath of God. By the end of chapter 9 around half of the world's inhabitants have died and yet, out of stubbornness, verses 20–21 say they still refuse to repent.

> ²⁰ The rest of mankind that were not killed by these plagues still did not repent of the work of their hands; they did not stop

worshiping demons, and idols of gold, silver, bronze, stone and wood—idols that cannot see or hear or walk. [21] Nor did they repent of their murders, their magic arts, their sexual immorality, or their thefts.

There are those people in life who are stubborn, and then there are those, like these in Revelation 9, that are extra stubborn.

You may have a family member or friend who is extra stubborn—not in all areas of life, just spiritually. You've tried talking to them, but they politely or rudely refused to listen. When they experienced an accident or illness, you thought surely this would get their attention, but it didn't. When their child was born, you believed it would soften their heart toward God—but, nothing. They want God and spiritual matters on their terms. Though the door to God will swing only one way, they keep pushing instead of pulling, wanting to live life on their terms. They are extra stubborn.

How do you handle that friend or family member who is extra stubborn to God? According to Revelation 10, you have to do something extra for the extra-stubborn. That's what God did.

God has already extended His grace to the stubborn. In Revelation 7, God commissioned 144,000 Jews to preach God's grace to those left behind. Now God's wrath reaches its greatest intensity as it moves from the blasts of seven trumpets to the out-pouring of seven bowls. As before, God extends His grace to the stubborn before He increases His wrath. In chapter 10, God does something extra for the extra-stubborn. He gives them an extra picture, an extra promise, and an extra message—three things you may want to do for the extra-stubborn person in your life.

AN EXTRA PICTURE

In Revelation 10:1–4, God gives an extra picture for the extra-stubborn.

> [1] Then I saw another mighty angel coming down from heaven.
> He was robed in a cloud, with a rainbow above his head; his face
> was like the sun, and his legs were like fiery pillars. [2] He was
> holding a little scroll, which lay open in his hand. He planted his
> right foot on the sea and his left foot on the land, [3] and he gave a
> loud shout like the roar of a lion. When he shouted, the voices of
> the seven thunders spoke. [4] And when the seven thunders spoke, I
> was about to write; but I heard a voice from heaven say, "Seal up
> what the seven thunders have said and do not write it down."

Remember, when John says "I saw" in Revelation, he's announcing a new vision. The focal point of this new vision is *another mighty angel.*" There are over sixty references to angels in Revelation, and as we have discussed, God has given them rank and order. This angel falls in the same rank as the one mentioned in Revelation 5:2.

Because the description of this angel is similar to John's description of Jesus in Revelation 1, some believe it is Jesus. One particular word, however, distinguished this angel from Jesus. It's the word *"another."* In the Greek it means "another of the same kind." This is another angel, not another representation of Jesus. However, John's description of this angel does give an extra picture of an important quality about Jesus—His impressive and unchanging nature. You see this when you look at each descriptor:

Robed in a cloud	God's presence and authority are associated with clouds throughout the Bible (Ex. 16:10; 19:9; 24:15; 34:5)	Authority of God's judgment
Rainbow above His head	Reminder of God's presence (Rev. 4:3) and His earthly judgment (Gen. 9:12–19)	History of God's judgment
Face like the sun	Like the holiness of Jesus as described in Revelation 1:16	Holiness of God's judgment
Legs like fiery pillars	Representing the firm and unbending justice of God throughout the earth (Rev. 1:14)	Jurisdiction of God's judgment
Roar of a lion	Both the roar of a lion and the sound of seven thunders have been the sounds of God's judgment (Jer. 25:30; Joel 3:14–16)	Intimidation of God's judgment

The thunderous statement and the picture given were intense, but John was told not to write it. He had already written enough to provide a compelling picture of God's unchanging nature and justice.

Though the spiritually stubborn would love for God to change His ways and reverse the hinges on His door to swing the way they want, in verses 1–4 God puts His foot down. He says, "I've never changed, and I'm not about to change now."

It's remarkable how much people will change when they realize the one in authority won't change. Before he retired from the Oklahoma Highway Patrol, my brother-in-law let me occasionally ride with him. From the passenger seat, I saw the numbers on his radar flashing the speeds of each driver. It surprised me that all the drivers were driving the speed limit. "When I'm in my car," I thought, "people drive crazy." Then it hit me: "I'm not in my car. I'm in a patrol car. No wonder they're obeying the law."

When drivers see a patrol car, they picture authority. They know the law will not change for them, therefore they change to obey the law. However, some among the extra-stubborn refuse to change, because they feel they are in authority. Maybe you are a self-made success story, or have come from family that's a self-made success story. Because your shrewd, hard decisions have paid off, others seek your advice. Your good family decisions have made your family life good as well. No wonder that, when it comes to surrendering your life to God, you're extra stubborn. When you're successful, it's hard to surrender any authority to God. However, that's why God gives you so many pictures of His authority. He provides multiple reminders of His ultimate authority.

For example, God is the ultimate authority when it comes to the law of the land, for Romans 13 says that He establishes and allows governments to rule. According to Romans 1, He's also the ultimate authority when it comes to nature. Just try to defy the law of gravity without a plane or parachute, and you'll see who's in charge. God is also the ultimate authority when it comes to life. No matter how many vitamins you take or how many parts of your body are cryogenically frozen, you can't defy death. Genesis 3:19 says the only one to defy death is Jesus, and the only reason He could do it is because He's the ultimate authority.

I guess that's why God gave this vision to John. The extra-stubborn need an extra picture that He remains the final authority. No matter how successful you become or how much clout you carry, your determination will never be strong enough to change God or His ways. No matter how long you pull on a door that must be pushed, the door won't open. God's authority and judgment will not change for you. You will have to change for God.

AN EXTRA PROMISE

Not all of the extra-stubborn have authority issues. Some stay extra stubborn because of a lack of trust. It could be due to your wits or because you've been hurt, but you refuse to trust anyone other than yourself—not even God. So for you, God provides an extra promise in Revelation 10:5–7.

> [5] Then the angel I had seen standing on the sea and on the land raised his right hand to heaven. [6] And he swore by him who lives forever and ever, who created the heavens and all that is in them, the earth and all that is in it, and the sea and all that is in it, and said, "There will be no more delay! [7] But in the days when the seventh angel is about to sound his trumpet, the mystery of God will be accomplished, just as he announced to his servants the prophets."

Decades ago when our reverence for God and His Word was higher, witnesses in a court of law went through a common exercise. Before taking the stand, they placed their left hand on the Bible, raised their right hand and promised to tell the truth, "so help me God." Making that vow before speaking gave weight to the truthfulness of their words.

The angel's vow in verses 5–7 surpasses any made in a court of law. The same practice appears in Deuteronomy 32:40–42 and Daniel 12:5–7. There, hands are raised to heaven and vows are made as though God endorses what's being said. Yet when the angel announces God's endorsement, he describes God the same way the twenty-four elders did in Revelation 4:11. This is not the vow of someone distant from God. It comes from an angel who's part of the inner circle with God. Therefore, you can trust what he says is true. You can trust his promise.

Then what promise has God's support? In verses 6 and 7, the angel says, *"There will be no more delay."* The seventh angel will blow his trumpet and the mysteries of God will be accomplished, just as the prophets foretold. The martyred saints, I'm sure, cheered hearing this. They had asked God in Revelation 6:10, *"How long…until you judge the inhabitants of the earth and avenge our blood?"* In Revelation 8:3–5 they have been praying for this day, and now God announces no more delay. As the saints celebrate in heaven, the extra-stubborn on earth say, "I'll believe it when I see it."

The extra-stubborn attest, "Preachers since the first century have been saying Jesus is coming soon." I have a book in my library titled *88 Reasons why Jesus is Coming in 1988*. Obviously, it didn't happen.

It did, however, add to an ever-growing list of reasons why they shouldn't believe us when we say Jesus is coming.

We believers keep trying to predict when God will fulfill His promise, instead of trusting Him to do so and praising Him for it. When we spend more time predicting than praising, we miss seeing God's promises fulfilled. That happened to the first century Jews as they watched for the coming Messiah.

Conservatively-speaking, there are 125 Old Testament prophesies that were fulfilled in the birth, life, death, and resurrection of Jesus.[42] Amazingly, these 125 promises of God were made by thirteen different individuals over the span of a thousand years. These promises were being fulfilled before the eyes of those living in the first century, and yet only a few of those people realized it. However, just because so many missed seeing God's promises fulfilled shouldn't take away from the truth that God fulfilled them. He kept His promises.

Sadly, the extra-stubborn focus all their attention on those who often get God's promises wrong, instead of focusing on the God who fulfills every promise He's made. Therefore, when you talk with the extra-stubborn, emphasize the fact that God keeps His promises.

For me, it helps to use Zig Ziglar's approach, and point to American football. Zig Ziglar would tell the extra-stubborn,

> What would you say if a quarterback, who was just drafted, told the press that for the first ten years of his career he'd play as a back-up quarterback, and would throw only twelve to thirteen passes a season? You'd probably say, "Doesn't sound like much of a career." Yet the quarterback goes on to say that every time he's

---

42   Tim LaHaye, ed., *The Tim LaHaye Prophecy Bible* (Chattanooga, TN: AMG, 2001), 1547–1551.

put into the game to throw a pass, it will be completed. Now you'd say, "The guy's crazy."

Well, in his first season, this quarterback completed all twelve passes in ten different games, and you're thinking, "He had a good season." What if, for the next five seasons, he averaged throwing twelve to thirteen passes a season, without a single incompletion. You'd probably say, "Why isn't he starting?" After ten years, he's now done what he said he would do. He's thrown 125 passes without an incompletion.

Remembering what the quarterback said ten years ago, the press now surrounds him and asks, "What do you predict for the remainder of your career?" He tells them, "I don't know how many more seasons I'll last or how many more games I will play, but this I know. I'm going to throw another 329 passes without an incompletion."

Having spent ten seasons completing every pass he threw, how confident would you be that the next time he enters a game to throw a ball it will be completed?

Over the span of 1,000 years, God made well over 125 promises regarding the first coming of Jesus Christ. Regarding the second coming of Jesus, it's conservative to say that God made 329 promises.[43] Realizing God's flawless record at keeping His promises, you can be sure that He will not miss one. If God promises it, you can be confident He will fulfill it.

---

43   Ibid, 1576–1599.

Thus, God provides an extra promise to the extra-stubborn. In Revelation 10:5–7, He promises them that there will be no more delay. The wrath He has promised is imminent. His promised second coming of Jesus now takes place. That which has been a mystery to so many for so long will unfold before their eyes.

By giving the extra-stubborn an extra promise, God says, "I have never broken a promise yet, and I won't start now. This is your last chance to trust me."

AN EXTRA EFFORT

Thus far, the extra-stubborn have been those who find it hard to trust authority. But not all of the extra-stubborn are that way. Some of the extra-stubborn simply find it hard to see life any other way. According to John 12:40 and 2 Corinthians 4:4, Satan has blinded them to their need for Jesus.

That seems hard to fathom, considering all they've seen to this point. Thus far in the book of Revelation they've seen:

- The deception of the Antichrist that leads to war (6:2–4)
- War that leads to famine (6:5–6)
- War and famine that lead to death (6:7–8)
- A black sun, a blood-red moon, and world leaders running to hide (6:12–17)
- Hail mixed with fire that burns a third of the world's foliage and fruit (8:7)
- A third of the seas turn to blood, killing a third of the sea life (8:8–9)
- A third of all spring water becomes poisonous, killing many (8:10–11)
- A third of the sun, moon, and stars becoming dark (8:12)

- Ungodly insects whose sting is worse than scorpions (9:3–5)
- An army of 200,000,000 killing one-third of earth's inhabitants (9:13–19)

Looking back, Revelation 9:20–21 records that even though the people saw all of this, they still failed to repent and surrender to God. How is that possible? Well, it's possible if you've never seen life any other way. Wearing blinders all your life makes it hard to see God and your need for Him. That's why in John's vision, God underscores the need for an extra effort for the extra-stubborn in Revelation 10:8–11.

> [8] Then the voice that I had heard from heaven spoke to me once more: "Go, take the scroll that lies open in the hand of the angel who is standing on the sea and on the land."
>
> [9] So I went to the angel and asked him to give me the little scroll. He said to me, "Take it and eat it. It will turn your stomach sour, but in your mouth it will be as sweet as honey." [10] I took the little scroll from the angel's hand and ate it. It tasted as sweet as honey in my mouth, but when I had eaten it, my stomach turned sour. [11] Then I was told, "You must prophesy again about many peoples, nations, languages, and kings."

In order to understand the extra effort needed for those blinded to their need for God, you need to grasp the details of these verses.

A voice tells John to take the little scroll from the hand of the angel. Some might confuse this scroll with the title deed of earth mentioned in Revelation 5, but it's not. Only Jesus was worthy to take that scroll of the title deed from God's hand. John reaches for a scroll from an angel. Furthermore, the Greek word used for this scroll is a diminutive form of the one used in Revelation 5. It's also called "little." The only place in the Bible that you will find this type of scroll is in Revelation 10.

If this scroll is not the title deed mentioned in chapter 5, what is it? I believe it represents the Word of God. I gain this conviction seeing John's experience with the scroll. In verses 9–11, the Voice orders John to eat the scroll. It will be sweet as honey in his mouth, but it will make his stomach bitter.

God never intended His Word to be a book for good reading. He meant it to be food for life. Just as food becomes a part of your life physically, God's Word does so spiritually. Furthermore, its message is bitter-sweet.

None of us wants to hear that we have sinned and fallen short of the glory of God (Rom. 3:23). Neither do we want to hear that we can't live good enough lives to earn our way into heaven (Eph. 2:8–9). And we especially don't want to hear that unless we surrender our life to Jesus, we will spend eternity in hell (Luke 13:23–30). That's the bitter truth that must be shared. However, don't forget the sweet.

The sweet message on our tongue says that, though the wages of sin is death, the gift of God is eternal life in Jesus Christ our Lord (Rom. 6:23). Did you hear that? God knows we can't earn our way into heaven. That's why He offers it as a gift (Eph. 2:8–9). And God's gift comes with His promise that, if we surrender all to Him, we will spend eternity in heaven with Him (John 3:16).

There's one other reason why I believe the little scroll is God's Word. What John is told to do with His scroll is the same charge we are given with God's Word. John is charged in verse 11, *"Then I was told, 'You must prophesy again about many peoples, nations, languages, and kings.'"* In Acts 1:8, we are told, *"But you will receive power when the Holy Spirit comes on you; and you will be my witnesses in Jerusalem, and in all Judea and Samaria, and to the ends of the earth."*

Writing this chapter, two stories came to mind—Jesus' and mine. I thought of Jesus on the cross. His face is probably unrecognizable from the blows He's received. His body is matted with bloody mud as the dust from the crowd became pasted on His open wounds. The sounds around Him were a mix of laughter and anger, both at His expense. Somehow, in the midst of His pain, fatigue, and misery, Jesus overhears the thieves crucified beside Him. One wants Jesus to rescue him first, and then he might believe. The other says to Jesus, "Lord, remember me when you come into your kingdom."

The lives of both thieves had been shaped one decision at a time. Their view of themselves, others, and life in general had been forged by decisions that led to actions, and actions that led to decisions. Suddenly, without realizing it, they were blindly living life in a rut, never realizing their lives could be different. Now with Jesus between them, one stays blind, but the other finally sees the truth and opens up to Jesus. I love what Jesus says. He tells the thief, "Today, you will be with me in paradise." Bloodied, belittled, and hurting, Jesus finds enough within himself to offer one extra effort for the thief beside Him.

As I thought of Jesus' story, I considered mine. I wrote on a piece of paper the names of individuals I had considered extra stubborn, but who I later saw surrender their lives to Jesus Christ. Their ages ranged from fifteen to seventy-four. Some wanted nothing to do with church, while others had attended church for years. Each of the names I wrote had three things in common. First, they were extra stubborn. They may have each been that way for different reasons, but make no mistake, they were extra stubborn about surrendering to Jesus. Second, each of them required extra effort, and not just by me. I learned that others had prayed for them and talked with them. Finally, each person whose name I wrote did eventually surrender to Jesus, even though there were times I wondered if they ever would.

I share this not to pat myself on the back, but actually to kick myself. In comparing my story to Jesus', I began to wonder how many opportunities God had given me to give an extra effort, but I was too tired, too busy, too scared, or just too plain frustrated from all the times others had rejected my efforts. How many times had I failed to give the extra effort, because I thought an extra-stubborn friend or family member was too stubborn to change?

If Jesus could give one more effort before His last breath, surely I could make an extra effort. I could offer an extra picture of God's authority, reminding my stubborn friend that God is not going to change His ways to fit theirs. I could share an extra promise of God to my friend who finds it hard to trust. If he could finally grasp the volume of promises that God has made and kept, maybe he could finally trust God with his life. And when I'm tired of praying, tired of caring, tired of sharing with my extra-stubborn friend, maybe I can still find that extra effort needed to help open their eyes to their need and God's love.

TWO RULES

Whenever I have the urge to give up on an extra-stubborn person, I remember the story of George Mueller. Born in Prussia in 1805, Mueller lived to be 92 years old. Most of his life was lived in England, where he served as a pastor and built orphanages that served over

10,000 orphans. After turning seventy, Mueller began a career as a travelling evangelist. Without the availability of an airplane, he traveled over 200,000 miles and preached in nearly forty countries. In my opinion, the reason for Mueller's remarkable accomplishments was his prayer-life. From his prayers we learn two important rules regarding our extra effort with the extra-stubborn.

Mueller recorded 50,000 answers to prayer. Remarkably, 30,000 of those answers were individuals who he prayed would surrender to Jesus. Five of those 30,000 were dear friends—friends who were extra stubborn. Mueller recorded that it took eighteen months of praying before the first friend became a Christian. It then took five years of prayer for the second, and twelve and a half years for the third. The remaining two friends were the most stubborn. After praying for them for fifty years, Mueller believed that both would surrender at any moment. Yet after continuing to pray for them for another twenty years, the fourth friend finally surrendered to Christ shortly before Mueller's death, and the fifth one year after Mueller's passing.

Because of his extra effort with his extra-stubborn friends, Mueller inspires us to remember two rules when dealing with the extra-stubborn in our lives.

RULE #1:
DON'T GIVE UP ON THEM UNTIL GOD SAYS SO!

I realize that Jesus instructs His disciples in Matthew 10:11–16 to shake the dust off their feet and move on, if a home does not receive them or their message. Tragically, many shake the dust off to move on before Jesus has given His approval. We are far quicker to give up on our stubborn friends than is Jesus. Therefore, don't give up on them until you have a firm conviction from God to move on. Besides, if it came to whether you would spend eternity in heaven or hell, you wouldn't want a friend or family member to give up on you.

RULE #2:
DON'T FOCUS ON THEM ALONE WHEN THERE ARE SO MANY MORE TO BE SAVED!

What I love about Mueller's example is that while he never gave up on his stubborn friends, he also never stopped looking for others who needed to surrender to Christ. If he had remained focused only on his five stubborn friends, he would have missed seeing 30,000 others surrender to Jesus. Though the extra-stubborn friend or family member is an important part of your world, there are many more who need Jesus. Therefore, don't let the extra-stubborn of your life blind you to how God wants to use you to help others throughout the world surrender to Him.

CHAPTER 13

THE PLAN WORKS
... IF YOU WORK THE PLAN
REVELATION 11:1-14

BY REVELATION 11, THOSE LIVING on earth have experienced earthquakes, wars, famine, hail and meteor showers, poisonous insects, poisonous water, and more. Surprisingly, many still living have yet to express any form of repentance—that is, until Revelation 11:13. It records the first act of repentance in the book of Revelation.

Because it took so long, you wonder, "What did God finally do to get them to repent?" Since I've not encountered hearts as hard as those in the tribulation, you'd think He did something never done before to get them to repent. But He didn't. He stayed with the same plan He employed throughout scripture. God used witnesses.

One of the reasons it's difficult for many to trust God's plan is because we seldom work it. As believers we would rather do anything and everything except witness. We would rather help in the nursery, teach children, go to youth camp, usher at church, sing in the choir, serve on a committee, lead a Bible study group, or even preach a sermon—anything but witness.

So when churches want to see more people surrender to Christ, we look for the newest and latest program. We bring in muscle teams, monster truck rallies, comedians, and special speakers who share how to surrender to Jesus. They do their part and we do ours. We put out flyers, host pizza rallies, set up chairs, and pass out programs. We feel good about our part because we feel that through our participation someone may surrender to Jesus. And no doubt, because of the effort of a group, some do come to Jesus. The problem with our plan, however, is that it is not as effective as God's.

It's revealing to look at the number of church members compared to the number of those being baptized. In the church I pastor, it takes sixty members to see one person saved. That's what happens when you try to reach people by programs.

Acts 2–6 describes what happens when believers work God's plan (every believer witnessing) instead of doing programs. Six months transpire between Acts chapters 2 and 6. In that time 120 witnesses grow to 8,000. At our current rate of doing evangelism by programs, it would take my church around 150 years to do what the early believers did in just six months.

Our programs are far less effective than God's plan. The fact that Revelation 11 shows God utilizing His plan, even in the last days, should compel us to get back to working God's plan, because God's plan works. Every believer is to be a witness. And when you look at the impact of God's two witnesses in Revelation 11, you see what makes God's plan so effective. Furthermore, their efforts reveal six timeless qualities that should make every believer more effective as a witness for God.

THE TWO WITNESSES

As in Revelation 11:2–3, this chapter covers the first 3½ years of the seven years of tribulation. The rapture of believers has occurred, and those remaining begin to experience God's wrath. In chapters 7, 10, and now 11 we see that even in His wrath, God offers grace. Two significant voices of God's grace during the first half of the Tribulation period are God's two witnesses. Revelation 11:1–6 introduces them to us:

> [1] I was given a reed like a measuring rod and was told, "Go and measure the temple of God and the altar, and count the worshipers there. [2] But exclude the outer court; do not measure it, because it has been given to the Gentiles. They will trample on the holy city for 42 months. [3] And I will give power to my two witnesses, and they will prophesy for 1,260 days, clothed in sackcloth." [4] These are the two olive trees and the two lampstands that stand before the Lord of the earth. [5] If anyone tries to harm them, fire comes from their mouths and devours their enemies. This is how anyone who wants to harm them must die. [6] These men have power to shut up the sky so that it will not rain during the time they are prophesying; and they have power to turn the waters into blood and to strike the earth with every kind of plague as often as they want.

Their Focus, Identity, and Impact

According to verses 1–2, the two witnesses focus their attention solely on the Jews. When John is told to measure the temple of God and the altar and to count the worshippers, the numbers aren't recorded. In Revelation 21, John takes a golden measuring rod and measures the Holy City of God. In that chapter, he provides the dimensions and a description of heaven. However, John's task of measuring the temple of God in chapter 11 is different. It has nothing to do with us as viewers. With these two measurements, God wants us to know the temple is His and so are the Jews.

In verse 2, John measures the areas of the temple for Jews alone (not the court of the Gentiles). John does this to reveal that the two witnesses will not focus on the Gentiles but on preaching God's grace to the Jews. They do this to fulfill God's promises in Romans 11:25–27 and Zechariah 12:1–14 that, in the end times, all of Israel will be saved. Yet, I believe that not only Israel will be saved, because Revelation 7:9 states that individuals *"from every nation, tribe, people and language"* will be saved as well.

What an important lesson for us. Even though we may be focused on sharing Jesus with a dear friend or loved one, others watch and overhear our conversations. Throughout history, countless people have surrendered to Jesus by overhearing a witness talking with someone else.

Many people wonder, "Who are the two witnesses in Revelation 11?" Some say they are the priest Joshua and the prince Zerubbabel. In Zechariah 4:2–6, this priest and prince reformed Israel, and were referred to as a lampstand and two olive trees. The early Church Fathers such as Tertullian, Irenaeus, and Hippolytus believed the two witnesses were Enoch and Elijah, for they were two men who never experienced death while on earth. More recently, however, convictions lean toward the two witnesses being Moses and Elijah. Here's why:

- The two witnesses will perform miracles similar to Moses and Elijah. (Exodus 7–11; 1 Kings 17:1; 2 Kings 1:10,12)

- Jewish tradition expected Moses and Elijah to return. (Deuteronomy 18:15, 18; Malachi 4:5; John 1:21; 6:14; 7:40)

- Both Moses and Elijah appeared at Jesus' transfiguration. (Matt. 17:3 – perhaps representing the Law and the Prophets)

- Both Moses and Elijah left the earth in unusual ways. (Moses body was supernaturally buried – Deuteronomy 34:5–6 and Elijah left the earth on a fiery chariot – 2 Kings 2:11–12)[44]

Who these witnesses are, however, is not as important as the impact of their lives. They were seen as the cause of famines, turning water into blood, and other plagues. They did this not to draw attention to themselves but to their message. Throughout their 3½ years, they never stopped prophesying.

Their Death, Resurrection, and Impact

Consider this. If people get upset when you mention Jesus today, the reaction will be far worse during the tribulation. It was doubtless the constant prophesying of these two witnesses that led to their deaths. What the world didn't know, though, was that their death was all part of God's plan . . . as was their resurrection. Verses 7–14 describe the impact of these events.

> [7] Now when they have finished their testimony, the beast that comes up from the Abyss will attack them, and overpower and kill them. [8] Their bodies will lie in the street of the great city, which is figuratively called Sodom and Egypt, where also their

---

44   This comes from a more detailed explanation found in John MacArthur, *Because the Time is Near* (Chicago: Moody, 2007), 183.

Lord was crucified. [9] For three and a half days men from every people, tribe, language, and nation will gaze on their bodies and refuse them burial. [10] The inhabitants of the earth will gloat over them and will celebrate by sending each other gifts, because these two prophets had tormented those who live on the earth.

[11] But after the three and a half days, a breath of life from God entered them, and they stood on their feet, and terror struck those who saw them. [12] Then they heard a loud voice from heaven saying to them, "Come up here." And they went up to heaven in a cloud, while their enemies looked on.

[13] At that very hour there was a severe earthquake, and a tenth of the city collapsed. Seven thousand people were killed in the earthquake, and the survivors were terrified and gave glory to the God of heaven.

[14] The second woe has passed; the third woe is coming soon.

Verse 7 records the first of 36 references in Revelation to the Antichrist as "The Beast." It's important to recall that Daniel 9:27 foretells of the Antichrist making a seven-year agreement with Israel and others. Halfway through this time, though, he breaks his agreement, thus revealing his true nature (2 Thessalonians 2:8–12). When the Antichrist kills God's two witnesses, it marks the turning point in his leadership and raises the intensity of his persecution of believers.

It is sobering that verses 8–9 describe an experience that could happen today. The bodies of the two witnesses lie dead in the streets of Jerusalem for three and a half days, and the entire world sees it. When I was a boy, that couldn't have happened, as the technology wasn't in place. But today, any event in the world can be captured at any moment and broadcast worldwide. Jesus could come and the Tribulation period could begin today.

John uses evil colors to paint the world's reaction to the execution of God's witnesses. Author Warren Wiersbe aptly calls the world's reaction in verse 10 a "Satanic Christmas." People are exchanging gifts over the deaths of the two witnesses.[45] But their celebration is short-lived. After laying dead in the streets for three and a half days, God breathes life into His two witnesses. He raises them to life, calls them home to heaven, and the world hears it and sees it all.

Residents of Jerusalem are the first to repent. Verse 13 says that *"they gave glory to God in heaven."* Four other times in Revelation this expression marks an act of repentance (Rev. 4:9; 14:7; 16:9; 19:7). Therefore, finally, after three and a half years of wars, famines, and plagues, we see the first expression of repentance by anyone on earth—and it took the lives of two witnesses to make it happen.

Neither One was "Superman"

In Revelation, we've read of living creatures and angels in various ranks and order. All of them possess supernatural abilities. Therefore some would assume these two witnesses were super-human as well—like "Superman."

Years ago I heard Paul Harvey's radio program "The Rest of the Story." He talked of two cartoonists named Joe and Jerry. It was 1938 and Hitler was beginning his tyrannical move to annihilate the Jews. Joe and Jerry, along with DC Comics, created Superman that year. In many of the comic books, Superman's enemies were Nazis.

---

45   Wiersbe, *Be Victorious*, 91.

What many didn't know was that Joe Shuster and Jerry Siegel were Jewish. Thus, the discussion for years has been the similarities between Superman and Moses. Superman came from a different planet, while Moses in Egypt came from a different culture. Superman was discovered as baby and raised by Jonathan and Martha Kent, while Moses was discovered and raised by Pharaoh's daughter. Both Moses and Superman saved nations from oppression.

The influence of Moses on Superman is still being debated, as is whether Moses is one of the two witnesses. However, one issue can be settled right now. The two witnesses are not superhuman like the angels, living creatures, or Superman: they are human just like you and me. The only reason they will be able to perform these supernatural acts is because they are acting on behalf of God. Everything they do as witnesses in the end times we have the potential to do in our time—not because of who we are and what we can do, but because of who God is and all that God can do. We are to be like these witnesses.

SEVEN TIMELESS QUALITIES OF GOD'S WITNESSES

Looking closely at the words used to describe these two witnesses and then comparing them to the other witnesses in scripture, seven timeless qualities emerge. The degree to which you embody these qualities determines the level of God's extraordinary activity in and through your life.

#1 – They are Sent with Authority

Verse 3 opens with the phrase, *"And I will give power to my two witnesses."* Translations differ on whether to use the word "power" or "authority" here. But I found that the American Standard Version doesn't use either word. According to the Greek manuscripts, the American Standard Version is literally correct. Neither the word "power" nor "authority" appears in this statement; translators inserted one or the other for clarity. For so many translations to do so, there must have been a good reason, and there was.

In verse 6, you find the word "power" used twice. Thus, the translator must have felt that it also fit the statement in verse 3. Then why have some translations used the word "authority"? It's because the Greek word used twice in verse 6 is *exousian*. It comes from the word *exousia* which means "authority in legitimate hands." It's the same word Jesus used in Matthew 28:18–19 when He tells His followers, *"All authority in heaven and on earth has been given to me. Therefore go and make disciples of all nations."* Because Jesus alone is the sole and legitimate authority in heaven and on earth, He commissions His followers to go and act on His behalf. The two witnesses do that in Revelation 11, and the world takes notice.

A good picture of those who act and speak with legitimate authority are police officers. When they tell a criminal to stop running or a suspect to open the door, they tell them to do so "in the name of the law." Officers understand that without the law their authority is no different than anyone else. But because of the law, they have the legitimate authority to act and speak.

As an individual, your opinion and beliefs are (possibly) no more legitimate than anyone else's. But as a believer in Jesus Christ, you should live, speak, and act differently, for you are under the highest authority. You should live, act, and speak with confidence because you do so in the name of Jesus Christ—the true and legitimate authority in heaven and on earth.

#2 – They Deliver God's Message

Verse 3 adds, *"And I will give power to my two witnesses, and they will prophesy for 1,260 days."* When most hear the word "prophesy," they think of someone foretelling the future. But that's not the purest meaning of the word. The role of the Old Testament prophet was to "speak forth" the message of God. Though some of the messages had future implications, the prophets were to speak forth whatever message God gave them.

Think for a moment how valuable your role is as a courier of God's message. Think of your value to the recipient. If you are carrying the message of a prisoner's pardon, the prisoner wants you to deliver it as soon as possible! If you are carrying the message of a hospice patient's cure, they don't want you to stop for coffee on the way. As God's witness, you carry news that will set people free from the guilt of their sin. You carry with you the lone message that gives life.

As God's messenger, you are important to the recipient, but you are also important to the sender. God has entrusted you with that which is important to Him—the costly message of salvation and life. The message you carry came at a high price. God sacrificed His only Son to create the message you carry. It's precious to God. We usually keep items that are valuable and precious under lock and key, but the price God paid for the message we carry will be wasted if we don't deliver it.

#3 — God Numbers Their Days

We also see in verse 3 how John was told that God's two witnesses would testify for 1,260 days. We would calculate that to be 3½ years. God knew how long He ordained them to testify. He knew to the day that it was 1,260 days.

There would likely be a greater urgency in our efforts to witness if we remembered that God has numbered our days as well. Psalm 139:16 and Job 14:5 both assert that God has numbered our days. Therefore, we need to see each day lived as one less day to witness.

Loree reminded me of this some time ago. Living far from family makes it special when they all decide to come and visit—hectic, but special. What makes it hectic is trying to get the house in order. "To Do" lists for another day suddenly become a priority. It was in the middle of a day when Loree and I had more on our list than hours in the day that she said something profound. She said, "If I knew Jesus was coming tomorrow, cleaning my house wouldn't be the most important thing for me to do today. I would want to be telling as many people as I could about Jesus."

Too often we have too much to do and too little time to accomplish it—which means we spend time doing everything else but witnessing. However, if we remember that with each passing day we have one less day to share Christ, we will regain our urgency to witness.

#4 — They are Broken before God and for Others

Before we leave verse 3, there's one more lesson to learn. It's seen in what the two witnesses were wearing. Verse 3 says they were prophesying for 1,260 days in "sackcloth." Wearing sackcloth in the Old

Testament signified brokenness. Either the individual in sackcloth was broken before God in repentance, or broken for others in mourning (Gen. 37:34; 2 Sam. 3:31; 1 Chron. 21:16; 2 Kings 6:30). Regardless of why they were broken, these references prove that God uses best those who are broken the most. Furthermore, I believe that being broken for others will come naturally once we are broken before God.

The great wordsmith Vance Havner said it well, "God uses broken things. Broken soil to produce a crop, broken clouds to give rain, broken grain to give bread, broken bread to give strength."[46] Havner then pointed to Simon Peter as an example. Here was a man broken over his failure before Christ, who yet rose from his brokenness to accomplish great things with Christ.

I'm sure Havner was referring to Peter's encounter with Jesus in John 21:15–19. Peter's encounter underscores three prerequisites to brokenness before God. First, you must *BE STILL* to be broken. Peter was having breakfast with Jesus, when Jesus confronted him. Many of us stay too busy to ever be still before God. Second, you must *BE OPEN* to be broken. Jesus asked Peter if he loved Him with the love of God. Peter was open, and confessed that he only loved Jesus like a good friend. Sadly, too often even when we get still with God, we can still remain closed to God. As a result, many of us aren't open enough to be broken enough for God to use.

The third prerequisite for brokenness is to *BE READY.* With each open confession, Jesus was willing to put Peter to work, telling him to "Take care of my lambs," "Take care of my sheep," and "Feed my sheep." Furthermore, Jesus told Peter that He would have to carry

---

him in the work. It would be too much for Peter to handle alone. That is why Peter would have to stay broken before God.

Again, this is why many of us fail to be broken enough for God to accomplish great things. In our hearts we are not truly ready to serve, not ready to be stretched, and not willing to be broken in a way that God can use best.

However, if more of us were still and open before God, if more were ready to serve, stretch, and stay open, can you imagine all that God could do? I can. More of us would be like the two witnesses in Revelation 11.

#5 – God Displays His Power through Them

In verse 6 the word "power" is used twice to point to the abilities of the two witnesses to cause famines and unleash plagues. As was stated earlier, the Greek word for "power" used both times in verse 6 is *exousian*. It means "authority in legitimate hands." Thus, under God's authority, we should have God's abilities to act in ways that validate us and the message we deliver.

People today are looking for authentic believers, not professional Christians. Yet it seems that people have always been looking for authenticity from those claiming to belong to God.

There are three epochs in scripture where God's power stands out more than others. The first appears during the plagues and miracles recorded in Exodus. Here God makes it clear that Israel belongs to Him. The second occurs during the ministry of Jesus described in the Gospels. The miracles He performed point to Him as the Messiah. The third was at the birth of the church in the book of Acts. Through the signs and wonders they performed, God wanted all to know that these witnesses and their message belonged to Him. In these examples,

God's authority gave His followers and His Son godly abilities to act in ways that authenticated Israel as His people, Jesus as His Son, and the New Testament believers as His witnesses.

Seeing God's power at work through believers in scripture forced me to ask myself an uncomfortable question: "What have I done that nonbelievers can't, that would cause them to see I truly belong to God—that I am an authentic witness for Him?" I thought of some answers, including:

- Going to Church – nonbelievers do that
- Reading the Bible – nonbelievers do that
- Helping the Less-Fortunate – nonbelievers do that
- Living an Ethical Life – nonbelievers do that
- Raising a Good Family – nonbelievers do that

So these answers don't work. The correct short answer is, "BE LIKE JESUS!" That means I will love like Him, forgive like Him, and sacrifice like Him. Nonbelievers can't do that, not like Jesus.

Furthermore, if we want to be like Jesus, we need to DO WHATEVER GOD SAYS! It's when we do whatever He says, that God does what only God can do—and He'll do it through us. That's when the authority of God reveals the abilities of God in and through our lives. And that's when nonbelievers will see us as authentic witnesses.

#6 – God Predetermines Their Death

The sixth quality can be easily overlooked. Verse 7 clearly discloses that God predetermined the death of His two witnesses. This is more than the day they will die, for we've already discussed how God numbers our days. This refers to the fact that God also predetermined how they would die: He allows the Antichrist to kill them. Their deaths will be public and ugly. For 3½ days their bodies will decay on the streets of Jerusalem for a godless world to see and celebrate.

When listening to believers talk about dying, most scenarios sound like this: "I just want to go to sleep one night and wake up in heaven." That may be what we want, but have we considered that God may want more from our death?

In 1935, Dr. Bill Wallace began serving as a medical missionary in Communist China. Though the Communist takeover of China put him at great risk, he stayed to care for the people and to witness to them about Jesus. On December 19, 1950, Communist officials raided his home, arrested him, beat him, and accused him of being a spy. After two months of torment, the police claimed that Dr. Wallace had hung himself. His body was buried in an unmarked grave. At risk to their own lives, Chinese believers removed his body from the unmarked grave and gave Dr. Wallace a proper burial. Above his grave they placed this sign: "For me to live is Christ."[47]

The statement over Dr. Wallace's grave comes from Philippians 1:21. There, the verse reads, *"For to me, to live is Christ and to die is gain."* I've often interpreted Paul's words here to mean that while he lives he wants to be like Christ, but when he dies that will be even better because he will enter heaven. That still may be the way Paul meant it, but after viewing the deaths of the two witnesses and the death of Dr. Bill Wallace, I see the verse meaning even more. It also means that while I live I want to live like Christ, but when I die I want my death to gain even more for God's Kingdom.

---

47   Dan Graves, MSL, "Bill Wallace Arrested in Early Morning Raid," Christianity.com, last updated June 2007, http://www.christianity.com/church/church-history/time-line/1901-2000/bill-wallace-arrested-in-early-morning-raid-11630801.html.

The death of the two witnesses and of Dr. Wallace should cause us to rethink how we want to die. Instead of simply wanting to go to sleep and wake up in heaven, maybe our prayer should be, "Lord, use my life—and even my death—in ways that will be a great witness for you."

#7 – God Uses Their Home-going

One more quality emerges from the passing of the two witnesses. Verses 11–13 portray how God uses their home-going.

After the two witnesses have lain dead for 3½ days, the world becomes the unexpected observer at their funeral service. The one officiating the funeral will be God, and I like the way God conducts it. First, God WAKES THE WITNESSES UP by breathing life back into them. Then, God CALLS THEM UP. The entire world hears God in a loud voice say, "Come up here." Finally, God SNATCHES THEM UP as, before the eyes of the world, they ascend to heaven in a cloud, just as Jesus did in Acts 1:9.

Witnessing the funeral of the two witnesses, something happens that did not happen in the first 3½ years of the tribulation. In verse 13, the Bible states that *"the survivors were terrified and gave glory to the God of heaven."* In the 3½ years that the two witnesses lived and prophesied, the people endured God's wrath through wars, famines, plagues, and more. In chapter 6, they ran from God instead of to Him. In chapter 9, they returned to their rebellious ways instead of repenting and turning to God.

Apparently, 3½ years of faithful witnessing wasn't enough. It took their faithfulness in death and God's faithfulness to raise them to life to finally crack open a hardhearted world.

In my decades as a pastor, I've seen this happen several times. For years, faithful witnesses shared their faith with family, friends, and co-workers, with little results. It's not until the witness dies they acknowledge the authenticity of their life and message. At the funeral service, they come to grips with their need and surrender to Jesus. It happens because, I believe, God speaks to those present at the home-going of His witnesses.

A TIMELY PERFORMANCE REVIEW

Most professions conduct what is called a "performance review." Though I want to stress that the world needs authentic witnesses, not professional Christians, it wouldn't hurt to conduct an occasional performance review on our effectiveness as witnesses. The following is a list of questions we can use as a personal performance review:

As a Witness . . .

- Do I live life confident that I have God's authority to act on His behalf?
- Do I frequently represent God and deliver His message?
- Do I act with urgency, because I realize that my days are numbered?
- Do I speak passionately, because of my brokenness before God and for others?
- Do I display the power of God, thus making me a credible witness?
- Am I willing for God to use my death in a way to draw more people to Him?
- Am I living in a way that will cause others to surrender to Jesus at my passing?

I've never met Dan Greene, but I like what he said: "Witnessing is not a spare-time occupation or a once-a-week activity. It must be a quality of life. You don't *go* witnessing; you are a witness."[48]

Witnessing is not simply another program for the church. Being a witness is God's plan for reaching the world. Both the past and the future prove that God's plan will work, if we as believers will work God's plan.

48   Draper, *Quotations*, entry 3344.

CHAPTER 14

GOD WILL MAKE EVERYTHING RIGHT

REVELATION 11:15-19

CERTAIN PASSAGES IN THE BIBLE cause the reader to look back and forward. Acts 1:6–8 does that. Looking back upon their previous three years with Jesus, and realizing that He has now been raised from the dead, His disciples ask Him,

> ⁶ "Lord, are you at this time going to restore the kingdom to Israel?"

> ⁷ He said to them: "It is not for you to know the times or dates the Father has set by his own authority. ⁸ But you will receive power when the Holy Spirit comes on you; and you will be my witnesses in Jerusalem, and in all Judea and Samaria, and to the ends of the earth."

Looking back, you can understand why Jesus' disciples ask the question. But Jesus' answer causes them to look forward. His answer paints a picture of what is about to happen. Before the book of Acts is finished, the good news of Jesus will have spread from Jerusalem to Judea, Samaria, and to the ends of the earth.

Like Acts 1:6–8, Revelation 11:15–19 causes us to both look back and forward. Looking back we see:

- In Revelation 2 & 3, the believers within the seven churches in Asia Minor are under persecution.

- In Revelation 5, Jesus takes the scroll (the title deed to earth) from God.

- In Revelation 6, Jesus begins opening the seven seals on the scroll allowing for deception, war, famine, and death to ride over the earth (the four horsemen of the apocalypse).

- In Revelation 8, Jesus opens the last seal, which summons seven angelic trumpeters. With each trumpet blast, God acts to reclaim the earth both physically and spiritually.

- In Revelation 11:15–19, the seventh angel sounds the trumpet. The tide has turned in the battle for earth. Heaven celebrates, knowing that the war is now won and God is going to make everything right.

Looking back, you can see why Revelation 11:15–19 describes a great celebration in heaven. However, when you look closely at the celebration, what is recorded causes us to look forward. Like Acts 1:6–8, Revelation 11:15–19 outlines what transpires before the end of the book. It summarizes what God will do to make everything right.

The more we study the book of Revelation, we realize it's more than simply an announcement of what happens in the future. It also reminds us of the way God has been, is, and will always be. Its message is a message for today, for even today we want the assurance that God will make everything right.

When I was thirteen, I sensed God calling me to serve Him in the ministry. That's when Dad began mentoring me. He shared with me his emotions, experiences, and thoughts as a pastor. There wasn't much that Dad didn't use as a teachable moment. I remember him sharing of an experience when he was being mistreated. Blatant lies were told to attack Dad. With calm resolve he said, "Son, just because others act ungodly, that doesn't mean you should in return. Besides, remember this. God, who sees all and knows all, will in time even everything out." I knew Dad wasn't wishing harm on those who were hurting him. He knew God saw his faithfulness and would bless him for it. Inevitably, a blessing would come and Dad would smile at me and say, "You see, Son, God is evening everything out."

There are times when each of us feels mistreated, even persecuted. Revelation 11:15–19 assures us that God, who sees and knows all, will even everything out. In fact, these verses explain why you can trust God to make everything right.

. . . ACCORDING TO HIS PROMISES

You can trust God to make everything right because He promises to do so. Revelation 11:15 records the fulfillment of a promise made by God long ago:

> [15] The seventh angel sounded his trumpet, and there were loud voices in heaven, which said:

> "The kingdom of the world has become the kingdom of our Lord and of his Christ, and he will reign forever and ever."

The seventh trumpet sounds, announcing that God has fulfilled a long-standing promise. The announcement is: *The kingdom of the world has become the kingdom of our Lord and of his Christ.* Though the King James Version translates it as "kingdoms," the correct translation is the singular "kingdom."

Back in Genesis 3, Satan altered the world God created. Furthermore, 1 John 5:19 makes it clear that since Genesis 3 the ways of *"the whole world is (have been) under the control of the evil one."* In the last days, however, the Antichrist forms a single world government. It becomes the unmasked expression of a godless world order. That's what makes the seventh trumpet blast so exciting. It signals a change in control. It announces that the kingdom of the world now belongs to God. God has won...just as He promised!

This trumpet blast represents God keeping the promise He made to Satan in Genesis 3:15. There He promised Satan a day would come when a woman would give birth to the Messiah. Though Satan would try to stop Him, the Messiah would crush him. The trumpet blast also signals God fulfilling the promise He made through Daniel around 530 BC and through David around 1000 BC. God's promise through them was that He, through His Son, would set up a kingdom that would endure forever (Dan. 2:44; 7:13–14, 27; and Psalm 2). Heaven has known it. Believers have known it. But now with this trumpet blast, Satan and those left on earth will realize it. God has won...just as He promised!

There is a time in warfare when one battle turns the tide, assuring victory. Even though the fighting continues, you know you've won. That's the emotion expressed in verse 15. Though the fighting will soon come to an end, God has reclaimed the kingdom of earth and He will never lose control again. You see that in the expression, *"and he will reign forever and ever."* Literally, it says *"and he will reign for ages to ages."*

Scripture measures time in ages. They include the Old Testament ages of the patriarchs, judges, kings and prophets, as well as the New

Testament ages of Jesus' ministry, the church, and Christ's second coming. The seventh trumpet announces that though ages have changed over time, the reign of God on earth will never change. That's God's promise.

Though the seventh trumpet has not yet sounded, believers wait with excitement. Someone said, "Prophesy is simply history written in advance." Therefore, as believers we trust that, no matter what we endure for our faith, a time approaches when God will make it right. He's made the promise in advance. And, in time, God will make it right.

Though my gentle and godly friend Fred Meier is now with the Lord, he still inspires me. Even in his nineties, Fred passionately shared his faith and prayed for revival. When he was 92, Fred published his first book, a book on Revelation entitled *Understanding the Times*. One day, before his book was published, Fred fell at his house and couldn't get up. Hours passed as he lay on the floor and prayed, "Father, please help me get up." Later, when I visited him in the hospital, he told me, "Mark, after praying for hours for God to help me get up, it was pretty clear that wasn't His plan. So, I changed my prayer. I prayed, 'Lord, then please help me get through this.'" With a soft smile, while lying in his hospital bed, Fred told me, "Mark, God is helping me get through this."

When living to honor Jesus, there will be times we will offend others. As a result, we might be mistreated at work. We might be overlooked for promotion or wrongly dismissed. Family members might distance themselves from us, and friends could even spread lies about us. Worldwide, believers are losing far more than their jobs or relationships. Their lives are on the line for being a follower of Christ.

Thus, when mistreated or persecuted for your faithfulness, you might wonder, "Does anyone know the truth? Will anyone make it right?" Remember then the prophecy found in Revelation 11:15. It's God's promise in advance. Either immediately or ultimately, God will make it right. Either He will lift you up from it or get you through it, but inevitably, God will make it right.

. . . BECAUSE HE IS GOD

When others repeatedly let us down, we can become cynical and jaded. We might even ask, "How can I be confident that God will keep His promise and make everything right? Because, others don't. People change their minds. Judges' rulings are overturned. Even friends and family go back on their word." That's true. However, we need to remember that God is not like others we know or anyone we'll ever meet. He keeps His promises and will make everything right…because He's God. God makes this point emphatically in Revelation 11:16–18a.

> [16] And the twenty-four elders, who were seated on their thrones
> before God, fell on their faces and worshiped God, [17] saying:

> "We give thanks to you, Lord God Almighty,
>   the One who is and who was,
>   because you have taken your great power
>   and have begun to reign.
> [18a] The nations were angry;
>   and your wrath has come."

This marks the third time in Revelation that the twenty-four elders have left their thrones and fallen on their faces to worship God (Rev. 4, 5, 11). And why wouldn't they? They've just heard a heavenly rendition of the "Hallelujah Chorus"! In case you missed it, look at verse 15 again and read the words that inspired Handel:

Revelation 11:15	Handel's "Hallelujah Chorus"
"The kingdom of the world	"The kingdom of this world
has become the kingdom of our Lord	Is become the kingdom of our Lord,
and of his Christ,	And of His Christ, and of His Christ,
and he will reign for ever	And He shall reign forever and ever,
and ever."	Forever and ever, forever and ever."

Though Handel's piece moves us greatly, it still fails to capture all that John experienced and wrote about in verses 16–18a. To Handel's well-deserved credit, he praises God with the refrain, "King of Kings and Lord of Lords." Handel's work has inspired us since 1749, but when heaven worships God, it's more stunning! It's more inspiring because heaven's description of God is more exhaustive than Handel's. Verses 16–18a recognize and praise God for His four majestic attributes.

God Almighty: He has the power!

Verse 17 opens with, *"We give thanks to you, Lord God Almighty."* Somehow, when we stopped calling God "Almighty," we stopped seeing God as all-powerful. The Old Testament labels Him "Almighty"

333 times, but the New Testament calls Him this only 12 times. As I scratched my head, wondering why, I realized that in the New Testament the all-powerful God became personal. Elohim, the God of the universe, became Immanuel, God with us. The God who was feared in the Old Testament took on flesh in the New Testament, and so became familiar.

This was what God wanted, but not at the loss of being feared. God doesn't want to be seen as so powerful that He's not personal. But neither should He be seen as so personal that we forget that He is all-powerful. That's why I'm thrilled that the book of Revelation recasts our image of God as "Almighty." All but three of the twelve New Testament references to God as "Almighty" occur in Revelation. We are once again reminded that our personal God is all-powerful. He is Almighty.

Therefore, when our persecutors seem larger than life and the abuses we've endured seem beyond healing, we look to the Almighty God of heaven. Seeing Him as He is, we realize there are no injustices, mistreatments, abuses, or persecutions that God can't make right. He's the Lord God Almighty!

God All-Knowing: He has the knowledge!

Furthermore, verse 17 assures us we'll never face an injustice or mistreatment that God hasn't seen, hasn't experienced, or doesn't know about. It says, *"We give thanks to you, Lord God Almighty, the One who is and who was…."* Though our hardships may be new to us, they are not new to God. Though they surprised us, they didn't surprise God. Though we don't know how to make them right, God does. He's done it many times before. He's not only the One who is, but He's also the One who was. He's seen it all many times, and He knows what we are going through. Because He knows all, He alone can make it all right.

Sovereign Lord: He has the authority!

The elders are also thankful that God has the authority to use His power and knowledge. Praising God, they say, *"We give thanks to you . . . because you have taken your great power and have begun to reign."* Only Jesus has the final say in heaven and on earth. He made that clear just before He ascended to heaven in Matthew 28:18. As was previously explained, *exousia* is the Greek word for authority and it refers to "authority in legitimate hands." Not only does Jesus possess God's knowledge and power, but He has been given the authority to use these to make things right.

God of Wrath: He has an attitude!

The elders praise God in verse 17 because of His abilities and authority to make everything right. However, in verse 18 the elders reveal there are times God makes things right "with an attitude." The elders say, *"The nations were angry; and your wrath has come."* Two Greek words describe God's anger and wrath in Revelation. The word used in verse 18 is *orge*. It's used four times in Revelation, and it describes God's wrath as "indignation, a fixed attitude of wrath." Here, God locks His jaw in anger. The other word for anger is *thumos*. It appears seven times in Revelation, and it describes God's anger as "rage." It portrays God exploding with anger to make things right.

Deep within, most of us like it when God gets angry on our behalf. Early in our ministry, Loree and I served a challenging church. On occasion I'd come home after a meeting and share with her how some of the people were ugly toward me. Sharing it with Loree helped me keep my emotions under control . . . because I knew she'd get angry enough for both of us.

When others mistreat you, lie about you, or hurt you with their words or actions, place yourself with the elders. Stop and praise God that He has the power, knowledge, and authority to make everything right. And when it comes to "attitude," it's far better when you let God get angry for you.

. . . IN HIS TIME

For those who have endured hardships and injustices for a long time, you may wonder, "When will God make everything right?" We want it to happen sooner than later.

It helps to remember that the book of Revelation was sent to the seven churches persecuted by Rome. Rome's persecution of the church lasted for 250 years! That means some believers lived and died never experiencing relief on earth from Rome's persecution. Even today, there are believers throughout the world who have not lived a day without fearing persecution. In such times we want to ask God, "When will You make everything right?" The remainder of verse 18 answers the question.

> [18b] "The time has come for judging the dead,
> and for rewarding your servants the prophets
> and your saints and those who reverence your name,
> both small and great—and for destroying those who
> destroy the earth."

The short answer is, "God will make everything right in His time." Verse 18 announces this saying, *"The time has come."* There are two Greek words translated as "time." One is *chronos.* It refers to a span of time. The other is *kairos* and it identifies a decisive point in time.

If you are weary beneath the weight of hardships, you might think that God's timing for making everything right is *chronos*—"He'll get around to it eventually." But, that's not true. According to verse 18, God's timing for making everything right is *kairos*. He has already ordained a specific time for making everything right. When that time comes, look at what God will do.

God will Judge

Verse 18 states, *"The time has come for judging the dead."* Earlier we learned that these verses not only looked back, but they also pointed forward to what is to come. Revelation 20:11–15 describes what has been called "The Great White Throne Judgment." All who have died and have not surrendered to Jesus stand before God to be judged. Because they have not surrendered to Jesus, Revelation 20:15 orders them to be *"thrown into the lake of fire."*

This should not surprise those being judged. Jesus warned them repeatedly. In Matthew 13:24–30, He said a day would come when He would separate the saved from the unsaved just as a farmer separates wheat from the weeds. The wheat (the saved) will be gathered and stored while the weeds (the unsaved) will be gathered and burned.

Still, even Jesus knew that many being judged would be surprised. He said in Matthew 7:22–23,

> [22] "Many will say to me on that day, 'Lord, Lord, did we not prophesy in your name, and in your name drive out demons and perform many miracles?' [23] Then I will tell them plainly, 'I never knew you. Away from me, you evildoers!'"

Make no mistake; in His time God will judge those who have died and have not surrendered to Jesus.

God will Reward

Since God judges the unsaved at the Great White Throne Judgment, what about those who surrendered their lives to Jesus on earth? 2 Corinthians 5:10 explains that believers are judged as well. Paul writes that we are judged by Jesus at the "*judgment seat*."

> [10] For we must all appear before the judgment seat of Christ, that each one may receive what is due him for the things done while in the body, whether good or bad.

The Greek word Paul used for "judgment seat" was familiar to Corinthian believers. According to Roman custom a *bema* or "judgment seat" sat in a town square or coliseum. Civil cases were heard and resolved there. Furthermore, rewards were given to those who were victorious in games.

What an appropriate picture. As believers we will one day stand before the *bema*, the "judgment seat" of Jesus. The One who knows all will have seen all of our life. Every one of us will have issues to be resolved with God—areas where we failed Him. However, every one of us will also have moments worthy of receiving rewards from God. He will know the times we were wrongfully mistreated for our faith, and still we honored Him by remaining godly and faithful. When we felt everyone only heard the lies and no one knew the truth—God did. When we thought no one cared enough to know and make it right—God will. God promises a time when we will stand before Him to be rewarded for our faithfulness. He will make everything right.

God will Destroy

The last statement in verse 18 points to God's fairness. It says *"The time has come…for destroying those who destroy the earth."* The Greek word for "destroying" literally means "to cause to rot and ruin." Here, Revelation 11 takes us back to Genesis 1. It reminds us that God created the earth and we who live on it so that we could have a meaningful relationship with Him. Yet in Genesis 3, Satan deceives Adam and Eve causing them to sin against God. Satan's deception and their sin began the rot that ultimately ruined the earth. Those who never repented of their sins while on earth will get from God what they gave to God—spiritual rot and ruin. He will destroy them the way their unrepentant lives destroyed the earth. God will make it right.

. . . ACCORDING TO WHAT IS RIGHT

The final verse in chapter 11 assures us that when God makes everything right, He will do it mistake free. I wish I could say that about myself. There have been times I've done what is right, at the right time, but in the wrong way. What was meant for good turned out to be a mistake. Other times, I've done what is right, in the right way, but at the wrong time. Again, though my intentions were good, it turned out badly.

That's why I'm glad we are leaving it up to God to make everything right. Verses 15–18 tell us that God promises to make everything right, for He is God. Furthermore, He will do it in His timing. Finally, verse 19 assures us that He will do it the right way. God's standards for what is right have always been what is holy. You see this through John's eyes in verse 19:

[19] Then God's temple in heaven was opened, and within his temple was seen the ark of his covenant. And there came flashes of lightning, rumblings, peals of thunder, an earthquake and a great hailstorm.

John's vision of God's temple being opened and the ark of the covenant being seen was especially meaningful to the Jewish believers. They understood what the ark meant. It represented God's presence. Therefore, the ark was labeled and treated with one key word—"Holy!" How fitting, since God is supremely holy.

God Is Holy

The ark reminds all of the holiness of God, because it represented the presence of God. That's why in the Old Testament, whether it was in the tabernacle or the temple, the ark resided in a place called the Holy of Holies. Out of reverence for God's holiness, only the High Priest entered the Holy of Holies, and he did so only once a year. It was on the Day of Atonement. On that day, the High Priest sprinkled the blood of a sacrificed bull and goat over the ark according to God's strict specifications. This was done to atone for the sins of God's people. It was also an annual reminder that God not only is holy, but He also requires holiness of His people.

God Requires Holiness

The people were reminded of God's requirement of holiness by what the ark held. Inside the ark were the stone tablets of God's law (Exodus 25:21), a jar of manna (Exodus 16:33), and Aaron's staff (Numbers 17:10). The law represented the standards of holiness God required of His people. The jar of manna reminded the people of how God miraculously fed them over forty years until they entered the Promised Land. And Aaron's budding staff signified that God had set Aaron and his linage apart as priests to serve God and His people. Therefore the ark reminded God's people that not only is He holy, but He requires holiness if we are to have a relationship with Him.

Do we understand that if God left it up to us to make everything right, it would be a fiasco? It would be horrible because everyone would have a different opinion of what is right. God's opinion of what is right is summed up in one word—"Holy!" And God has the right to make everything right—not according to just anyone's opinion of what's right, but according to His standards of holiness.

Furthermore, God has the right to set and enforce those standards. He alone earned that right when He came as Jesus and became our ultimate sacrifice. Hebrews 9:24–28 makes it clear that His blood was placed on the ark in God's temple, giving us the opportunity to be holy before God.

> [24] For Christ did not enter a man-made sanctuary that was only a copy of the true one; he entered heaven itself, now to appear for us in God's presence. [25] Nor did he enter heaven to offer himself again and again, the way the high priest enters the Most Holy Place every year with blood that is not his own. [26] Then Christ would have had to suffer many times since the creation of the world. But now he has appeared once for all at the end of the ages to do away with sin by the sacrifice of himself. [27] Just as man is destined to die once, and after that to face judgment, [28] so Christ was sacrificed once to take away the sins of many people; and he will appear a second time, not to bear sin, but to bring salvation to those who are waiting for him.

Thus when we see the sacrifice Jesus has made for us, when we confess our sins and surrender our life to Him, we meet God's requirements for holiness. This allows us to also receive God's rewards of holiness.

God Rewards Holiness

In Revelation 11:19, John gives a picture of heaven's temple that would have excited Jewish believers. He saw the temple of God open, with direct access to the ark. Prior to Jesus' crucifixion, only the High Priests were allowed access to the ark, and only once per year. Yet Matthew 27:51 records that when Jesus died on the cross, the curtain in the temple separating the Holy Place from the Holy of Holies was ripped from top to bottom. God did this, signifying that all could now have direct access to Him. All could be forgiven and have a relationship with Him. Through Christ we are made holy.

When God makes things right, He does it right. Again, I wish I could say that. A lot of the things I fix don't stay fixed. That's not true of God. Jesus' sacrifice on the cross not only made it possible for us to have a relationship with Jesus while on earth, but in heaven as well. We get to experience a meaningful, everlasting relationship with Almighty God. There's no greater reward than that.

BECAUSE GOD WILL MAKE
EVERYTHING RIGHT . . .

A few years ago, a survey asked people to what degree they believed "we will all be called before God at the Judgment Day to answer for our sins." Sixty-four percent completely agreed with the statement. What was surprising was that ten years earlier only fifty-two percent had completely agreed.[49]

But even if only one percent completely agreed, God would still do it. He would fulfill His promise because His actions are not based on what we believe, but on who He is (Holy) and the promises He made. Therefore, because God will make everything right, let me make two important suggestions. First, make sure everything in your life is right with God. Make sure you have surrendered your life to Him and that you are living your life that way. Second, focus your life on living better, not bitter. If you are living your life surrendered to Christ, you will offend others. Don't let their ungodly focus on you take your godly focus from Christ. You can live so bitterly, over what others have said or done, that you end up doing nothing with God. Trust God to make everything right, and keep on living right with God.

---

49   McHenry, *McHenry's Stories*, 159.

CHAPTER 15

SURVIVING THE WAR
REVELATION 12

WAR RARELY AFFECTS ONLY THE countries that start it. In time, individuals and countries not involved in the start, start getting involved in the war—whether they want to or not.

Near the end of World War II there were two young men captured by the Americans in Germany. If it weren't so sad, their story could almost be a comedy. The two young men were sent to a POW camp, where it was noticed that they didn't converse with the other prisoners. In fact, they spoke a completely different language. Once it was discovered that the two men were actually from Tibet, a special translator was brought in, allowing the two men to finally tell their story.

In the summer of 1941, the two friends had left their small village in Tibet to see the world. Unknowingly, they wandered onto Soviet Russian territory. Russian authorities saw them and abruptly put them on a train, with hundreds of other young men, headed to an army camp. There they were given uniforms, guns, and training and sent to the Russian front.

Horrified by all the killing, the two young Buddhists, who didn't believe in killing, ran away. They were captured by the Germans and taken to Germany. As American forces approached Germany toward the end of the war, the Germans armed some of their prisoners and told them to fight. So again the two young Tibetans were given guns and told to fight. And, once again, they ran. This time they were captured by the Americans.

When the two finished their story, the interpreter asked them if they had any questions. They had only one: "Why were all those people trying to kill each other?"[50]

In many ways, the human race resembles those two young men from Tibet. We are caught in the middle of a spiritual war between God and Satan. We weren't involved in its start, but since Adam and Eve, it has involved us all. If you feel you've been able to remain neutral or unaffected by this war, think again. According to the Bible, there are evidences that you are being pulled to align yourself with one side or the other.

- When you want to know why you've been created and what is your purpose in life – *that's God drawing you to His side.* (John 3:16; 6:40, 44)

- When you use various pleasures and passions in life to keep you from thinking about God's purpose for your life – *that's Satan drawing you to his side.* (1 John 2:15–17; 5:19)

- When you know in your heart that certain acts or thoughts are ungodly, and that those ungodly acts separate you from a holy God – *that's God drawing you to His side.* (John 16:5–11)

- When you take those certain acts or thoughts and find a reason to say they're all right – *that's Satan drawing you to his side.* (Rom. 1:18–25)

---

50   Hewett, *Illustrations Unlimited*, 403.

- When you look at the life, death, and resurrection of Jesus and say, "He has to be the Savior, for no one else has ever done what He did" — *that's God drawing you to His side.* (John 16:5–11)

- When you see other religious beliefs in the world as viable, even though no one associated with them has ever done what Jesus did — *that's Satan drawing you to his side.* (John 4:19–26)

- When you silently think that one day Jesus will judge you according to whether or not you have surrendered your life to Him — *that's God drawing you to His side.* (John 16:5–11)

- When you hope or believe that if God judges you, He will do so according to your understanding of goodness — *that's Satan drawing you to his side.* (Matt. 7:21–23; Mark 10:17–22).

As you might imagine, it's dangerous to be caught in the middle of a spiritual war between God and Satan, especially when both sides want us to align with them. The two young Tibetans were able to survive being caught in the middle of their war. How can we survive being caught in the middle of ours? Well, it helps if we know the history behind the war.

A HISTORY LESSON

Revelation 12:1–6 provides a short history of the war between God and Satan. Though it might be hard to imagine, you are about to read the history of the world in less than 165 words.

[1] A great and wondrous sign appeared in heaven: a woman clothed with the sun, with the moon under her feet and a crown of twelve stars on her head. [2] She was pregnant, and cried out in pain as she was about to give birth. [3] Then another sign appeared in heaven: an enormous red dragon with seven heads and ten horns and seven crowns on his heads. [4] His tail swept a third of the stars out of the sky and flung them to the earth. The dragon stood in front of the woman who was about to give birth, so that he might devour her child the moment it was born. [5] She gave birth to a son, a male child, who will rule all the nations with an iron scepter. And her child was snatched up to God and to his throne. [6] The woman fled into the desert to a place prepared for her by God, where she might be taken care of for 1,260 days.

Imagine capturing the events of a particular era of history in just one book. Now consider summarizing the history of the world in just six verses. See the challenges? You couldn't address every day, only the major events or movements. God does this in verses 1–6. Trying to make His short account even clearer, God has put it into story form. Below are some of the major events in God's history of the world.

Betrayal in Heaven

The first major event actually takes place prior to the creation of the world. It involves a betrayal in heaven. Isaiah 14:12–20 provides a prophetic eulogy of the life and death of Satan. It explains that Satan was the best and brightest angel in heaven, but that wasn't good enough for him. He wanted to be like God, which led to his attempt to overthrow God. Satan is called the "Red Dragon" in Revelation 12 and the "Morning Star" in Isaiah 14. Both accounts record his failure to overthrow God. Consequently, Revelation 12:4 states that a third of the angels revolting with Satan are also cast from heaven to earth.

The Key is the Child

As the war continues between God and Satan, two aspects change. One is the location of the battle: it now moves from heaven to earth. The other is the strategy of the war. Satan knows God wants a relationship with those He created. Therefore, Satan does everything possible to keep that relationship from happening.

In Genesis 3, Satan deceives Adam and Eve, causing them to sin against God and thus breaking the relationship God wanted with them. Furthermore, 1 Corinthians 15:20–22 makes it clear that, because of that original sin, all people are born in sin and separated from God. It also says that through Christ sin can be forgiven, and the original relationship with God restored.

God knew that the Messiah had to be born and sacrificed to accomplish this. Because of God's statement to Satan in Genesis 3:15, Satan knew this as well. Both God and Satan understood that their success or failure in the war was dependent upon the birth of a child. You realize that before a child could be born, a mother had to be selected. Though it may surprise many, the woman giving birth to the child in Revelation 12 is not Mary. It's actually the nation of Israel.

The description of the woman in Revelation 12:1 resembles the description God gives to the nation of Israel in Genesis 37:9 where the twelve stars in her crown represent the twelve tribes of Israel. Israel gives birth to the Messiah, but as Revelation 12:2 points out, not without pain.

Satan knew that God's plan was for the Messiah to come from His chosen people Israel, particularly from the line of David (Dan. 9:6–7; Jeremiah 23:5; 33:15; Luke 1:32–33). Therefore, Satan understood that if he could destroy God's people and David's linage, he could destroy God's plan. That is why Israel was the center of Satan's attack, before and at the birth of Christ. Warren Wiersbe explains,

> Throughout Old Testament history, Satan tried to prevent the birth of the redeemer. There was always a "dragon" standing by, waiting to destroy Israel or the ancestors of the Messiah. Pharaoh is called a "dragon" (Ezek. 29:3), and so is Nebuchadnezzar (Jeremiah 51:34). At one particular point, the royal line was limited to one little boy (2 Kings 11:1–3). When Jesus Christ was born, Satan used King Herod to try to destroy Him (Matt. 2).[51]

Even after the birth of Christ, Satan's attacks on Israel are well documented. In my opinion, Satan has used world leaders such as Stalin and Hitler to do his work. Other world leaders after them have threatened and continue to threaten to annihilate Israel. Furthermore, Revelation 12:13–17 shows that, in the last days, the focus of Satan's one-world government will be to destroy the Jews. All this, over the birth of a child—but a child believed to be the Messiah.

Even today, people question whether or not Jesus is the Messiah, and for good reason. Dr. Charles Feinberg, a noted Messianic Jewish scholar, states that within Israel's history alone there have been sixty-four different individuals since the time of Christ claiming to be the

---

51   Wiersbe, *Be Victorious*, 99.

Messiah. Yet I believe Jesus is the true Messiah for the following reasons.

First, I believe Jesus is the Messiah because God proved it. There are over 100 distinct Old Testament prophesies about the Messiah, and Jesus fulfilled them all.[52] *Second, I believe that Jesus is the Messiah because on several occasions He openly admits it.* Jesus admits it to His disciples, other individuals, and even to the council wanting to crucify Him (Matt. 16:16–20; 26:62–64; John 4:21–26; 10:24–30). *Third, I believe that Jesus is the Messiah because Satan acts like it.* Satan tries to stop His birth by trying to destroy Israel. Furthermore, he tries to kill Jesus as a child and then tries to tempt Him away from God's plan as a man. Satan wanted the child to never be born, nor to become a man and fulfill God's plan. Because, as Satan would learn, the child who was the key would one day hold all the keys.

The Child Holds All the Keys

Satan's rampage against God's people and Jesus' followers continues for one reason. After Jesus' death and resurrection, the child who was the key now holds all the keys. In Matthew 16:18–20, Peter acknowledges Jesus as the Messiah. Immediately Jesus tells Peter He will give him the keys to the kingdom of heaven. Jesus can't give what He doesn't possess. Thus, He holds the keys to the kingdom of heaven. Furthermore, Revelation 1:18 explains that Jesus holds the keys to death and Hades as well. When it comes to a war between countries on earth, the winner is usually the one with all the weapons. When it comes to a war between Satan and God, the winner is the one with all the keys—and that's Jesus.

---

52   Tim LaHaye and Ed Hindson, eds., *The Popular Encyclopedia of Bible Prophecy* (Eugene, OR: Harvest House, 2004), 223.

A Question of Alignment

Though the war between God and Satan started as a fight over who will reign in heaven, it is something more. Having lost his campaign for heaven, Satan and God now fight over us. God fights to have the relationship He always wanted with us, the relationship He created us to have with Him. Satan fights to keep us from it. God's efforts are driven by love. He knows we will not be restored to and fulfilled by Him without a relationship with Him. Satan's actions are driven by arrogant pride. He's not fighting to help us, but to hurt God. At the core, God's fight is all about us, and Satan's fight is all about him.

Thus, in this ongoing war between God and Satan, we need to ask, "Whose side am I on?" God has done everything He can to draw us to His side. Satan has done everything he can to keep us from it. Do we want to align ourself with One who fights for us because He loves us, or with someone who fights over us because he loves himself? I pray you have surrendered your life to Jesus and have aligned yourself with Him. Remember, not only is He the one who loves you, but He's the one with all the keys.

SURVIVAL LESSONS

Just because you may have aligned yourself with God doesn't mean the fighting is over. God may have captured all the keys and essentially has won the war, but the fighting goes on. Revelation 12:6 alludes to this, but verses 7–12 make it clear.

> [7] And there was war in heaven. Michael and his angels fought against the dragon, and the dragon and his angels fought back. [8] But he was not strong enough, and they lost their place in heaven.

⁹ The great dragon was hurled down—that ancient serpent called the devil, or Satan, who leads the whole world astray. He was hurled to the earth, and his angels with him.

¹⁰ Then I heard a loud voice in heaven say:
"Now have come the salvation and the power
and the kingdom of our God,
and the authority of his Christ.
For the accuser of our brothers,
who accuses them before our God day and night,
has been hurled down.
¹¹ They overcame him
by the blood of the Lamb
and by the word of their testimony;
they did not love their lives so much
as to shrink from death.
¹² Therefore rejoice, you heavens
and you who dwell in them!
But woe to the earth and the sea,
because the devil has gone down to you!
He is filled with fury,
because he knows that his time is short."

The War Enters a New Phase

Certain statements in verses 7–9 and verse 12 show the war between God and Satan entering a new phase. Though Satan and his demons have been active on earth, Job 1 indicates that Satan still has access to heaven. In Job 1:6–12, Satan stands before God accusing Job of not being the godly man God thinks. Of course, the book of Job shows God and Job proving Satan wrong. Yet the point I want to make is in Job 1:6, *"One day the angels came to present themselves before the LORD, and Satan also came with them."* Satan still had access to heaven.

Revelation 12:7–9 says that in this battle, God sent His angel Michael to deal with Satan. Now Satan and his angels are cast out of heaven to the earth. This ultimate banishment occurs during the last half of the Great Tribulation. Verse 6 speaks of the 1,260 days that Israel rests under God's protection. Though written differently, verse 16 repeats it. Both verses talk about the last 3½ years of the Great Tribulation. Furthermore, verse 12 adds that now Satan's fury reaches new levels, for he realizes *"his time is short."*

A New Phase with the Same Tactics

It's baffling that, even though Satan realizes his time is short, he doesn't change his tactics. In verses 7–12 he is called "Satan" (the adversary), "the devil" (liar or slanderer), "the accuser" (another adjective for Satan), and "that ancient serpent." This last title alone reminds that he hasn't changed since Eden.

In these verses, however, he wears one label that appears only in the book of Revelation. He's called the "Red Dragon." "Dragon" refers to his menacing character. The color red displays intent—death, the same color given to the second horse of the apocalypse, whose rider brought bloody war to earth. The description of the dragon reveals how he has and will bring death. Pastor and author John MacArthur explains it well:

- The seven heads represent the seven world empires under Satan's leadership: Egypt, Assyria, Babylon, Medo-

Persia, Greece, Rome, and in the last days the one-world government of the Antichrist — Revelation 17:9–10

- The ten horns represent the ten kings who will rule under the Antichrist — Revelation 17:12

- The shifting of crowns that will take place from the Dragon's heads to the Beast's horns in Revelation 13:1 points to a shift in power from the previous world empires to the ten kings under the influence of the Antichrist.[53]

Satan's tactics, which had been subtle and indirect in the past, will be direct and ruthless in the last days.

Remember Your Survival Training

Though Satan's efforts become more ruthless, verse 11 states that those who surrender to Jesus in the last days will survive spiritually. Their survival will be like that of Air Force Captain Scott O'Grady in 1995.

When Bosnian Serbs shot down O'Grady's plane, his parachute landed him in hostile territory. For the next six days he survived by eating little, moving carefully, and avoiding enemy capture. Upon his rescue, he was asked how he survived. He said he simply tried to remember and do everything he was taught in survival school.

Since Satan's tactics in the end times will be little different from today, it would be good to see what the believers will do to survive. It would be good to use their experiences and other scripture passages as a crash course in spiritual survival. As a crash course, it's limited to five important lessons.

---

53   MacArthur, *Time*, 201–202.

LESSON #1
Trust the Blood

Revelation 12:11 assures that believers in the end times will overcome Satan *"by the blood of the Lamb."* Jesus' shed blood pays the price for our sins and enables us to have the relationship with God (Rom. 6:23). Because of Jesus' blood and by our full surrender to Him, we align with God. Jesus says in John 10:28 that we are in God's hand and nothing will cause Him to let us go. Our spiritual survival is assured when we realize that Satan can do nothing to separate us from God. Live confidently in Christ! Trust the blood!

LESSON #2
Dress for Battle

The next three lessons come from Ephesians 6. Verses 13–17 say our survival depends on being dressed for battle. The Apostle Paul was shackled to a Roman soldier while writing this letter. Paul says that—to survive the war between Satan and God—we need to be sure to wear the following pieces of armor.

- TRUTH, like a belt, will hold your life together.
- RIGHTEOUSNESS, like a breastplate, will protect your past, present, and future.
- A READINESS TO SHARE THE GOSPEL, like sandals, will keep you focused.
- FAITH, like a shield, will stop Satan's constant attacks.
- THE SECURITY OF YOUR SALVATION, like a helmet, will give you confidence in the fight.

I read somewhere that it costs our government a minimum of $40,000 to provide one infantry soldier a year of training. If our government sees the importance of dressing and equipping our troops for physical battle, we need to remember the importance of dressing ourselves daily for spiritual battle.

LESSON #3
Use the Book

The only offensive weapon listed in Ephesians 6 appears in verse 17. It says to take *"the sword of the Spirit, which is the word of God."* Global warfare has become so dominated by technology that many battles are fought from a distance. Missiles, shells, and shots are fired from a distance. That wasn't so in biblical times. Much of the fighting was face to face with swords. That makes it personal.

Calling the Bible a sword fits, because using it is always personal. Hebrews 4:12 teaches, *"For the word of God is living and active. Sharper than any double-edged sword, it penetrates even to dividing soul and spirit, joints and marrow; it judges the thoughts and attitudes of the heart."* When Satan attacks, it's personal. He attacks our emotions, thoughts, and attitudes about others and ourselves. We need God's Word to cut away lies with truth. And just as a first-century sword was ineffective if left in its sheath, God's Word will not be effective until it is placed in our mind and heart. Use the Book!

LESSON #4
Bend Your Knees

The fourth lesson in spiritual survival training comes from Ephesians 6:18. It says, *"And pray in the Spirit on all occasions with all kinds of prayers and requests. With this in mind, be alert and always keep on praying for all the saints."* A similar challenge appears in 1 Peter 5:8. It charges, *"Be self-controlled and alert. Your enemy the devil prowls around like a roaring lion looking for someone to devour."* Jesus gives the same charge to Peter, James and John in Matthew 26:40–41 when He found them asleep, saying, *"'Could you men not keep watch with me for one hour?'" he asked Peter. 'Watch and pray so that you will not fall into temptation. The spirit is willing, but the body is weak.'"* "Watch and pray" is the same as saying "stay alert."

What a lesson! Satan always prowls, looking to attack you, a family member, friend, or fellow believer. Constantly vulnerable to his unexpected attacks, we must remain alert and prepared. We do this by constantly bending our knees before God in prayer.

LESSON #5
Live Boldly . . . to the End!

This last lesson returns us to Revelation 12:11. It states, *"They overcame him (Satan) by the blood of the Lamb and by the word of their testimony; they did not love their lives so much as to shrink from death."* At the risk of their own lives, they remained faithful witnesses. Satan could not break them. He could not stop them from living boldly, even to the end.

Ten years after his rescue, Scott O'Grady was interviewed again. The interviewer knew his story and asked him, "What was it like to be camouflaged, and yet so close to somebody who mean[t] you harm?" O'Grady answered,

> When they're walking right by you, your heart is pounding. And I was scared. You know, and that's just normal. I mean, anybody that's in combat that says they're not, I kind of question that. But it's also where you are a professional, and you are an American soldier. And we have a code of conduct that you will not give up, you will not surrender

of your own free will, and that code of conduct really holds close to our hearts."[54]

If that's the code of conduct for American soldiers, it should be more so for believers. Regardless of Satan's attacks, we will not give up. Every day we will live trusting the blood, dressed for battle, using the Book, bending our knees, vowing to live boldly for Christ to the end.

AVOIDING A WAR OF DOUBLE WRATH

As believers, Satan attacks us daily. Every day he looks for some way to weaken us and make us ineffective for Christ. Though he attacks aggressively today, he becomes fiercer in the end times. Revelation 12:12 alludes to this saying, *"But woe to the earth and the sea, because the devil has gone down to you! He is filled with fury, because he knows that his time is short."* Verses 13–17 underscore it even more.

> [13] When the dragon saw that he had been hurled to the earth, he pursued the woman who had given birth to the male child. [14] The woman was given the two wings of a great eagle, so that she might fly to the place prepared for her in the desert, where she would be taken care of for a time, times and half a time, out of the serpent's reach. [15] Then from his mouth the serpent spewed water like a river, to overtake the woman and sweep her away with the torrent. [16] But the earth helped the woman by opening its mouth and swallowing the river that the dragon had spewed out of his mouth. [17] Then the dragon was enraged at the woman and went off to make war against the rest of her offspring—those

---

54   Scott O'Grady, interview by Miles O'Brien on *American Morning*, CNN, July 5, 2005, http://edition.cnn.com/TRANSCRIPTS/0507/05/ltm.05.html.

who obey God's commandments and hold to the testimony of Jesus.

During the last 3½ years of the Great Tribulation, God protects the Jewish believers. Some see America in these verses as the eagle protecting Israel, but it is God. He's always been Israel's protector or deliverer. Exodus 19:4 says that God delivered Israel from Egypt "on eagles' wings." Deuteronomy 32:11–12 states that God cared for Israel in the wilderness as an eagle would her young. In Isaiah 40:32, God delivered Israel from Babylonian captivity "mounting [her] up with wings as eagles."[55]

In the end times, Jewish believers will need protection beneath God's Wings. During the final 3½ years of the tribulation, the war between God and Satan reaches its greatest intensity. It's a time of double wrath. God unleashes His wrath on those left behind because they refused to repent. Satan unleashes his wrath on those who have repented. In world history, this is the harshest time to live.

The spiritual war described in Revelation 12 exceeds anything experienced today. But God gives us this glimpse into the future with the hope that we will avoid this time of double wrath. By surrendering your life to Christ today, you will not have to face the intense war of tomorrow.

---

55   Wiersbe, *Be Victorious*, 102.

CHAPTER 16

BEWARE THE GREAT COUNTERFEITER

REVELATION 13

THOUGH HE DIED BEFORE AMERICA officially claimed her independence, many consider Jonathan Edwards one of the greatest theologians America has produced. What you are about to read sounds as though he was introducing Revelation 13. With remarkable discernment, Edwards wrote,

> The more excellent something is, the more likely it will be imitated. There are many false diamonds and rubies, but who goes about making counterfeit pebbles? However, the more excellent things are, the more difficult it is to imitate them in their essential character and intrinsic virtues. Yet the more variable the imitations be, the more skill and subtlety will be used in making them an exact imitation.[56]

The Bible tells the story of an all-powerful God who moved among us as Jesus. Then Jesus died on the cross, but came back to life three days later. Upon His ascension to heaven, Jesus' apostles performed signs and wonders, proving that Jesus is the Messiah and validating their message.

---

56   Jonathan Edwards in *Religious Affectations*, Christianity Today, vol. 37, no. 3.

In Revelation 13, Satan imitates God's excellent plan. We read of a dragon—Satan, a great beast—the Antichrist, and a lesser beast—a false prophet. The Antichrist has all the power and authority of Satan while moving among us. He becomes fatally wounded but is miraculously restored to life. His false prophet performs signs and wonders that cause the world to listen to his message and worship him.

At a first reading of Revelation 13, it seems Satan merely copies what God did. But it's far worse. A copy is recognized as a copy and seen as less valuable. We don't pay as much for the print as we do the original. What Satan does in Revelation 13 should be considered counterfeiting. A counterfeiter tries to replace the original, and pass off the counterfeit as valuable.

Again, what we are reading in Revelation 13 takes place in the end times. However, it seems that in our time Satan continues honing his craft as a counterfeiter.

Looking at all the world's major beliefs, we find similarities. That's why many people assert that all beliefs lead to God. Yet somehow they forget that Jesus said, *"I am the way and the truth and the life. No one comes to the Father except through me."* (John 14:6) Even in Christianity you can find Satan's counterfeiting work. Matthew 5:18 and Revelation 22:18–19 say that nothing in God's Word should be changed nor shall it ever pass away, yet some sects of Christianity have created their own version of the Bible.

I don't know who said it, but I agree with the statement, "Men may make counterfeit money, but, in time, counterfeit money will make counterfeit men." That's why it's important to read and understand Revelation 13. If we don't stop and identify Satan's counterfeit lies, we will find ourselves living counterfeit lives—never achieving the value of life God intended.

SATAN'S AIM

Charles Colton coined the phrase, "Imitation is the sincerest form of flattery." Yet it wasn't flattery that caused Satan to imitate God's actions. Revelation 13:1–4 uncovers Satan's sinister aim behind his actions.

> [1] And the dragon stood on the shore of the sea. And I saw a beast coming out of the sea. He had ten horns and seven heads, with ten crowns on his horns, and on each head a blasphemous name. [2] The beast I saw resembled a leopard, but had feet like those of a bear and a mouth like that of a lion. The dragon gave the beast his power and his throne and great authority. [3] One of the heads of the beast seemed to have had a fatal wound, but the fatal wound had been healed. The whole world was astonished and followed the beast. [4] Men worshiped the dragon because he had given authority to the beast, and they also worshiped the beast and asked, "Who is like the beast? Who can make war against him?"

The last verse in Revelation 12 states that *"the dragon was enraged at the woman (Israel) and went off to make war against the rest of her offspring."* Such a statement would make us think Satan's rage was void of reason, that his actions had no aim. However, verses 1–4 identify three objectives behind his counterfeiting work.

To Weaken God's Influence

Satan's first aim is to weaken God's influence on earth. To do this, verse 1 says Satan gives leadership of his one-world government to the

Antichrist. In fact, when comparing Revelation 12:3 to Revelation 13:1, we see that everything that Satan is and has is given to the Antichrist. However, there is one difference worth noting. It says that the seven heads of the beast (the Antichrist) each bear a blasphemous name.

As reported in our study of Revelation 12, the seven heads represent the seven world empires under Satan's leadership. They include Egypt, Assyria, Babylon, Medo-Persia, Greece, Rome, and the one-world government of the Antichrist (Rev. 17:9–10).[57] Each of these world empires either worships something other than God, or has a leader that promotes himself as God. Daniel 9:27 and 2 Thessalonians 2:1–12 indicate that in the last 3½ years of the Great Tribulation the Antichrist breaks his covenant of peace with Israel. He stops the Jewish ceremonies held in the newly built temple and sets himself up as God.

Just as Satan has done in the past, he aims through the Antichrist to weaken God's influence among the people by presenting them with a counterfeit god.

A similar strategy was used in World War II. Lawrence Malkin made this known in his book *Krueger's Men: The Secret Nazi Counterfeit Plot and the Prisoners of Block 19.* Bernhard Krueger's idea was to use Jewish prisoners to produce 650,000 notes a month of British and, later, American currency. The plan was to use a flood of counterfeit currency to ultimately sabotage the economies of both governments.

Satan aims to flood the world with multiple counterfeit gods, and ultimately one lone counterfeit god, in order to sabotage the spiritual economy of the world. It's sad that we are seeing some of the effects

---

57   MacArthur, *Time*, 201.

of his sabotaging efforts even today. We not only see this in the thousands of differing world religions and beliefs, but it also surfaces in the new spiritual "fast-food plan."

Some fast-food establishments and restaurants now offer a list of options allowing us to create our own meal by picking two or three items from a list for a given price. By flooding the world with counterfeit gods, Satan now offers a "build-your-own belief option." You can create your own god, but Satan hides the true price. It costs us our opportunity to truly know God now and for eternity.

Satan's aim behind flooding the world with counterfeit gods is scary and simple. By flooding the world with all these counterfeit beliefs and experiences, it weakens God's influence in lives on earth.

To Offer Paper Power

The second aim behind Satan's counterfeiting efforts is to offer paper power. Verse 2 explains, *"The dragon gave the beast his power and his throne and great authority."* Satan made the same offer to Jesus when tempting Him in the wilderness. In Matthew 4:8–10, Satan shows Jesus all the kingdoms of the world and tells Him, *"All this I will give you if you will bow down and worship me."* Thankfully, Jesus commands Satan to leave and vows to only worship God. Jesus did this because He knew Satan's power, throne, and authority are all counterfeit. Like offering a bogus check, they aren't worth the paper they are written on.

Frank Abagnale Jr., understood the effectiveness of writing bogus checks. The movie *Catch Me If You Can* made his story popular. Between his sixteenth and twenty-first birthdays, Abagnale wrote bogus checks and pocketed over $2.5 million dollars: quite a large sum in the 1960s. Surprisingly, Abagnale didn't only deceive

Americans. His bogus checks were effective in twenty-six countries. People around the world took his checks, not realizing that what he wrote wasn't worth the paper it was written on.

The word "authority" in verse 2 underscores Satan's worthless paper power. It's the same Greek word Jesus uses for authority in Matthew 28:18. There, before His ascension to heaven, Jesus announces, *"All authority in heaven and on earth has been given to me."* Though verse 2 labels Satan's authority as "great," and though it's the Greek word *megas*, which would cause us today to call it "mega-authority," God knows Satan's authority is only on paper, and it's not worth the paper it's on. As was shared in the study of Revelation 12, Jesus has the keys of heaven, death, and Hades (Matt. 16:18–20; Revelation 1:18). Jesus' reign and resources back His authority and power. Satan has nothing in the bank to back what he says. What is sad is that many will wait too late to figure it out.

To Have What God Has

Verse 4 reveals Satan's ultimate aim behind all his counterfeit efforts. It says, *"Men worshiped the dragon because he had given authority to the beast, and they also worshiped the beast and asked, 'Who is like the beast? Who can make war against him?'"* Do you remember why Satan was cast out of heaven? Isaiah 14:14 records that he wanted to make himself *"like the Most High."* When he tempted Adam and Eve to sin against God, Satan dangled the same carrot in front of them that caused his fall. He told them in Genesis 3:5 that if they ate forbidden fruit they *"would be like God."* Then in Matthew 4:9 Satan wanted Jesus to bow down and worship him.

Every lie, every counterfeit effort by Satan, had this ultimate aim in mind—to have what God has. He wants God's position, God's power, and to be worshipped like God—but not at the same price. When Satan's deception in Eden led to our broken relationship with God, God was willing to come as Jesus Christ and die on the cross to pay the price for our sins. Out of love for us, He was willing to put His life on the line for us. Not Satan; he wants what God has, but never at the same price. He'll put our life on the line, but not his. That is why he will never have what God has. In the span of eternity he might have his fifteen minutes of fame, but it won't last—counterfeits never do.

GOD'S RESPONSE

As Satan works his counterfeit plans, it may seem that God is doing nothing. But that's not true, and we can see this from a careful reading of Revelation 13:5–10.

> [5] The beast was given a mouth to utter proud words and blasphemies and to exercise his authority for forty-two months. [6] He opened his mouth to blaspheme God, and to slander his name and his dwelling place and those who live in heaven. [7] He was given power to make war against the saints and to conquer them. And he was given authority over every tribe, people, language and nation. [8] All inhabitants of the earth will worship the beast—all whose names have not been written in the book of life belonging to the Lamb that was slain from the creation of the world.

> [9] He who has an ear, let him hear.
> [10] If anyone is to go into captivity,
> into captivity he will go.
> If anyone is to be killed with the sword,
> with the sword he will be killed.

This calls for patient endurance and faithfulness on the part of the saints.

When a grievous crime is committed, those doing the investigation wait until obtaining all the evidence before making any arrests. They build a case before presenting it to the judge. In the same way, God lets Satan's counterfeit run its course. He does so to build His case—a case not only against Satan, but against those who fall to his scam.

Building a Case

Verses 5–7 bring to mind the saying, "giving them enough rope to hang themselves." Three times in these three verses we find the word "given." In verse 3, the beast was given *"a mouth to utter proud words."* The Antichrist becomes a mesmerizing orator, whose blasphemous statements will go unpunished by God for 3½ years. In verse 7, the beast is given *"power to make war against the saints."* God does not withhold the Antichrist's attacks on the saints, save the 144,000 Jewish believers (Rev. 12:14). And in verse 7, the beast is given *"authority over every tribe, people, language and nation."* Referring to the authority of government, Romans 13:1 reminds us that *"there is no authority except that which God has established."* Thus, no authority exists on earth that God has not allowed. In the last half of the Great Tribulation, God allows the Antichrist to assume supreme authority over the world, because he is building a case.

Verses 8–11 announce that God's case will not only be against the Antichrist, but against those who fall prey to his counterfeiting ways. It will be 3½ years of winnowing. In Luke 3:17, John the Baptist pictures God with a winnowing fork in His hand. The purpose of the fork was to throw the harvested to separate the wheat to be stored from the chaff to be burned. The Antichrist becomes that winnowing fork in God's hand. His actions separate the believers from the blind—separating those who have surrendered to God from those who have succumbed to Satan.

I took a college class in business law, taught by a sitting judge. He opened our first class posing the question, "Which is better, to be innocent or to have a good attorney?" I was eighteen years old and sided with those in class who felt innocence always wins. Being a judge, he had the final say. Looking as though he was laughing at our innocence, he said, "It's better to have a good lawyer."

I'm afraid there are many who believe that when they stand before God, they will be able to plead their case well. They will speak of extenuating circumstances. They'll blame others, and will probably even try to blame God. But God the Judge is also the court clerk, and a perfect God has taken perfect records. Regardless of your plea, God will simply look for your name on a page. He will look to see if your name is written in the book of life. He will look to see if you ever surrendered your life to Jesus Christ.

Encouraging the Saints

For those with their name written in the book of life, God provides a special word of encouragement. In verses 9–10 God says,

> [9] He who has an ear, let him hear.
>
> [10] If anyone is to go into captivity,
>
> into captivity he will go.
>
> If anyone is to be killed with the sword,
>
> with the sword he will be killed.

> This calls for patient endurance and faithfulness on the part of the saints.

In the last days, God allows the beast to have authority in the world and to attack the saints. He tells believers, "If I allow you, a family member, friend, or fellow believer to be taken into captivity or to be executed, stand strong. Remember, I allowed it. Therefore endure it with patience, and be faithful."

God's encouragement to future saints speaks to us today. Even today, God allows us to endure unwanted experiences so He can build a case. Our earnest faithfulness to God piles up the evidence demanding a verdict. God sees the jurors surrounding us. He knows they are assessing the evidence of our lives. Some may be strong believers needing encouragement to remain strong. Other believers may have grown weak. Our faithfulness inspires them to stand strong once again. A different audience watches, too—unbelievers. They wonder if a life in Christ is all we say it is. By watching our faithfulness in unfair circumstances, we may help them surrender to Jesus.

Thus, Revelation 13:5–10 is more than God building a case against the Antichrist and his followers. It reminds us that God at times builds a case for and through His followers. The question to ask in the middle of your trial is, "Is God building a case for me or against me?" To answer this question, stop and review the degree of your faithfulness to God in the midst of the trial.

SATAN'S METHODS

Revelation 13 unveils Satan's sinister intent to weaken God's influence by counterfeiting His ways. He offers us worthless paper power, if we will worship him as God. God will allow Satan's counterfeiting scam to build His case—a case against the Antichrist and his followers as well as a case for God and His followers. Like stepping into a smoke-filled room, Revelation 12:11–88 enables us to overhear Satan's plans behind his scam.

> [11] Then I saw another beast, coming out of the earth. He had two horns like a lamb, but he spoke like a dragon. [12] He exercised all the authority of the first beast on his behalf, and made the earth and its inhabitants worship the first beast, whose fatal wound had been healed. [13] And he performed great and miraculous signs, even causing fire to come down from heaven to earth in full view of men. [14] Because of the signs he was given power to do on behalf of the first beast, he deceived the inhabitants of the earth. He ordered them to set up an image in honor of the beast who was wounded by the sword and yet lived. [15] He was given power to give breath to the image of the first beast, so that it could speak and cause all who refused to worship the image to be killed. [16] He also forced everyone, small and great, rich and poor, free and slave, to receive a mark on his right hand or on his forehead, [17] so that no one could buy or sell unless he had the mark, which is the name of the beast or the number of his name.
>
> [18] This calls for wisdom. If anyone has insight, let him calculate the number of the beast, for it is man's number. His number is 666.

For Satan's counterfeit to succeed, several aspects of his scheme must work together. According to Ephesians 6:11, the word "scheme" aptly describes Satan's efforts. It says, *"Put on the full armor of God, so that you can take your stand against the devil's schemes."* The Greek word for "schemes" is *methodeia*. We hear in it the English word "method." Verses 11–18 reveal Satan's well-planned methods behind his counterfeiting scam.

Counterfeiters Need Con Artists

The first method in Satan's scheme requires the use of a con artist. To be successful, counterfeiters need to be or have con artists. Verses 11–17 introduce a gifted con artist.

Verse 11 describes him as *"another beast."* The Greek word for "another" refers to another of the same kind. Verse 12 says he possesses the same kind of authority as the first beast. Verses 14–15 add he has the same kind of power as the first beast, yet he describes him differently. We are not told how many heads he has, but it's clear he has only two horns and no crowns. The absence of crowns may point to the fact that he's void of any political or governmental authority. However, it's disturbing that the beast has two lamb horns, making him seem gentle and unassuming. But when he speaks, verse 11 says he has the voice of a dragon. He plays the role of the lamb to fulfill the plans of the dragon. That's the epitome of a con artist.

Even Frank Abagnale understood the importance of being a con artist. To amass $2.5 million dollars in just five years, he posed as an airline pilot, a teacher, a doctor, and attorney.

Like a magician showing you one hand to distract you from the other, a con artist shows you a false role to hide his true motives. Satan did this in Eden. In Genesis 3, he played a beautiful serpent. The serpent was probably beautiful, for only after the deception did God change his form to make him slither on the ground. The serpent played the part to hide his plan, and he is still doing so today.

2 Corinthians 11:14–15 divulges how Satan masquerades as an angel of light. His servants also play the role of God's servants and deceive many. Sadly, the news only reports a portion of all that Satan has done through pastors, priests, and others to hide their ungodly plans. Satan's actions as a con artist continue even in the end times.

Revelation 13 reports that the false prophet appears as unassuming as a lamb, but using words of a dragon. Satan has been so successful as a con artist we may wonder, "How can I tell true character from a character actor? How can I tell if Satan is trying to con me?" We will look at that shortly. However, it's important that we identify Satan's second method behind his counterfeit plan.

Con Artists Need a Truth

Though it sounds ironic, a con artist needs to use a truth to promote his lie. Even good counterfeiters understood this. In one of his "The Rest of the Story" broadcasts, I heard Paul Harvey unveil the secret behind one of the most successful counterfeiters in history. For years this counterfeiter passed off phony bills in several countries, and only toward the end of his life did he reveal his secret: it was the paper. He said most counterfeiters are not caught because of poor printing skills, they are caught because they can't find paper like that of real bills. His secret was to take several $1 bills, remove their ink, then reprint them as $100 bills. He took the true paper in order to reprint and re-circulate a lie.

In Revelation 13:13–17, we find Satan using a truth to carry his lies. The false prophet takes the ways the Holy Spirit worked in the past and removes God's message from them to reprint and recirculate Satan's lies. When placed side-by-side, we see how the False Prophet uses the Holy Spirit's ways to spread Satan's lies:

Holy Spirit	False Prophet
Instrument of Divine Revelation (John 16:13)	Instrument of Satanic Revelation (Rev. 13:11)
Seals Believers to God (1 John 3:24)	Marks Unbelievers with the Number of the Antichrist (Rev. 13:16)
Builds the Body of Christ (John 7:37–39)	Builds an Empire of the Antichrist (Rev. 13:17)
Uses Miracles to Lead Mankind to the Truth (John 14:17, 26)	Uses Miracles to Lead Mankind away from the Truth (Rev. 13:13–15)
Points Men to Christ (John 15:26)	Points Men to Satan (Rev. 13:12, 14) [58]

As before, we might wonder, "How can I ever detect what Satan is doing, and so protect myself from his counterfeiting scam?" Again, we will get to that in a moment, but first we need to see the hidden agenda behind Satan's actions. Satan's well-planned methods have a preconceived end. Simply put, Satan lies to gain control.

He Lies to Gain Control

In Revelation 13:16–18, Satan's counterfeiting methods give him what he wants—control! Just as Revelation 7:2–3 says that God places His seal or mark on the foreheads of the 144,000 Jews who surrender to Christ, the Antichrist places his mark on an unbelieving world that surrenders to him. Those caught without the mark are put to death.

---

58   Hindson, *Revelation*, 142. (I modified the order and some wording. MB)

Those refusing the mark may hide, but they find it hard to survive. They won't be able to purchase food or supplies without the mark of the beast. The Antichrist and his false prophet have worked their scam and gained control.

That's the way Satan and his scams have always worked. He plays a part to hide his plan, and uses a truth to conceal his lie until suddenly we realize we are hooked. Through a philosophy, conviction, action, or addiction, he gains control of your life. It's a control that's hard, but not impossible, to break.

What God describes in the end times will take place. The vast majority of the world will fall to his diabolical scam. They will surrender control of everything to the Antichrist. We are not in the end times, and yet Satan is still counterfeiting and scamming to gain control of our lives. Therefore, we need to learn what to do to see his scam before it ever takes control.

COUNTERFEIT CONSULTATION

Isn't it amazing how those who know the scams best become consultants to protect others from falling prey? After spending five years in prison, Frank Abagnale founded a consulting firm called Abagnale and Associates. For over thirty years now, he has been a consultant for the FBI and over 14,000 companies. This former con artist now teaches others how to protect themselves from con artists.[59]

Satan will never become a consultant teaching us how to protect ourselves from him. However, God has an exhaustive knowledge of Satan's schemes. In Revelation 13, God discloses four protective measures against Satan's counterfeiting ways.

---

59   Abagnale and Associates website, http://www.abagnale.com/aboutfrank.htm

#1 – DON'T BE NAÏVE

The first protective measure is "Don't Be Naïve." Don't think Satan doesn't exist. Furthermore, don't think that Satan exists but acts like a mindless brute. Satan aims to (1) weaken God's influence in your life and in the world (2) by offering paper power: counterfeit things that may look good on paper but don't really exist and will never last. Satan will do all this at your expense to (3) achieve his ultimate aim— to be worshiped as God.

#2 – BE INFORMED

Therefore, to counter Satan's counterfeit, you need to be informed. Since Satan uses the truth to carry his lie, we need to have a firm grasp of the truth. When Satan tempts Jesus in Matthew 4, Jesus counters his counterfeit efforts by quoting scripture. Even when Satan uses scripture out of context to deceive Jesus, Jesus knows it. Realizing that Satan uses the truth to carry his lies, be well-read and well-informed regarding God's truth.

Realizing that Satan offers counterfeit solutions to life's true problems, gain a true perspective of the problem. The only way to do that is to see it from God's side. Seeing life from God's side, we see the difference between godly solutions and counterfeit ones. We become well-informed by spending time with God in His Word.

#3 – BE DETERMINED

It takes determination to counter Satan's counterfeit efforts. Be determined to live each day so God can build a case with you, not against you. Surrender your life to Jesus and live each day fully surrendered. That way when God allows hardships to come, those who are watching will see what a life surrendered to Christ looks like. God then builds a case through your life to draw others to Him. Living that way, we never have to worry about God building a case against us due to a lack of surrender.

#4 – BE ENCOURAGED

Finally, we need to remember this important protective measure—be encouraged. We may grow weary constantly looking for, discovering, and countering Satan's counterfeits. We may think, "It's hopeless; why do I keep doing this?" Here are some reasons to be encouraged in the effort. Be encouraged because:

- Others are watching who are being deceived. Your life reveals Satan's lies, and inspires them to surrender their lives afresh or for the first time to God. Your efforts to counter the counterfeiter make a difference.

- Others are watching who are growing tired in their efforts to counter Satan's counterfeits. Your faithfulness encourages them to stay faithful. Your efforts to counter the counterfeiter encourage others to do the same and make a difference.

- God is watching. He knows how hard it is to counter the counterfeiter. He knows the sacrifice you are making to remain faithful to Him. Though at times it seems that the counterfeiter is getting away with a lot, in the end he loses everything and you gain everything . . . because God is watching. Be encouraged!

CHAPTER 17

IT'S YOUR CHOICE
REVELATION 14

I HAVE ALWAYS BELIEVED IN growth by consequences. We grow by learning from our successes and our mistakes. Our children understand this through the video games they play. Their characters ultimately win by making a series of right choices. But they won't make the right choices until they learn from the wrong ones.

That makes growth by consequences an effective parenting tool as well. Explaining to children the consequences of right and wrong choices, and then holding them accountable for their choices, is crucial. When done consistently, they will in time consider the consequences before they act. Learning from wrong choices helps us make right ones.

Sadly, not everyone likes the concept of growing by consequences. We hear it in spiritual conversations when people say, "I just don't believe that a loving God would send anyone to hell." If they would look closely at John 3:16–18, they would see that God sends no one to hell. He clearly explains the consequences of surrendering or not surrendering one's life to Jesus. Then He lets us experience the consequences of our choice.

> 16 For God so loved the world that he gave his one and only Son, that whoever believes in him shall not perish but have eternal life.

[17] For God did not send his Son into the world to condemn the world, but to save the world through him. [18] Whoever believes in him is not condemned, but whoever does not believe stands condemned already because he has not believed in the name of God's one and only Son.

In these and other verses throughout the Bible, God explains the consequences of surrendering or not surrendering to Jesus. He explains it so well and up front that there shouldn't be any surprises. The consequences of our actions are clear, and the choice is left up to us.

Another important tool in good parenting is consistency—consistently saying what you mean and meaning what you say. We find that true of God throughout His Word. What Jesus says in John 3:16–18 resurfaces in the last book of the Bible. In Revelation 14, God identifies three choices and consequences explained repeatedly throughout scripture.

Revelation 14:1, 6, and 14 open with the same Greek phrase *kai eidon*. It means "and I looked" or "and I saw." God gives John three visions. These visions not only summarize what God is about to do in Revelation 15–19, they also repeat the choices and consequences that God explains time and again in His Word. Therefore, as we look at these choices and consequences, remember: it's your choice!

ENJOY WORSHIP WITH GOD
. . . Or Not!

The first choice, or consequence, explained in Revelation 14 is that you can enjoy worship with God . . . or not. The choice is yours. God explains this in verses 1–5.

¹ Then I looked, and there before me was the Lamb, standing on Mount Zion, and with him 144,000 who had his name and his Father's name written on their foreheads. ² And I heard a sound from heaven like the roar of rushing waters and like a loud peal of thunder. The sound I heard was like that of harpists playing their harps. ³ And they sang a new song before the throne and before the four living creatures and the elders. No one could learn the song except the 144,000 who had been redeemed from the earth. ⁴ These are those who did not defile themselves with women, for they kept themselves pure. They follow the Lamb wherever he goes. They were purchased from among men and offered as first-fruits to God and the Lamb. ⁵ No lie was found in their mouths; they are blameless.

These verses remind us of John's experience in Revelation 5:6. There, a worship experience in heaven takes place when John says, *"Then I saw a Lamb."* Just as in Revelation 5, the worship experience in Revelation 14 involves the twenty-four elders, the four living creatures, as well as all in heaven and earth. However, now a special group is added. With the lamb are the 144,000 Jewish believers He had sealed and promised to protect in Revelation 7:2–4.

Again, this vision foretells what will happen in the subsequent chapters. Those God protected are present, and it's time for them, and only them, to sing.

The Right to Sing

Some may wonder, "What gives them the right to have a special song in this heavenly worship experience?" One reason is no one else knew their song. No one else knew it because no one else in heaven had the exact same experience with God as did these 144,000. Though many believers other than these 144,000 surrendered their lives to Christ and are a part of the heavenly worship experience, the vast majority were raptured before the Great Tribulation. Though others beyond the 144,000 surrender to Christ during the Great Tribulation and are also there to worship, only the 144,000 were set aside for a unique service unto God. They were the *"firstfruits"* (v. 4) to surrender themselves to God during the tribulation, and through them, others followed. Out of their unique experience with God they offer a song in worship only they could sing.

This is a good place to be reminded what worship is and is not. Worship is not about what we can get out of the experience. That's what we expect when we go to a performance. Worship is all about what we express to God out of the overflow of our experience with Him. That's why many leave worship services empty. We leave empty if we expect the worship services to fill us, when in reality our service with God during the week should bring us full and ready to worship God out of the overflow of our life. Thus, 144,000 were full from their experiences with God and had a song only they could sing. Furthermore, they had earned the right to sing it.

Verses 3–5 list all they did to earn the right to sing their song. They were redeemed. The Greek root word means "to go to market." They understood that their sins amassed a bill with God they could never pay. Jesus went to the market of a holy God and with His very life paid their bill in full. They understood this and surrendered their lives to Him.

This made them pure before God, and they made the effort to remain pure. Reviewing pagan beliefs in scripture, most emphasized promiscuity. Sexual promiscuity will likely reach new lows in a world governed by the Antichrist. Though culture around them said it was all right, they knew that in God's eyes it was all wrong. Thus, the 144,000 remained sexually pure.

Furthermore, they were "wherever" followers. Wherever God asked them to go, they went. Whatever God asked them to do they did. They were obedient without question or hesitation. No wonder they could worship God out of the overflow. Their lives were full of experiences that gave them reason to worship.

As a result, God looked on them with holy pride as He considered them His firstfruits. They surrendered first, spoke first, and served first. Though most of us wait for someone else to step out first, they obeyed God without waiting for others to go first. And when they spoke out, there was no lie in them. They spoke the truth and lived the truth. Therefore, in a single word, God calls them blameless.

Recognizing Jesus' sacrifice and surrendering to Him, resisting the culture and remaining pure, remaining obedient to whatever God asked even when it meant being the first to do it and doing all blamelessly before God...no wonder God gave the 144,000 a special place in the worship in heaven. They earned it, and they were ready for it.

Singing Because of Right Choices

Though we often don't see it this way, experiencing God in worship is the result of making right choices. Like most pastors, I have individuals who have been members for years. They served in the church seldom missing a service. Tragically, though, they gave their time to the church, but never truly gave themselves to Jesus. Once they realized this and genuinely surrendered to Him, their worship experience changed dramatically. Though none ever voiced it this way, they could have said, "I've attended worship services all these years but never really got it, and now I know why. I never really got it because I never really had it. I never really had a relationship with God until I surrendered my life to Jesus." When you make that right choice, you discover that you now have the right to sincerely worship. Realizing Jesus has forgiven your sins, and that His spirit now lives in you, you not only have the right to sing, but you want to sing.

However, to keep ourselves in full voice, we need to keep making right choices. When we make right choices to stay pure, go wherever Jesus says even if it means being the first, our choices keep us close to God. Being close to God, we can't help but want to worship Him and sing.

In case you missed it, here's how right choices lead to a life of sincere and meaningful worship.

- A right choice leads you to surrender your life to Jesus.
- Surrendering your life to Jesus leads you to seeing and worshipping God in a close and meaningful way.
- Worshipping God in a close and meaningful way helps you make more right choices with God.
- Making more right choices with God produces even more meaningful worship experiences with God.

Seeing the worship experiences of the 144,000 in Revelation 14 reminds us that in life we can enjoy worship with God or not...the choice is ours.

HEED GOD'S WARNING
. . . Or Not!

In Revelation 14:6–11, John's second vision reveals a second choice and consequence. John sees three angels delivering three messages.

Through their messages, God makes a strong statement. He says, "You can heed My warning...or not! The choice is yours."

First Angel: "You Can Still Repent."

The message of the first angel in verses 6–7 appears throughout the New Testament. Even in the last days, God says, "You can still repent!"

> ⁶ Then I saw another angel flying in midair, and he had the eternal gospel to proclaim to those who live on the earth—to every nation, tribe, language and people. ⁷ He said in a loud voice, "Fear God and give him glory, because the hour of his judgment has come. Worship him who made the heavens, the earth, the sea, and the springs of water."

Verse 6 records the first angel proclaiming the eternal gospel for all on earth to hear. This Greek word for "gospel," *euangelisai*, is translated as "gospel" or "good news" over 100 times in the New Testament. Though this is its only occurrence in the book of Revelation, it comes at a significant moment.

Chapter 14 represents a summary of God's final judgment. He knows the time is near. That's why God sends His angel to deliver the same good news He delivered again and again—"You can still be forgiven. You can still be saved. You can still have an immediate and everlasting relationship with me...if you will repent!"

Some may say, "I see the word 'gospel' in verse 6, but I don't see the word 'repent' anywhere." It's in the phrase *"Fear God and give him glory."* Forms of this idiom appear elsewhere in scripture, describing acts of repentance (Josh. 7:19–21; Eccles. 12:13–14; Luke 23:40–43). This is just like God. In His last minutes on the cross, Jesus promised salvation to a repentant thief, and now in the last minutes before His final judgment, God again offers salvation to those who repent.

Second Angel: "The Ways of This World are Wrong."

We can all probably identify several individuals in our lives who see no need to repent. We might have tried having a spiritual conversation with them, but ended up walking away scratching our heads and wondering "Where do they get these ideas? How could they be so blind?" Scripture says their bizarre ideas come from Satan (2 Cor. 4:4). He makes them spiritually blind (John 12:40). This becomes even worse in the end times. Thus, a second angel is needed. John sees him and records his message in verse 8.

> [8] A second angel followed and said, "Fallen! Fallen is Babylon the Great, which made all the nations drink the maddening wine of her adulteries."

In subsequent chapters, "Babylon the Great" describes the one-world government of the Antichrist. Just as the purpose and personality of an organization is channeled from the top down, the one-world government's purpose and personality comes from Satan himself. Through the deceptions of the Antichrist and the False Prophet (Rev. 13), people blindly think the ways of the world are right and will prevail. God knows otherwise and makes it known. God knows that the ways of the world are wrong and that the one-world government of the Antichrist is already fallen. He wants others to see it, before it's too late.

Third Angel: "The Ways of This World Lead to Hell."

Many of us have a friend or loved one who is so blind and stubborn that we think God will have to do something dramatic to get their attention. That is God's intent with the message delivered by the third angel in verses 9–11.

> ⁹ A third angel followed them and said in a loud voice: "If anyone worships the beast and his image and receives his mark on the forehead or on the hand, ¹⁰ he, too, will drink of the wine of God's fury, which has been poured full-strength into the cup of his wrath. He will be tormented with burning sulfur in the presence of the holy angels and of the Lamb. ¹¹ And the smoke of their torment rises forever and ever. There is no rest day or night for those who worship the beast and his image, or for anyone who receives the mark of his name."

Through this message God says, "If you don't surrender your life to me, you will experience the extent of my full wrath—eternity in hell." Listen to the words God uses to make this warning. Unless you repent you will be *"tormented"* in a place of *"burning sulfur"* and *"smoke...forever and ever."*

This is not a new warning from God. In Matthew 7:13–14, Jesus warns that the ways of this world lead to destruction. And when talking about hell, He describes what that destruction looks like.

Three words are translated in the Greek New Testament as "hell." The one used most by Jesus is *Gehenna*. This was a valley southwest of Jerusalem with a violent past and a gruesome image. In 2 Kings 23:10, under the godless rule of King Manasseh, Gehenna was the evil place where babies were placed in heated metal images and burned as an act of pagan worship. Godly King Josiah stopped all that and turned Gehenna into a city dump, to burn trash. The corpses of criminals were also thrown there to be burned. Gehenna in Jesus' day was the picture of perpetual fire carrying the smell of burning flesh. It was the clearest picture Jesus could give when describing hell.

God uses such imagery to underscore the message of the third angel in Revelation 14:9–11. Even at the last, God wants to make it clear that the ways of this world are wrong, and ultimately lead to hell. That is why it is imperative that we know the facts and choose to repent.

Know the Facts and Choose

My son John Mark and I had a wonderful experience diving the Dos Oios caverns in Mexico. Our guide's name was Victor. Since neither of us had ever dived in caverns, we had a lot of questions. Victor explained that the difference between a cave and a cavern is that caverns have periodic openings. Since we were in a cavern, we would never be more than 45 seconds from fresh air, in case something went wrong. In a cave, on the other hand, you can go for a long time before finding fresh air. "How long?" we asked. Victor said, "There are 47 miles of underground caves and caverns filled with water. That is why you need to listen to my instructions before we start, and follow my lead on the dive." With that said, Victor had our full attention.

Before our dive, Victor gave us two warnings. He said that during our dive we would see the spot where the cave's fresh water meets and mixes with the ocean's saltwater. Smiling, he explained, "The visibility in these caverns is crystal clear. You will be able to see 600 feet in front of you. However, when we get to the place where the two water sources meet and mix it becomes blurry. I'll point it out to you, so that when you see it you won't think something's wrong in your head."

I was glad Victor had told us before this happened, because when he pointed to the blurred spot underwater, I knew what to do. I had to turn away and follow my guide. Victor would keep us in clear water.

That's what God does in verses 6–11. He lets those in the end times, and us today, know that Satan will do everything he can to blur our eyes and mind. Satan mixes his lies in with God's truth. If we don't turn from the mixture and follow Jesus and His truth alone, we won't survive spiritually. In fact, we will experience something else Victor warned us about.

The second warning Victor gave was about choosing between two openings. One would keep us on our cavern dive. The other would lead us on a long cave dive. We asked Victor, "How long?" He said we would go for over three hours before being able to surface. Because of our limited air supply, we knew if we took that opening it would be the last decision of our life. To make sure we didn't mistakenly take the wrong opening, a sign was posted underwater in front of it. Though I don't read Spanish, the image of the grim reaper on the sign said enough. I heeded the warning, followed my guide, and went the other way.

God's vivid description of hell lets those in the end times and us today understand the importance of making the right choice. Everyone born has two great openings before them. One leads to a full life with God on earth and everlasting life with Him in heaven. The other leads to a life blurred by Satan on earth and an everlasting life without God in hell. God has placed all this in His Word so that we can know the facts. His hope is that once we hear the facts, we will heed His warning and make the right choice. If not, God knows that the grim reaper is waiting.

EXPERIENCE GOD'S WRATH
. . . Or Not!

Though it seems inappropriate for Jesus to be called the grim reaper, those who have chosen not to surrender to Him will likely give Him that title. Verses 14–20 explain:

> [14] I looked, and there before me was a white cloud, and seated on the cloud was one "like a son of man" with a crown of gold on his head and a sharp sickle in his hand. [15] Then another angel came out of the temple and called in a loud voice to him who was sitting on the cloud, "Take your sickle and reap, because the time to reap has come, for the harvest of the earth is ripe."[16] So he who was seated on the cloud swung his sickle over the earth, and the earth was harvested.
>
> [17] Another angel came out of the temple in heaven, and he too had a sharp sickle. [18] Still another angel, who had charge of the fire, came from the altar and called in a loud voice to him who had the sharp sickle, "Take your sharp sickle and gather the clusters of grapes from the earth's vine, because its grapes are ripe." [19] The angel swung his sickle on the earth, gathered its grapes and threw them into the great winepress of God's wrath. [20] They were trampled in the winepress outside the city, and blood flowed out of the press, rising as high as the horses' bridles for a distance of 1,600 stadia.

This is John's third vision recorded in chapter 14. Though we marvel over Jesus in a manger and are humbled by Him on the cross, we don't like to consider Jesus on a cloud coming with a sickle in His hand. Yet for those who choose not to surrender to Jesus, He acts as their grim reaper. Sadly, those who experience Jesus this way should not be surprised: God warns them in verses 9–11, and Jesus fulfills the warning in verses 14–20.

Verse 14 says the One on a white cloud wearing a gold crown is *"like a son of man."* These qualifiers identify Him as Jesus. Verses 15–19 reveal that Jesus is not alone. Three angels soon join Him. The first angel calls to Jesus and says it's time to swing His sickle and begin the harvest (v. 15). The second angel emerges from the temple holding a sickle as well (v. 17), followed by a third angel (v. 18), who then compels the second angel to join Christ in harvesting those who remain on earth.

This passage describes Jesus' judgment as a grape harvest, and it is gruesomely fitting. In the first century, grapes were cut from vines and placed in large vats. There the grapes were stomped until their juices flowed. According to verse 20, this winepress of God's wrath occurs *"outside the city."* This means it happens near but not at Jerusalem. Realizing that chapter 14 is a summary of events to come, looking ahead to Revelation 16:16 we find John identifying the final battle on earth as the battle of Armageddon. It's located around fifty miles northwest of Jerusalem. That makes it near, but not at, Jerusalem. Verse 20 also says that the blood from the winepress of God's wrath will flow 5 feet deep ("as high as the horses' bridles") for 200 miles ("1,600 stadia"). Furthermore, God knows that those who experience His wrath didn't have to—they chose to.

Earlier I mentioned how choices and consequences are a part of parenting. James Dobson has been a friend to parents for decades. He said something once that helped me get through this harsh picture of God's wrath. He said that God gave us a free choice because there is no significance to love if there is no alternative.[60] God made it known through His word that He created us to have a loving relationship with Him. And to be certain that our love for Him was real and not divinely programmed, He gave each of us the freedom to make choices. That meant when we chose to surrender our lives to Him, it was meaningful.

Throughout creation, God has tried a variety of ways to communicate His love for us. The most dramatic was when He put on skin and sacrificed Himself for our sins as Jesus. In Romans 5:8, the Bible says God displayed His love for us with the hope that we would choose to love Him in return. It adds in 2 Corinthians 5:15 that He sacrificed Himself for us with the hope that we would choose to surrender our lives to Him. God created us with the freedom to choose and to face the consequences of our choices. If we choose to surrender our lives to Him, we experience a full life with Him on earth and an eternal life with Him in heaven. If we choose not to surrender to Him, our experience will be different. We will never know the life with God we were created to have on earth, and we will spend eternity without Him in hell when we die.

The choices and consequences are so dramatically different that God has tried every way possible to communicate them to us. He's done this with the hope that we heed His warning, avoid His wrath, and enjoy a life with God that will cause us to worship Him out of the overflow of our experiences with Him.

---

60   Draper, *Quotations*, entry 1141. The exact quote is, "God gave us a free choice because there is no significance to love that knows no alternative."

We can experience or avoid God's wrath. Revelation 14:14–20 says it's our choice. But don't think we can wait until the battle of Armageddon to decide. God can swing His sickle for any one at any time. That's His choice.

A TIME OF REST
...or Not!

There is one passage in chapter 14 that I saved until now. On my first reading, I thought it was a parenthetical thought in the chapter. But the more I read it, the more it became personal.

At the end of God's warning to repent in verses 6–11, God speaks to those who have repented. He knows they are living in a time when

- Believers face a worldview that has turned away from God (Rev. 13:4);
- Believers feel the wrath of Satan who has targeted them for persecution (Rev. 13:7);
- Believers live at a time when the world feels God's undiluted wrath (Rev. 14:10).

Therefore, in verses 12–13, God encourages them to make choices that reward them with rest. God says that, in such times,

> [12] This calls for patient endurance on the part of the saints who obey God's commandments and remain faithful to Jesus.

> [13] Then I heard a voice from heaven say, "Write: Blessed are the dead who die in the Lord from now on."

> "Yes," says the Spirit, "they will rest from their labor, for their deeds will follow them."

Though Loree and I are not experiencing all that the believers in the end times will, that doesn't make our pressures *feel* any lighter. Trying to live for Christ and lead others to do the same in this day and time is hard. One evening, Loree and I were watching a television program that explained how the witness protection program worked. Before being admitted into this program, the individuals are told,

> "You will be relocated to another state, given a completely different occupation with a new name, identity, phone number, and email address. It will be as though you have disappeared from the face of the earth."

Hearing that, Loree touched my arm and wistfully asked, "Mark, how can we get in on that?"

Honestly, it's hard to live as a believer in an unbelieving world. Furthermore, it's hard to stand with Christ when so many want to knock us off our perch. It will be exponentially harder in the end times, but that doesn't mean we don't feel the pressure as a believer today. That's why God's words to the believers in verses 12–13 are important to hear.

God says there are choices we make when wearied from living as a believer that He rewards with rest. In verse 12 God says, "Choose to patiently endure." Though we want to quit, God says to choose to keep going.

Also in verse 12, God says we might think that if we compromise a little we can stand a little longer. God has always said that compromise, no matter how small, is a huge mistake. Though we might prefer compromise, God says to keep His commandments.

Finally in verse 12, God helps us choose not to quit or compromise by reminding us that our choices in life are personal to God. His charge is to *"remain faithful to Jesus."* What a reminder. On the eve of His crucifixion, Jesus was faced with the desire to quit, or at least to find some other way to fulfill God's plan. Yet, under pressure that none of us will ever fully experience, Jesus remained faithful to God for us. Therefore, regardless of the pressure we may feel for being faithful to God, we should be faithful to Jesus.

Above all, God adds that when we choose to patiently endure, obey His commands, and remain faithful to Jesus, God promises a consequence worth waiting for. He says in verse 13 that there will come a day when believers will experience *"rest from their labor"* and *"their deeds will follow them."* When God puts it that way, I choose to stay faithful to Him now, because He has promised me that a rest comes later

BETTER, OR BITTER?

REVELATION 15, 16

⁴³ *"You have heard that it was said, 'Love your neighbor and hate your enemy.'* ⁴⁴ *But I tell you: Love your enemies and pray for those who persecute you,* ⁴⁵ *that you may be sons of your Father in heaven. He causes his sun to rise on the evil and the good, and sends rain on the righteous and the unrighteous."*

— MATTHEW 5:43–46

DURING HIS SERMON ON THE Mount, Jesus shares that God allows good experiences (the sun) and bad experiences (the rain) to affect the lives of the righteous and unrighteous alike. We see this repeatedly during the Great Tribulation.

For example, in Revelation 6 the righteous and unrighteous alike experience the deception, war, famine, and death brought on by the four horsemen of the apocalypse. In Revelation 8 and 9, seven trumpet blasts signal seven severe acts of God to reclaim the earth physically and spiritually. Both the righteous and unrighteous feel these. However, Revelation 15 and 16 record dramatically different responses to these shared experiences. The righteous respond one way, and the unrighteous another.

The study of Revelation 15 and 16 offers two important insights for today. First, *WE WILL NEVER HAVE AN EXPERIENCE THAT GOD HAS NOT ALLOWED OR INITIATED.* Some see

God as a great clockmaker and the earth as His clock. In their view, God creates the earth, sets it in motion, then sits back and watches it work without any further involvement. The Bible gives a different picture of God. In scripture, God either initiates our experiences, or allows our actions or the actions of others to dictate our experiences. Again, we never have an experience that God has not allowed or initiated.

Second, our experiences in the past often teach us how to respond to experiences today. *REVELATION 15 AND 16 SHOW US EXPERIENCES IN THE FUTURE THAT TEACH US HOW TO RESPOND TO EXPERIENCES ALLOWED OR INITIATED BY GOD TODAY.* Furthermore, these chapters not only teach us how to respond to the good experiences (when the sun shines), they also teach us how to respond to the painful experiences (when the rain falls). According to Revelation 15 and 16, we can respond to painful experiences one of two ways. We can allow them to make us better, or bitter.

BETTER, NOT BITTER!

Revelation 15 records the response of the righteous. They faced bitter times, yet emerged better. Verses 1–4 record both their story and their song.

> [1] I saw in heaven another great and marvelous sign: seven angels with the seven last plagues—last, because with them God's wrath is completed. [2] And I saw what looked like a sea of glass mixed with fire and, standing beside the sea, those who had been victorious over the beast and his image and over the number of his

name. They held harps given them by God [3] and sang the song of Moses the servant of God and the song of the Lamb:

"Great and marvelous are your deeds,

Lord God Almighty.

Just and true are your ways,

King of the ages.

[4] Who will not fear you, O Lord,

and bring glory to your name?

For you alone are holy.

All nations will come

and worship before you,

for your righteous acts have been revealed."

The first two verses carry two distinct visions. The first vision in verse 1 discloses what remains in fulfilling God's wrath. In Revelation 6, God's wrath begins with the opening of the seven seals. In Revelation 8 and 9, it grows with each blow from the seven trumpets. And now, in Revelation 15 and 16, God's wrath is completed as He pours out His wrath from the seven bowls.

The second vision, in verse 2, captures those who surrender to Christ during the Great Tribulation. Like all living on earth, they experience a world under God's wrath. Yet unlike most earth's inhabitants, they turn to God instead of from Him. They refuse to receive the mark of the beast, so they suffer bitterly for it. God's wrath on the earth makes food scarce. And without the mark of the beast, they won't be able to buy any food that is available (13:17). Some are placed in prison (13:10). Many are martyred (12:11). They experience bitter treatment from those who despise God. In John's vision, however, these believers don't emerge from their bitter times with bitter lives. Instead, the bitter times make them better.

Look where they are. Verse 2 states they are standing beside a sea of glass and fire. We first read of this sea of glass in Revelation 4:6. It represents those who now stand holy before the throne of God.[61] However, the sea of glass is now mixed with fire. This particular group has come through the fires of God's wrath during the Great Tribulation, and now stand holy before Him in heaven.

To their credit, instead of being cynical about God, they can't wait to sing before God. Verse 3 acts as the program for their concert. It says they sing the songs of Moses and the Lamb. The song of Moses refers to Exodus 15 as the people sing to God after being delivered from their bondage in Egypt. The song of the Lamb takes us back to Revelation 5. There Christ appears in heaven and all heaven celebrates. These two songs explain the reason and emotion behind their singing. They have been delivered by God from their bitter times, and they are not bitter with God. They know they are better because of God. Thus, they celebrate.

Though these verses describe what will take place in the future, they also help us deal with bitter experiences today. They remind us that God allows bitter times, not to make us bitter, but to make us better.

I confess there was one bitter experience that almost left me bitter, not better. My dad had been a pastor for forty-three years. He and Mom endured and sacrificed a lot in the ministry. Dad was forced to retire early when a disc in his back ruptured, thus causing his

---

61   See explanation in study of Revelation 4:6.

retirement years to be years filled with pain. When the pain became unbearable, the surgeons opened Dad up to see how they could help. But when the surgery revealed that Dad's body was consumed with cancer, they sent him home with hospice care.

I was with Dad for nearly a month before he died. While watching him suffer, I prayed a lot—but it didn't seem that God was answering my prayers. Unconsciously, I was making a list of unanswered prayers; like keeping a ledger, I was adding up reasons to be bitter with God. The night after we buried Dad, I became fearful that if I didn't lance the bitterness festering in my heart, I would always remain bitter with God. At other times, writing poetry had helped me get the poison out of my system. I thought no one would ever read this, but it's too honest and too real not to share. It's called "A Graveside Prayer."

A Graveside Prayer

I sat on the front row
Praying the rain would stay away.
But I had my doubts
As unanswered prayer had caused
  My faith to fade.

When I prayed for his cancer to go,
It quickly spread.
When I prayed for his mind to stay clear,
It became worse instead.
And when he struggled to take a breath,
I prayed, "God, take him now!"
But God said, "Not yet,"

And he struggled on somehow.

As anger gripped my heart,
I asked God, "Why?"
"Why would a minister
who gave so much
    have to suffer before he died?"

Then the answer came to me
From 2 Corinthians 12, Isaiah 40,
    And Ecclesiastes 3.
They spoke of God's
Sufficient grace, renewing strength,
    And perfect timing.

But anger's grip was tight,
And the war within was fierce,
    Till the anger was let go
    By looking at Dad's life
    Through the years.

Dad's life had not been easy.
He had been challenged a lot.
Yet with each mountain claimed,
Or Red Sea crossed,
No matter the valley passed through
Or burden of his cross,
He faced each test

With the same strong resolve,
To show the greatness of God,
Whatever the cost.

Through it all, Dad never
Blamed God, cursed God,
   Or asked, "Why?"
In fact, he led us all
In singing praises to God
   A few nights before he died.
And Dad died the way he lived
Giving glory to God,
   In every circumstance of life.

But for me,
Guilt and questions still remained.
Could my life with God
Ever be the same?
I was angry at God.
It was God that I blamed.
And through it all, my faith
Had been drained.
Would He forgive me and answer me
the next time I prayed?

Then I smiled as I thought
of the forecast for the day.
Sixty percent chance of rain.

Yet God had answered my prayer
And kept the rain away.
The only drops to fall
Were the tears we shed
When we buried Dad that day.
And I was reminded that God is always faithful,
Even if he doesn't answer every prayer
The way we want when we pray.

© Mark Becton 2003

By looking back on Dad's life with God, I could see the bitter experiences he endured. But they made him better with God, not bitter against Him. As he mentored me, Dad would say, "Son, I will tell you about my good and bad experiences in ministry. That way when you get knocked up against the ropes, you will remember that your Dad was, too. He survived, and so will you."

Dad was right, and God was right. By giving us the picture of the Tribulation saints singing to God in heaven, God gives us the same lesson Dad gave me. Throughout Revelation, God vividly describes the ropes the believers are knocked against, ropes many of us may never touch. Now, in Revelation 15, God shows us they survived. In fact, they've done more than just survive: they've come from the bitter times, better. In heaven, they sing and praise God for His deeds, His ways, and His character. There's not one note of bitterness against God in their song. It's all praise, because God has brought them through the bitter experiences in life and made them better.

BITTER, NOT BETTER!

Not everyone responds to bitter experiences on earth like the end-time believers. Many allow bitter experiences in life to make them bitter against God. In Revelation 15:5–16:1, God hides nothing. He openly confesses that He is the one behind the bitter experiences.

> [5] After this I looked and in heaven the temple, that is, the tabernacle of the Testimony, was opened. [6] Out of the temple came the seven angels with the seven plagues. They were dressed in clean, shining linen and wore golden sashes around their chests. [7] Then one of the four living creatures gave to the seven angels seven golden bowls filled with the wrath of God, who lives forever and ever. [8] And the temple was filled with smoke from the glory of God and from his power, and no one could enter the temple until the seven plagues of the seven angels were completed.
>
> [16:1] Then I heard a loud voice from the temple saying to the seven angels, "Go, pour out the seven bowls of God's wrath on the earth."

Seven angels carrying seven bowls come from God's temple in heaven. They pour from the bowls seven plagues.

The root word in the Greek for "plague" refers to a wound caused by a blow or a punch. In the last days, those that remain feel the closed fist of God's wrath much like the Egyptians did in Exodus. Revelation 16 lists the seven plagues poured out on the earth. An Egyptian in Exodus could say, "I experienced that!"

END TIMES	PLAGUE	EGYPT
Revelation 16:2	"malignant sores"	Exodus 9:9–11
Revelation 16:3	"seas to blood"	Exodus 7:20–24
Revelation 16:4	"rivers and springs to blood"	Exodus 7:20–24
Revelation 16:8	"intense heat from the sun"	
Revelation 16:20	"darkness"	Exodus 10:21–29
Revelation 16:12	"Euphrates River dries up"	
Revelation 16:17–21	"earthquake and hail"	Exodus 9:23–24

Though an Egyptian in Exodus could say, "I experienced that," one living in the end times could accurately reply, "But you didn't feel it like we have. You only felt one round of God's wrath. This is our third."

In the first round, God opens the seven seals to the title deed of earth. Those living on earth feel the blows of God's wrath through deception, war, famine, death, earthquakes, and darkness. In the second round, God sounds a trumpet before each punch. Many of God's blows with the seven bowl judgments in round three are repeats of His seven trumpet judgments from round two.

SEVEN BOWLS	PLAGUE	SEVEN TRUMPETS
Revelation 16:2	"malignant sores"	
Revelation 16:3	"seas to blood"	Revelation 8:8–9
Revelation 16:4	"rivers and springs to blood"	Revelation 8:10–11
Revelation 16:8	"intense heat from the sun"	
Revelation 16:20	"darkness"	Revelation 8:12
Revelation 16:12	"Euphrates River dries up"	
Revelation 16:17–21	"earthquake and hail"	Revelation 8:7

Enduring the multiple rounds of God's wrath not only wears the people down, but the combination of His punches in round three seems unbearable. Watch how one punch is followed by another.

First, all who wear the mark of the beast are covered by festering and incurable sores. Already painfully uncomfortable, God turns the oceans, rivers, and springs to blood. Not only do they smell the death from the rotting marine life, but they can't get a fresh drink of water. They long for a drink of water, because God turns up the heat. The intense heat not only causes a drought, but flooding as well. What a strange combination of drought in the fields combined with raised water levels from the melting of the polar icecaps and snow-capped mountains. Crops can't grow under either condition, making food scarce.

Hope is scarce as well. Hopelessness grows worse as God sends darkness over the earth. An earthquake in daylight is bad enough, but consider trying to survive the worst earthquake the world has ever seen—in the dark. The city of Jerusalem splits into three sections. Cities throughout the world collapse. Think about it. Where do you find shelter, especially as God bombards the earth with hailstones that weigh over 100 pounds?

What is often overlooked is that believers will experience this (except for the malignant sores) and draw closer to God. They emerge from these bitter times, and are better. However, the vast majority of the world takes a different position. Their hard times make them harder against God. These bitter times will make them even more bitter than before.

Bitter about God's Judgments

After the first three angels pour out God's wrath upon the earth, the third angel makes a profound statement. With that statement, we learn why people are so bitter against God. Revelation 16:5–7 states,

> [5] Then I heard the angel in charge of the waters say:

> "You are just in these judgments, you who are and who were, the Holy One, because you have so judged; [6] for they have shed the blood of your saints and prophets, and you have given them blood to drink as they deserve."

> [7] And I heard the altar respond:

> "Yes, Lord God Almighty, true and just are your judgments."

The people are bitter against God because of His judgments. The bitter think God is acting out of character. They always pictured God as good and loving. Yet the angel makes it clear that God is more than good. He is, always has been, and always will be holy. Since God is holy, He is both good and just.

It is hard for many in the end times to see God as just. Doing so means they have to change His position in their lives. C. S. Lewis explains how this has always been a problem for mankind.

> The ancient man approached God (or even the gods) as the accused person approaches his judge. For the modern man the roles are reversed. He [modern man] is the judge: God is in the dock. He [modern man] is quite a kindly judge: if God should have a reasonable defense for being the god who permits war, poverty, and disease, he is ready to listen to it. The trial may even end in God's acquittal. But the important thing is that Man is on the Bench and God in the dock.[62]

Lewis saw this problem with mankind years ago. Not only will many in the end times have a problem with God's judgments, but many today do, as well.

This may be your story. Witnessing or experiencing something bitter may have made you bitter with God. You thought God should only be loving, not just. You felt He acted out of character—at least the character you wanted Him to have. Furthermore, because of your position with God you felt you could be bitter with Him. From your position, you get to judge God. He doesn't get to judge you. From your position, you felt you had the right to be bitter with God.

---

62   C. S. Lewis in "God in the Dock," *Christianity Today,* vol. 35, no. 13, April 1, 1998, http://www.preachingtoday.com/illustrations/1998/april/2648.html.

Yet just as our understanding of God's character is often wrong, so is our view of His position. God is both loving and just. And, as a just God, He's on the bench. We are on the dock. He judges us. But unlike our quick judgments of God, His judgments of us are often delayed by grace.

God has been telling us for years that the wrath we see in Revelation 16 is coming. Listen to this short roll call of prophets. Joel spoke of it around 825 BC (Joel 1:15), as did Amos around 750 BC (Amos 5:18). Isaiah announced it around 700 BC (Isa. 61:2), followed by Zephaniah around 625 BC (Zeph. 1:15–18). Jesus alluded to it in Matthew 24. Even the martyrs who had been faithful to God called out for God's justice in Revelation 6:10. Still, in Revelation chapters 7, 10, 11, and 14, God offers opportunities to turn to Him. Even as God renders His justice in chapters 15 and 16, it's understood that anyone at any time can turn to God and come through these bitter times better, not bitter, with God. Yet many won't.

Bitter over God's Control

Most in the end times endure their bitter experiences by becoming more bitter with God. They do so not only because they don't agree with God's judgments, but also because they don't like that God is in control. This is evident in Revelation 16:8–11.

> [8] The fourth angel poured out his bowl on the sun, and the sun was given power to scorch people with fire. [9] They were seared by the intense heat and they cursed the name of God, who had control over these plagues, but they refused to repent and glorify him.

These two verses show how bitterness produces a fatal form of psychosis. It causes us to lose touch with reality, and leads to a bitter end.

Verse 9 states that, after the fourth plague, the people become so bitter they curse God's name. The Greek word for "curse" literally means "to blaspheme." The act of blaspheming God means to talk to or about God as though He were equal or even less than equal to you. Those experiencing the bitter times in Revelation 16 do this.

Verse 9 also explains why they did it. They were bad-mouthing God because they knew He controlled their experiences. The Greek word for "control" is *exousia*. It means having both the ability and authority to do something. They knew God was behind their malignant sores, bloody water, intense heat, world-wide darkness, earthquakes, and hailstorms. Still, their bitterness caused them to think they could talk down to God and get away with it.

Our family has a miniature dachshund named Oscar, who will on occasion bark at bigger dogs from within the protection of the house. Meeting them on the street, though, he has enough sense to greet them with his tail tucked. Oscar fully grasps the reality of the moment. By pure size and strength, he knows he's not the one in control, and so he succumbs to the one that is.

Many living in the end times won't have the sense God gave Oscar. Because it is evident that God has the authority and ability to shake the world, many (out of bitterness) will shake their fist at God. Furthermore, their bitter psychosis causes them to think their bitter experiences are all God's fault. Sure, God is the one behind them, but He is not to blame for them. We are.

It's human nature to cast blame. When God confronted Adam and Eve with their sin in the Garden of Eden, Genesis 3 records how they quickly blamed someone else. Though Adam was there the whole time watching Satan tempt Eve, Adam blamed her for handing him the fruit. Then she blamed the serpent for tempting her. Though she knew what God said about the forbidden fruit, she listened to Satan instead. As a result, we live in a world altered by sin and we continue to impact our lives by our sins.

However, when our sins produce bitter experiences for us, we blame God. We blame Him because we know deep down that He's in control and He holds us accountable. We are bitter at Him because we would rather be in control, so no one can hold us accountable.

Bitter Enough to Fight

By Revelation 16:12–16, the psychosis of bitterness has grown so strong that those bitter with God are ready to fight Him.

> [12] The sixth angel poured out his bowl on the great river Euphrates, and its water was dried up to prepare the way for the kings from the East. [13] Then I saw three evil spirits that looked like frogs; they came out of the mouth of the dragon, out of the mouth of the beast, and out of the mouth of the false prophet. [14] They are spirits of demons performing miraculous signs, and they go out to the kings of the whole world, to gather them for the battle on the great day of God Almighty.

> [15] "Behold, I come like a thief! Blessed is he who stays awake and keeps his clothes with him, so that he may not go naked and be shamefully exposed."

[16] Then they gathered the kings together to the place that in Hebrew is called Armageddon.

Armageddon comes from two Hebrew words meaning "the hill of Megiddo." The word *Megiddo* means "place of troops" or "place of slaughter." Today it is identified as the Plain of Esdraelon and the Valley of Jezreel. From Mount Carmel, it spreads twenty miles long and fourteen miles wide. Napoleon called it "the most natural battle-field of the whole earth."[63] Historically, over two hundred battles have been fought there.[64] None, however, will come close to matching the last battle to take place there. There the nations of the world join forces to fight God. It will live up to its name and become a place of troops and slaughter (Rev. 19:11–16). It will be Armageddon.

I believe bitterness plays a significant role in causing the nations to join forces against God. As explained earlier, extreme bitterness can become a psychosis that causes us to lose touch with what is real. This leaves us vulnerable to listen to others who feed us with more lies. Verses 13 and 14 divulge that evil spirits persuade the kings of the world to combine their armies against God. They cause these kings to think they can defeat God.

Even today, people bitter against God live on edge, ready to fight. They gladly listen to the spiritual delusions of others who share their bitterness against God. Those voices increase their bitterness, stirring their eagerness to fight. They now look for an argument, or worse yet, to actually hurt someone. Yet if they would stop and look deep within, they would see that their argument or fight is not with someone else: it's with God. Some have grown so confident in their position against

63   Wiersbe, *Be Victorious*, 117.
64   MacArthur, *Time*, 256.

God that they think they can argue with or fight against God and win. Yet unless they can get beyond the bitterness, in the end they will experience their own Armageddon with God. And like the armies of the world in the end times, they will lose.

Bitter and Blind to the End

The armies of the world will have their fight with God at Armageddon. A single statement summarizes their defeat—"They were bitter and blind to the end."

Before leaving chapter 16, it's important not to overlook verse 17. It states,

> [17] The seventh angel poured out his bowl into the air, and out of the temple came a loud voice from the throne, saying, "It is done!"

This three-word announcement, *"It is done,"* sounds familiar. You may recall in John 19:30 that just before Jesus dies, He cries from the cross, *"It is finished."* After His announcement and death there was an earthquake (Matt. 27:51). It's meaningful to see that the announcement in Revelation 16:17 comes from God's throne, not the seventh angel. Revelation 5:6 places Jesus *"standing in the center of the throne."* It is likely that Jesus, who cried *"It is finished"* from the cross, is now the One who cries *"It is done"* from the throne. Just as Jesus' statement from the cross was soon followed by an earthquake, His statement from the throne is followed by an earthquake that will topple the cities of the world.

There is a difference, though, between Jesus' announcement from the cross and the one He makes from heaven. His statement from the cross is one of *GRACE*, while His statement from the throne is one of *JUDGMENT*. From the cross, Jesus says He has accomplished everything God requires to restore our relationship with Him. From the throne, Jesus says He has accomplished everything God requires regarding judgment. That makes Jesus' statement from the cross one of *OPPORTUNITY*, and His statement from the throne one of *FINALITY*. From Calvary to Armageddon, God offers the opportunity to experience His grace. But once we die or Armageddon takes place, if we haven't surrendered our life to Jesus, God's judgment is final. Jesus says, "It is done."

My encouragement is not to be like those who gather and die at Armageddon. Don't live bitter and blind to the end.

HOW WILL YOU RESPOND?

Revelation chapters 15 and 16 give two different experiences in the end times. Though all who live in the end times go through bitter experiences, chapter 15 spotlights the believers who go through them and emerge better. Chapter 16, on the other hand, explains how the rest of the world allows the bitter times to make them even more bitter with God. Tragically, they experience a double loss. Not only do they lose the opportunity for God to make them better, but they also lose the chance for a better life with God in heaven.

Without question, we all experience bitter times in life. God either allows or initiates them. Whether we emerge from them better or bitter is determined by our response. Few speak to this truth as clearly as Joni Eareckson Tada.

A diving accident at age seventeen has confined Joni to a wheelchair, and without significant use of her arms or legs. Joni's autobiography honestly portrays her early struggle with bitterness against God. Yet it was her surrender to Jesus that enabled her to make a bitter experience better. Joni's personal journey gives her a unique insight on the two sides of suffering and bitterness. Joni says,

> With profound potential for good, suffering can also be a destroyer. Suffering can pull families together, uniting them through hardship, or it can rip them apart in selfishness and bitterness. Suffering can file all the rough edges off your character, or it can further harden you. It all depends. On us. On how we respond.[65]

We don't have to be in the end times to experience bitter times. And we don't have to be in the end times to know that bitter times present a choice. On one hand, we can surrender to Jesus and draw close to Him so that He can help us make the bitter times better. On the other hand, we can let the bitter times make us even more bitter with God. Like those in Revelation 16, we run the risk of living bitter and blind to the end.

Therefore, remember this. How we respond to bitter experiences in life is critical. Our response determines how we live and how we end.

---

65   Draper, *Quotations*, entry 10933.

CHAPTER 19

GOD'S EULOGY FOR RELIGION
REVELATION 17

Re-li-gion (ri lij'en): "any specific system of belief, worship,
conduct, etc., often involving a code of ethics and philosophy"

— WEBSTER'S NEW WORLD DICTIONARY [66]

USING THIS DEFINITION—*"ANY* SPECIFIC SYSTEM of belief"—statisticians have recorded around 4,200 religions that currently attract the attention and allegiance of people worldwide.[67]

I would think that God would define religion differently. His definition might read:

> Re-li-gion (ri lij'en): "a tactic Satan uses to keep people from experiencing and enjoying what God has always wanted with humanity, and what humanity has always longed for with God—a relationship."

This prompts an important question, "Is your spiritual life shaped by a religion, or by a relationship with God?"

To answer this, ask yourself this diagnostic question from Dr. D. James Kennedy: "If you were standing before God and He asked you,

---

66   David B. Guralnik, editor, *Webster's New World Dictionary of the American Language* (New York: The World Publishing Company, 1970), 1200.
67   George Weigel, "World religions by the numbers," Catholic Education Resource Center online, http://www.catholiceducation.org/articles/printarticle.html?id=3353.

'Why should I let you into my heaven?', what would you say?" I've asked that question to many over the years. Some of the common responses include, "Because I've tried to live a good life," "Because I've attended church," or "Because I was baptized." Then there are the abrupt answers such as, "I really don't believe in heaven," or "I don't believe in organized religion."

All these answers point to lives that have been influenced more by religion than by a relationship with God. Even the last two answers of "I really don't believe in heaven" or "I don't believe in organized religion" indicate the influence of religion, for you have to form some system of belief to support and explain what you don't believe.

In Genesis chapters 1–2, God creates humanity for a relationship with Him, not for religion. By Genesis 10, Satan begins offering religion instead. By Revelation chapter 17, God says, "Enough is enough!" The book of Revelation describes what happens in the end times. Within Revelation 17 we not only find the end of Satan and all who have been deceived by him, but also the end of religion.

Revelation 17 sounds sort of like a eulogy. Just as funeral eulogies usually describe the birth, life, and death of the deceased, Revelation 17 reads like God's eulogy for religion.

THE BIRTH OF RELIGION

[1] One of the seven angels who had the seven bowls came and said to me, "Come, I will show you the punishment of the great prostitute, who sits on many waters. [2] With her the kings of the earth committed adultery and the inhabitants of the earth were intoxicated with the wine of her adulteries."

³ Then the angel carried me away in the Spirit into a desert. There I saw a woman sitting on a scarlet beast that was covered with blasphemous names and had seven heads and ten horns. ⁴ The woman was dressed in purple and scarlet, and was glittering with gold, precious stones and pearls. She held a golden cup in her hand, filled with abominable things and the filth of her adulteries. ⁵ This title was written on her forehead:

MYSTERY

BABYLON THE GREAT

THE MOTHER OF PROSTITUTES

AND OF THE ABOMINATIONS OF THE EARTH.

⁶ I saw that the woman was drunk with the blood of the saints, the blood of those who bore testimony to Jesus.

When I saw her, I was greatly astonished.

Now you are likely thinking, "Where is religion mentioned in these verses? I don't see it, nor any reference to religion's birth."

Though you might not see it at first, Revelation 17:1–6 actually speaks of the birth of religion. Verse 1 characterizes religion as *"the great prostitute."* It's a fitting description, for religion does to our relationship with God what prostitution does to the relationship between a husband and wife. Religion, like prostitution, offers something illegitimate for something real. It replaces something meaningful with something momentary. Religion, like prostitution, is all about having what you want, the way you want it, when you want it. It takes that which was meant to be special, and destroys it with something that can only be described as selfish. Make no mistake; religion is like prostitution, for both carry a price.

Throughout much of world history, religion has stood on the world's street corner, enticing people away from a fulfilling relationship with God. Thus, God labels religion *"the great prostitute."*

In verse 5, we discover when and where it all began. All that is needed is to read the inscription on the forehead of the great prostitute.

MYSTERY
BABYLON THE GREAT
THE MOTHER OF PROSTITUTES
AND OF THE ABOMINATIONS OF THE EARTH.

In biblical times, the Greek word for "mystery" was synonymous with the word "secret." Most only see the glamour and glitter of the great prostitute—religion. They live unaware of the secret behind her birth, or her secret aim. These secrets are revealed in her name, *"BABYLON THE GREAT."*

The word "Babylon" appears 290 times in the Bible. Throughout the Bible, the word refers both to a location and a lifestyle. The historic location of ancient Babylon is in Iraq, forty-fifty miles south of modern-day Baghdad. The lifestyle attributed to Babylon, and thus to religion, goes all the way back to its birth.

Genesis 10:8–11 recognizes Nimrod, the great-grandson of Noah, as the founder of Babylon. In Genesis 11:1–4, the city receives her name. Wanting to build their own reputation by building an impressive city and tower, the people begin erecting a great tower reaching toward the heavens. Therefore, they named the city *Bab-El*, which means "gate of God." Though they mentioned God in the name, their relationship with God in this endeavor was in name only, and God knew it.

That's why God did something that would forever change the name of the city and give it a name befitting the actions of the people. In Genesis 11:5–8, God causes the people to speak different languages, and then scatters them throughout the world. Looking back to *Bab-El*, they called it *Babel*, which meant "confusion."[68]

How fitting. Think about it. When our actions for God are in name only, when it's all about us and not about God, we have a religion, not a relationship. What God intended to be clear now becomes confusing. History proves that confusion gives birth to more confusion.

Babel becomes Babylon, and Babylon embraces a myriad of gods. History cites Nimrod's wife as the one who brought a variety of mystery religions to Babylon. Thousands of years later, when the Babylonians conquered the Jews in 586 BC, they brought the Jews back with them to Babylon. There the Jews were introduced to the worship of Marduk and a pantheon of gods. Looking beyond Babylon to the five other world empires of Egypt, Assyria, Medo-Persia, Greece, and Rome, we will find each of them consumed with religion. They weren't consumed with a relationship with God, but with religion—strange beliefs that fulfilled their wants but not their lives—strange beliefs that made life and a relationship with God more confusing than clear.

---

68   Much of the information in these paragraphs can be found in Tim LaHaye, *Revelation Illustrated and Made Plain* (Grand Rapids, MI: Zondervan, 1975), 234. LaHaye is quoting from Harry A. Ironside, *Lectures on the Book of Revelation*, 12th ed. (Neptune, New Jersey: Loizeaux Brothers, 1942), 287–291.

I once saw a photograph of a family of five generations. Seated in the front was the couple who started it all. They were surrounded by about seventy-five others. Though they didn't all look exactly alike, there was one common feature shared by them all—their eyes! Looking into their eyes you could tell they all came from the same couple. You knew they were family.

Though there are around 4,200 world religions, if you look closely at each of them, it seems they come from the same place—Babylon. Furthermore, if you aren't sure if you are involved in a religion or in a relationship with God, ask yourself these questions.

- Do I believe what I believe and do what I do because it's cultural, comfortable, or convenient?
- Do I believe what I believe and do what I do because it's what I and others like me have always done?
- Do I believe what I believe and do what I do because it makes me feel good, and because I want others to know that I'm a good person?
- Do I believe what I believe and do what I do, but still wonder if I really have a relationship with God and if I will spend eternity in heaven with Him when I die?

If you answered "yes" to these questions, then you are among those building the tower of Babel. Like them, you are working hard at building a religion, not a relationship with God. In a religion, all you believe and all you do will always be about you. But in a relationship, all you believe and all you do will always be about God.

Before we move on to the life of religion, there's one more lesson to learn from its birth. Don't forget that Nimrod, who built Babylon, was the great-grandson of Noah. God used Noah and his family to restart human history. Yet just four generations removed from Noah, his great-grandson helped people build a religion instead of a relationship with God.

Therefore, if you have a relationship with God, make sure you explain to your children why you believe what you believe and why you do what you do. If you don't, they won't know that it's because of your relationship with God. After a while, they may believe what you believe and do what you do simply because you did. That means they will have a religion, but not a personal relationship with God. Nimrod reminds us that our families are never more than a generation away from having a religion instead of a relationship with God.

THE LIFE OF RELIGION

Thousands of years pass between Genesis 11 and Revelation 17 During religion's long life, it had many affiliations. Verses 7–8 reveal some of them.

> ⁷ Then the angel said to me: "Why are you astonished? I will explain to you the mystery of the woman and of the beast she rides, which has the seven heads and ten horns. ⁸ The beast, which you saw, once was, now is not, and will come up out of the Abyss and go to his destruction. The inhabitants of the earth whose names have not been written in the book of life from the creation of the world will be astonished when they see the beast, because he once was, now is not, and yet will come."

When John sees *"the great prostitute,"* the woman representing religion, verse 6 says he *"was greatly astonished."* The word "astonished" fails to convey the fullness of John's experience. In fact, translators have had a hard time agreeing on how to translate it. The Greek word used for "astonish" in verses 6 and 7 has also been translated as "admire" (KJV), "wonder" (NAS), and "marvel" (NKJV). Evidently, John was overwhelmed by both the impressive and imposing sight of religion. It's as though he thought, "No wonder people are so tempted to choose religion over a relationship with God!"

In verse 7, I picture the angel seeing John in this awestruck stare. Slowly he leans toward John's ear and says, "John, have you ever wondered why religion can be so impressive and imposing to people? I'll tell you her secret: it's all in her affiliations."

Religion and Well-being

The first secret behind religion's alluring nature appears in her affiliation with well-being. Verse 4 describes her as *"dressed in purple and scarlet, and… glittering with gold, precious stones and pearls."* In John's day, the colors of purple and scarlet were the colors of royalty, nobility, and wealth. Wearing these colors, others knew you had your act together. You had position, popularity, and money. Surprisingly, John saw these colors wrapped around religion.

Many today are attracted to one religion or another for the same reason. They don't want a relationship with God. Instead, they want the prospects of position, popularity, and money. They want wealth, health, and well-being. In their mind, religion provides it.

That's why some attend one church over another. They think, "That's where I can have the best business contacts." If you're single, you may attend church for the sole reason that church may be your best opportunity to find a husband or wife. Some choose one denomination over another because they preach that God blesses good Christians. In everyday language that means they preach, "If you are good to God, He'll be good to you. He'll make you rich." (If that's

true, then the apostles must have been bad Christians.) Then there are
those who will accept a particular belief system over another because
it promises inner peace.

If you listen to these reasons for joining a church, denomination,
or belief, they sound like the same reason Nimrod had for building
Babylon: "It's all about you." If you believe what you believe and do
what you do to benefit yourself, then you've been attracted to the
colors of a religion instead of involvement in a real relationship with
God.

Religion and Power

Another secret behind religion's imposing nature lies in her affiliation with power. According to Revelation 13:8–18, in the end
times all the religions of the world are placed under a single umbrella.
That umbrella rests in the hand of the false prophet of the Antichrist.
Furthermore, verses 1, 3 and 7 describe *"the great prostitute...sitting on
the scarlet beast...which has the seven heads and ten horns."* That means the
one-world religion and the one-world government not only wear the
same impressive color, scarlet, they will also share the same power.
Verses 3 and 7 say the Antichrist's one-world government carries the
one-world religion, and verse 13 explains that the one-world religion
supplies the one-world government of the Antichrist with power.

Historically, it is imposing when religion gives power to government and when government gives power to religion. This currently
occurs in governments run by militant Islamic extremists, who carry
out their executions in public. Historically, Christianity has done the
same. From 1540–1570 AD, the Roman Catholic Church carried out

her inquisitions on reformers. During that 30-year period, no less than 900,000 reformers were put to death.[69]

Make no mistake; having a relationship with God is powerful. The word "power" appears over 120 times in the New Testament. The majority of those references refer to the power of God to save the lost and strengthen the saved. However, being involved in a religion, instead of in a relationship with God, may cause you to want and use power for different reasons.

In a religion, you want power so you can intimidate others. You hear it in the religions that say, "If you don't believe what I believe, I'll take your life." But if you have a relationship with God, you know you have the power to save life, because God saved yours. Furthermore, you are willing to use that power to save others the way God saved you. That's why you would say, "I'll give my life if you will believe what I believe," not "I'll take your life if you don't."

Religion and Worldwide Influence

When you look at the life of religion, you can't help but recognize its worldwide appeal. Verses 1 and 3 state that *"the great prostitute"* who rides *"the scarlet beast"* is sitting *"on many waters."* Verse 15 then explains, *"The waters you saw, where the prostitute sits, are peoples, multitudes, nations, and languages."* In the end times, as throughout history, religion carries a worldwide appeal. The only difference is that, during the end times, all the world's religions are united under the religion of the Antichrist and his false prophet.

The reason religion has and always will have a worldwide appeal is that it plays on the worldwide need to have a relationship with God.

---

69   LaHaye, 234. LaHaye is quoting from Henry H. Halley, *Halley's Bible Handbook*, 24th ed. (Grand Rapids, MI: Zondervan, 1965), 291–292.

Genesis 1–3 tells us that God creates everyone in His image to have a relationship with Him. Those chapters also reveal that our sin marred that image and separated us from God. Here is the great tragedy. Instead of acknowledging that God came to earth as Jesus, died on the cross for our sins, and rose from the dead to restore our relationship with God, most people choose to create their own religion instead of restoring their relationship with God. Romans 1:18–23 explains.

> [18] The wrath of God is being revealed from heaven against all the godlessness and wickedness of men who suppress the truth by their wickedness, [19] since what may be known about God is plain to them, because God has made it plain to them. [20] For since the creation of the world God's invisible qualities—his eternal power and divine nature—have been clearly seen, being understood from what has been made, so that men are without excuse.
>
> [21] For although they knew God, they neither glorified him as God nor gave thanks to him, but their thinking became futile and their foolish hearts were darkened. [22] Although they claimed to be wise, they became fools, [23] and exchanged the glory of the immortal God for images made to look like mortal man and birds and animals and reptiles.

Since Genesis chapters 1–2 record that all are created in the image of God, and Romans 3:23 asserts that all have sinned and fallen short of the glory of God, we clearly have two choices. We can restore our relationship with God. That happens by confessing our sins and surrendering to Him through Jesus. Sadly, many choose differently, and create a religion that satisfies their mind, but not their need. As long as there is a worldwide need for a relationship with God, people will create their own religions—to try to meet their needs their way, instead of God's way.

Religion and Results

Remember, John stares awestruck when he first sees the great prostitute. She offers a life of well-being, is powerful, and has worldwide influence. Yet anything can look good from a distance. Take a closer look at religion, and you will realize it promises a lot, but delivers very little.

When I was a sixth grader, my school held a magazine subscription campaign. Each of us was given a pamphlet with pictures of the prizes we could win. Of course, the prizes were placed in groups. If you sold 5 to 10 subscriptions, you picked from one group of prizes. If you sold 10 to 20 subscriptions, you selected from another group. There was one prize that caught my eye. It was a combination safe. It looked strong and sturdy, and I was impressed with its size.

So for the next week, I went from house to house selling magazine subscriptions. When I had the number needed to order the safe, I filled out all the forms, turned them in to the school, and waited for my prize. On the day the prizes came in, we all gathered in our homerooms. My teacher lifted a huge box onto his desk. I knew that my safe took up at least half the space in that box. As he called a few names and handed out a few prizes, I snickered at how small the other students' prizes were. Then, he called my name. As I walked up to the box, I saw my teacher reach in with one hand and remove a SMALL, PLASTIC, SAFE!

I had had such dreams for my safe. There were so many things I had planned to put in it. But what my teacher handed me wasn't big enough to hold my thoughts, much less any stuff. Needless to say, I was angry with the magazine company for taking advantage of me. Their pictures had promised me so much, and I did everything they had asked me to do. Yet what I received in return was so little.

All who choose a religion over a relationship with God will experience the same betrayal. Religion gives you a glamorous picture of all it offers—well-being, power, and worldwide appeal. Then it asks you to do a lot to receive all that it offers. At some point, you ask religion to pay up. You have fulfilled all that it asked, and now you want all that it promised. It's then you learn that religion always promises more than it can deliver.

Having a relationship with God, however, is far different. In a relationship with God, God delivers more than you ever pictured. One reason for this is that you get to walk with the One who actually made all the promises.

THE DEATH OF RELIGION

As we said earlier, eulogies usually cover the birth, life, and death of the deceased. In Revelation 17:9–18, God explains how religion dies. Though religion's death seems unusual, when you hear God's explanation, it becomes understandable.

A Deadly Condition

Verses 9–18 read like a coroner's report. Though verses 15–18 record how religion dies, verses 9–14 unpack the pre-existing conditions leading to religion's death.

> [9] "This calls for a mind with wisdom. The seven heads are seven hills on which the woman sits. [10] They are also seven kings. Five have fallen, one is, the other has not yet come; but when he does come, he must remain for a little while. [11] The beast who once

was, and now is not, is an eighth king. He belongs to the seven
and is going to his destruction.

[12] "The ten horns you saw are ten kings who have not yet received a kingdom, but who for one hour will receive authority
as kings along with the beast. [13] They have one purpose and will
give their power and authority to the beast. [14] They will make
war against the Lamb, but the Lamb will overcome them because
he is Lord of lords and King of kings-and with him will be his
called, chosen, and faithful followers."

A friend of mine nearly died of a heart attack in his early for-
ties. Doctors discovered that his left anterior descending artery was
blocked. The medical field has a non-medical term for this condition.
They call it "the widow-maker." It's called this because those who
have this condition usually don't know it until it's too late.

Religion's condition could be described as a spiritual widow-
maker. Just as a medical mind is needed to see the physical widow-
maker, verse 9 states that you need a spiritual mind to see the spiritual
widow-maker at the heart of religion.

Verses 9–11 identify the beast as the spiritual widow-maker of
religion. Verse 9 explains that the beast has seven heads that are on
seven hills. This causes many to think that the beast refers to Rome,
which was built on seven hills. However, verse 10 says that these seven
hills represent seven kings. Verse 10 also announces that *"five have
fallen."* This makes the kings the empires of Egypt, Assyria, Babylon,
Medo-Persia, and Greece. Of the seven kings, verse 10 adds *"one
is."* This represents Rome, the empire in place at the time of John's
visions.

Finally, verses 10b–11 add, *"the other (king or empire) has not yet come; but when he does come, he must remain for a little while. The beast who once was, and now is not, is an eighth king. He belongs to the seven and is going to his destruction."* The seventh empire will be the one under the rule of the Antichrist. At the time of John's vision, it had not yet come. When the Antichrist establishes his rule, it will last for only a short while—seven years. During his reign, the Antichrist will appear to be fatally wounded, but then will be physically restored and returned to power. Thus, according to verse 11, this will make him the one *"who once was, and now is not."* He will reign as the seventh and eighth king.

According to verses 12–14, the ten horns represent the ten rulers who will follow the Antichrist's lead and make war against the Lamb. Revelation 5 identifies Jesus as the Lamb. Jesus' purpose has always been to restore our relationship with God. Satan's objective has always been to stop Him. Revelation 17 finally exposes religion as the mysterious, or secret, weapon that Satan uses to counter God's desire of having a relationship with us. The heart of religion, however, has a condition that will ultimately kill it.

A Fatal Day

Don't be fooled: Satan is the ultimate spiritual widow-maker. Lying at the heart of religion, his aim is to kill everyone's chance for a relationship with God. Surprisingly, when Satan no longer has any use for religion, verses 15–18 show him turning on it. Just before God destroys Satan, Satan, through the efforts of the Antichrist, will destroy religion. Verses 15–18 give an account of religion's fatal day.

[15] Then the angel said to me, "The waters you saw, where the prostitute sits, are peoples, multitudes, nations, and languages. [16] The beast and the ten horns you saw will hate the prostitute. They will bring her to ruin and leave her naked; they will eat her flesh and burn her with fire. [17] For God has put it into their hearts to accomplish his purpose by agreeing to give the beast their power to rule, until God's words are fulfilled. [18] The woman you saw is the great city that rules over the kings of the earth."

In the last days, God causes the Antichrist and his ten rulers to turn on the one-world religion. Religion—the very instrument used in the end times and throughout time to keep us from a relationship with God—is destroyed.

Since life can only come through a relationship with God, religion never really had a life to offer. There is no doubt that religion has existed. If you treat religion's existence as a life, then the Bible has recorded its birth, its life and now, in Revelation 17, its death. God has given His eulogy for religion.

DECISIONS AT A CEMETERY

After hearing the eulogy for the deceased, we often at a funeral begin evaluating our own lives. We ask ourselves, "How does my life compare to the deceased? What experiences have I had compared to the one who passed?"

Having heard the eulogy for religion, let's compare. Are you living a life marked by religion, or one that is moved by a relationship with God? Put the two side-by-side, and decide which describes your life.

LIFE WITH RELIGION	LIFE WITH A RELATIONSHIP
...is all about you	...is all about God (2 Cor. 5:15)
...delivers less than promised	...delivers more than promised (Eph.3:20)
...still troubles you	...assures you still (1 John 5:13)

Placing these two lives side-by-side doesn't make any changes or decisions for you. It just helps you with the decision you need to make.

There's one more piece of advice I would like to offer. It comes from a dear friend who once told me, "Mark, if I have to make a major decision in life, I make it in a cemetery." For him, seeing the finality of life put everything in perspective. You never have a decision more important than, "How do I know and experience life with God?"

Revelation 17 and Matthew 28 allow you to make that decision in a cemetery. In Revelation 17 you stand over the future grave of religion. Religion is not the answer. But as you walk from Revelation 17 to Matthew 28, you move from a full grave to an empty tomb. At the empty tomb you hear the announcement, *"He is not here; he has risen, just as he said"* (Matt. 28:6).

Standing in this particular cemetery, you need to ask yourself, "What do I want? Do I want a religion about God or do I want a relationship with God?" Each will cause you to experience life and end life differently. Now it's up to you to choose wisely.

CHAPTER 20

WEEPING FOR HUMPTY DUMPTY

REVELATION 18

ONE OF THE REQUIREMENTS OF my PhD program was to take four semesters of German. We were not taught to speak German, but only to read it for research. I remember coming home frustrated and telling Loree, "I'm so tired of all the 'Frankenstein' words." The German language has the tendency of sewing several words together in order to give life to a new word. Such a word walks among us today. It is *weltanschauung*. The Germans have sewn together the words *welt*, meaning "world," and *anschauung*, meaning "outlook." In doing so, they produced a term that continues to grow in popularity. It is the word "worldview."

When a political figure runs for office, reporters and readers want to know his or her worldview. We realize that how someone sees the world affects their decisions, because our worldview encompasses how we see the world theologically, scientifically, politically, economically, and in every area of life. Furthermore, we don't have a different pair of glasses for each of these disciplines. We don't take off our theology glasses in order to see and have an opinion on the economy. Our worldview fuses together our thoughts in all these areas and creates a single pair of glasses through which we view the world. It's our view of the entire world. The question we need to ask ourselves is, "WILL MY WORLDVIEW STAND THE TEST OF TIME?"

Revelation 18 shows a dominant worldview permeating the end times. Furthermore, in the end times, the term "worldview" has two meanings. It not only represents how you view the world, but it will also describe how the world views you.

Revelation 17 foretells that the one-world religion and the one-world government of the Antichrist are woven together, and give power and authority to each other. Furthermore, their union produces a single worldview that proves to be personally and financially successful (17:3–4: *"dressed in scarlet"*). As a result, most of the inhabitants of the world will hold to the single worldview created by the Antichrist. Those who don't hold to it will find the world turning on them (Rev. 12:11; 13:10, 17).

It's understandable that with the world backing a single worldview, those supporting it will think their worldview is right. Fortified by popular opinion, people in the end times will believe that their worldview will never fall. And why not? In their mind, they represent the first generation to persuade the whole world to agree to a single worldview. Yet when God pours His seven plagues upon the earth (Rev. 15, 16), and when the Antichrist destroys the one-world religion he created (Rev. 17), the worldview of the end times will prove to be as fragile as Humpty Dumpty. I'm sure you remember the nursery rhyme,

> Humpty Dumpty sat on a wall.
> Humpty Dumpty had a great fall.
> All the king's horses and all the king's men
> Couldn't put Humpty together again.

Like Humpty Dumpty, the dominant worldview of the end times will fall, and tragically, those who adopted that worldview will fall because of it.

BEFORE READING REVELATION 18

Even though we are not living in the end times, the message of Revelation 18 speaks to the following. First, WHETHER YOU REALIZE IT OR NOT, YOU HAVE A WORLDVIEW. You have a conviction about God, government, morals, money, and more. Right now you are living your life according to your worldview.

Second, WHETHER YOU ACKNOWLDGE IT OR NOT, GOD HAS A WORLDVIEW. Even if you say God does not exist, that doesn't make it so. People all over the world have never met you or heard of you. Still, you exist. You can't wish God away. You can't make Him disappear by saying He doesn't exist. He exists, and He is here to stay. That means His worldview is the only one that is true and lasts forever.

Third, WHETHER YOU WANT TO THINK ABOUT IT OR NOT, YOUR WORLDVIEW WILL ULTIMATELY CAUSE YOU TO END LIFE EITHER WEEPING OR SINGING. Revelation 18 shows if you live by God's worldview you will end life singing. But if you live by a different worldview, you will end life weeping.

Thus when you read through Revelation 18, ask yourself, "IS MY WORLDVIEW GOD'S WORLDVIEW?" It needs to be. If it's not, then your worldview will fall and be just as fragile as Humpty Dumpty. And, tragically, you will fall with it.

THE FALL

Revelation 18:1–3 journals the fall of the worldview of the end times. Witnessing this fall, John writes,

> [1] After this I saw another angel coming down from heaven. He had great authority, and the earth was illuminated by his splendor. [2] With a mighty voice he shouted:

> "Fallen! Fallen is Babylon the Great!
> She has become a home for demons
> and a haunt for every evil spirit,
> a haunt for every unclean and detestable bird.
> [3] For all the nations have drunk
> the maddening wine of her adulteries.
> The kings of the earth committed adultery with her,
> and the merchants of the earth grew rich from her excessive luxuries."

With a thunderous voice of authority, an angel from heaven announces the fall of the worldview that dominates the end times. We hear the name given to the worldview when the angel cries in verse 2, *"Fallen! Fallen is Babylon the Great!"*

Understanding Babylon the Great

In Revelation 17, Babylon the Great is the name given to the harlot resting on the beast that is sitting on the many waters of the world. There, the harlot represents the one-world religion that shares power and authority with the beast, who stands for the one-world government of the Antichrist (Rev. 17:1–5). Together, they create a worldview embraced by every nation on earth (v. 15).

In Revelation 18, John adds something to the picture painted in Chapter 17. His last brush-stroke in Revelation 17:18 reads, *"The woman you saw ("the harlot"—the one world religion of the Antichrist) is the great city that rules over the kings of the earth."* Seven more times in Revelation 18, John picks up the brush and refers to Babylon the Great as a great city that influences the world.

In verse 2, John adds detail to his painting by identifying this city as *"a home for demons and a haunt for every evil spirit."* We find this reference one other time in the book of Revelation. It's in Revelation 16:13–14. There it talks about three evil spirits looking like frogs. They are the demons performing miraculous signs enticing the kings of the world to fight against God at Armageddon. The three demons are sent from a place recognized throughout the world as the head-quarters for the one-world religion and one-world government of the Antichrist.

The final touches of John's portrait appear in verse 3. It states that the kings and business leaders of the world look to this city for leadership and direction.

It is not new for a city to be seen as the holy headquarters for a particular religion. Some cities today are known for their religious significance. A short list includes

- Rome and Catholicism
- Mecca and Islam
- Salt Lake City and Mormonism
- Varanasi and Hinduism
- Jerusalem and Judaism
- Bodhgaya and Buddhism

The difference is that in the end times there will be one city recognized as the holy and capital city of the one-world religion and one-world government of the Antichrist. People all over the world believe she will never fall. Yet she does.

Why It Falls

Verses 1–3 portray how the world sees Babylon the Great before she falls. She is the religious, political, and financial hub of the world. The world thinks she will never fall. Yet she falls. She falls because God doesn't see her the way the world does. God's view of Babylon the Great is give in verses 4–8.

> [4] Then I heard another voice from heaven say:

> "Come out of her, my people,
>   so that you will not share in her sins,
>   so that you will not receive any of her plagues;
> [5] for her sins are piled up to heaven,
>   and God has remembered her crimes.
> [6] Give back to her as she has given;
> pay her back double for what she has done.
> Mix her a double portion from her own cup.
> [7] Give her as much torture and grief
> as the glory and luxury she gave herself.
> In her heart she boasts,
> 'I sit as queen; I am not a widow,
>   and I will never mourn.'
> [8] Therefore in one day her plagues will overtake her:
> death, mourning, and famine.

She will be consumed by fire,

for mighty is the Lord God who judges her."

Until recently, I was unfamiliar with the story behind the Humpty Dumpty nursery rhyme. The label "Humpty Dumpty" goes back to 15th century England. It was used to describe someone large and heavy. During the English Civil War of 1642–1649, the label was ascribed to a large and heavy cannon mounted on the protective wall of St. Mary's Wall Church in Colchester, England.

A round from an opposing cannon struck the wall beneath Humpty Dumpty, causing it to fall. Even though all the king's horses and men tried to lift and repair the great cannon, their efforts were in vain. Within eleven days, Colchester fell to her foes.[70]

Prior to her fall, the people of Colchester likely walked by St. Mary's Wall Church and felt secure, seeing Humpty Dumpty in place. With Humpty Dumpty on the wall, they lived their lives feeling that all was in order and safe. But when the great cannon fell, so did the city and all those under her protection.

This is a good time to ask, "What is your Humpty Dumpty?" What is it in life that you look to and think, "As long as that is in place, I feel safe"? Is it your job? You may think, "As long as I have my job, I can take care of my needs or that of my family." Is it your marriage, or if you are still living at home, is it the marriage of your parents? As long as your marriage or your parents' marriage seems strong, you feel secure. Is it your health? With a strong body and mind, you feel you can overcome any challenge.

---

70   "Humpty Dumpty," last accessed July 13, 2013, http://www.powerfulwords.info/nursery_rhymes/humpty_dumpty.htm.

When you tie all of these together along with your religious beliefs, (and remember, God is not interested in religion, He's looking for a relationship with you), then you have formed a formidable worldview, one you believe is right and will never fall. Yet if God can cause the single worldview of the end times to fall, what makes you think your worldview will stand against God's judgment?

Just as a single well-placed round caused the great cannon Humpty Dumpty to fall, a well-placed round of God topples the city and worldview of Babylon the Great. Verse 8 identifies that round as the blast of God's judgment. Verses 5–7 describe the forces that make God's judgment so powerful.

The Force of Unforgiven Sins

Verse 5 explains that God's judgment carries with it the force of unforgiven sin. It reads, *"for her sins are piled up to heaven, and God has remembered her crimes."* The word "piled" comes from a Greek word that means "glued together." God had seen, stacked and glued together all the sins of Babylon the Great. No wonder the blow of God's judgment has such force.

Even before the end times come, verse 5 should be a sobering statement for all of us living today. It is frightening to think that our sins are stacked and glued together by God. Unless we confess and repent, they stand as a monument reminding God of our rebellion. And like the fate of Babylon the Great, they add to the ever increasing force of His righteous judgment.

The Force of Ungodly Acts

Verse 6 interjects that the force of God's judgment on Babylon the Great is directly proportionate to the force of ungodly acts they committed. Verse 6 states, *"Give back to her as she has given…Mix her a double portion from her own cup."* Revelation 17:4–6 records that the cup of Babylon the Great is full of her abominable acts and that she has become drunk from the blood of the saints. Knowing every ungodly act in her cup, God now pours out upon her a double portion of all she has poured out against God.

For a moment, move the statement of verse 6 from the end times to the end of your life. Make no mistake, an all-knowing God knows all about you, and He will judge you with a force double to the ungodly acts you lived before Him. Therefore, how important is it for you to seek God's forgiveness and make sure you have a clean record with God before you face Him?

The Force of a Misspent Life

Another force behind God's judgment appears in verse 7. It's the force of a misspent life. Verse 7 announces, *"Give her as much torture and grief as the glory and luxury she gave herself."* As we learned in Revelation 17, God has always wanted a relationship with us, but many would rather be involved in a religion than in a relationship with God. The reason many choose a religion over a relationship is that a relationship requires surrender and sacrifice. It's about giving yourself to the one you love. All a religion requires is a little extra time. That means we can spend more of our time fulfilling our dreams, our desires, and our wants: it's all about us.

God knows what we could have had in a relationship with Him, and what we settled for in a misspent life all about us. Therefore when God judges us, we receive as much attention from God in the end as we gave ourselves as we lived. That was the force behind God's judgment of Babylon the Great, and it will be the force behind His judgment of us.

The Force of Misplaced Trust

Finally, verse 7 reveals one more force generating the impact of God's blow on Babylon the Great. It's the force of misplaced trust. You hear it in the arrogant statement, *"I sit as queen; I am not a widow, and I will never mourn."* A queen who is not a widow achieved her position on her own merits. And a queen who never mourns is confident that her reign will never be challenged or ended. She trusts in herself alone, for in her mind there is no one greater.

I'm sure all whose worldview led them to trust in Babylon the Great were surprised when she fell. Though Babylon the Great said she would never mourn, and though her followers thought she would never fall, the force of God's judgment has caused her fall. And now in Revelation 18:9–19 we see a world in mourning.

EARTH WEEPS

As a boy, I remember reading the Humpty Dumpty nursery rhyme, but I don't remember seeing a cannon. Instead, Humpty Dumpty was characterized as a large egg wearing a crown and a smile. In fact, Humpty Dumpty was all smiles until he fell off the wall, broken beyond repair.

There are two reasons Humpty Dumpty came to mind when reading Revelation 18. One was the cry in verse 2, *"Fallen! Fallen is Babylon the Great!"* For some reason, hearing that statement brought to mind "Humpty Dumpty had a great fall." The other reason this nursery rhyme came to mind is because verses 9–24 make it clear that Babylon the Great is broken beyond repair. The single worldview of the end times, that once seemed unbreakable, proves to be as fragile as an egg—as fragile as my childhood picture of Humpty Dumpty. With her worldview smashed, verses 9–19 record how the earth weeps, while verses 20–24 describe how heaven sings.

Weeping over Broken Security

Revelation 18:9–10 explains how and why the kings of the earth weep when Babylon the Great falls by the hand of God.

> ⁹ "When the kings of the earth who committed adultery with her and shared her luxury see the smoke of her burning, they will weep and mourn over her. ¹⁰ Terrified at her torment, they will stand far off and cry:
>
> "'Woe! Woe, O great city,
> O Babylon, city of power!
> In one hour your doom has come!'"

The weeping over Babylon the Great will be worldwide. Verse 9 says *"the kings of the earth…will weep and mourn over her."* The reason for their weeping is heard in their dirge. They sing, *"Woe! Woe, O great city, O Babylon, city of power! In one hour your doom has come!"*

Earth's kings see Babylon as a city of power. The Greek word for "power" in this verse refers to "a force." Its root meaning points to a force that holds things together. No king submits himself or his rule to another if he didn't think he was submitting to something stronger than himself and his country.

All of earth's kings and religious leaders will submit to the world-view of the one-world government, believing it will hold everything together for them. And for seven years it does. All the religions and rule of the earth are under the leadership of the Antichrist. The government of the Antichrist makes decisions that cause most people throughout the world to feel secure. It isn't until the end that the world realizes they have placed their security in the wrong worldview. And now they weep.

Weeping over a Broken Lifestyle

Revelation 18:11–17a joins the mourning of the merchants with the tears of the kings, as the lament throughout the earth grows.

> [11] "The merchants of the earth will weep and mourn over her because no one buys their cargoes any more—[2] cargoes of gold, silver, precious stones, and pearls; fine linen, purple, silk, and scarlet cloth; every sort of citron wood, and articles of every kind made of ivory, costly wood, bronze, iron, and marble; [13] cargoes of cinnamon and spice, of incense, myrrh, and frankincense, of wine and olive oil, of fine flour and wheat; cattle and sheep; horses and carriages; and bodies and souls of men.

> [14] "They will say, 'The fruit you longed for is gone from you. All your riches and splendor have vanished, never to be recovered.' [15] The merchants who sold these things and gained their wealth from her will stand far off, terrified at her torment. They will weep and mourn [16] and cry out:

> "'Woe! Woe, O great city,
> dressed in fine linen, purple, and scarlet,
> and glittering with gold, precious stones and pearls!
> [17] In one hour such great wealth has been brought to ruin!'"

John MacArthur keenly identifies twenty-eight different commodities mentioned in verses 12–13.[71] Just as decisions made by world leaders affect the world's markets today, the merchants of the end times earn their livelihood and lifestyle from the one-world view emanating from Babylon the Great. In their mind, it was good business: verse 15 says they gained their wealth by buying into the one-world view. As a result, verse 16 describes them dressed in the colors of success worn in Babylon the Great.

These verses act as a warning to those with a rags-to-riches story today. Like merchants of the end times, they run the danger of buying into a worldview that has been strong and successful for them and others. However, it is as fragile as eggshells to God's touch. Rags-to-riches stories are lived by pragmatists, who create or adopt whatever worldview is most effective. In their minds they think, "If it's effective, it must be right." Furthermore, since it has proved effective for you, then surely it must be effective and right for others as well. You hold to your worldview purely on the successes you have experienced without asking "the God question." You haven't asked yourself, "Is my worldview God's worldview?" Revelation 18 emphasizes that in the end, God's worldview wins. Those who have gone from rags to riches without a relationship with God, now go from riches to rags.

Weeping over Broken Hopes

By the time described in Revelation 18:17b–19, God's judgment causes Babylon the Great to fall. The city that established a single worldview is gone. Kings of nations and rulers of commerce now

---

71   MacArthur, *Time*, 278.

share the same experience as the common man; they all now weep over their broken hopes.

> "Every sea captain, and all who travel by ship, the sailors, and all who earn their living from the sea, will stand far off. [18] When they see the smoke of her burning, they will exclaim, 'Was there ever a city like this great city?' [19] They will throw dust on their heads, and with weeping and mourning cry out:
>
> "'Woe! Woe, O great city,
> where all who had ships on the sea
> became rich through her wealth!
> In one hour she has been brought to ruin!'"

As merchants look upon the charred remains of Babylon the Great, verse 14 depicts them looking toward the fallen city saying, *"The fruit you longed for is gone from you. All your riches and splendor have vanished, never to be recovered."* The phrase "never to be recovered" is a double negative in the Greek.[72] It is the strongest way to say "All that this city and worldview provided you will never be provided again. What you have lost because of the one-world view will never be recovered."

Verses 9–10 show the effects of loss on the rulers. Verses 11–17 reveal the impact of loss on the merchants. Now verses 17–19 unveil the results of loss on everyday life. Captains and sailors depended on Babylon and her worldview for their business; they needed Babylon in place to help them meet and fulfill their dreams.

Now the one-world choir is complete. Kings, merchants, captains, sailors, and tradesmen weep together over their broken hopes. The one-world religion and government, that had established a one-world

---

72   Ibid.

view from one city, is gone—and the earth weeps. Tragically, they weep for the wrong reasons.

Weeping for the Wrong Reasons

Most parents understand that children cry for different reasons. Therefore their cries have different sounds. For example, consider the cries of children sitting in timeout. Parents can tell when their child cries because he is mad for being in timeout, or when he is sorry for what he has done.

When our boys were small, I remember listening to the sounds of their cries. I wanted to hear the sounds of "I'm sorry." Good comes from those tears. Hearing the sounds of "I'm sorry" in their weeping, I knew the boys understood that what they had done was wrong. They were now ready to listen to instruction, and Loree and I were trying to help them adjust their worldview. They were also eager to hear how much we loved them, and were ready for a hug.

Good comes when weeping carries the sounds of "I'm sorry." But God doesn't hear those sounds in Revelation 18. He hears the sounds of "I'm scared because I've lost my sense of security;" "I'm mad because I've lost my former lifestyle;" "I'm panicked because I've lost all my hopes." The world is weeping over everything they lost because of their fallen worldview, which means they are weeping for the wrong reasons.

If they were weeping for the right reasons, they would cry over being lost instead of what they lost. They would weep over all that God had to forgive instead of what had been taken away. They would weep over experiencing the open arms of God instead of the empty promises of a fallen worldview. If they truly were weeping for the right reasons, the sounds of their tears would change to the sounds of a tearful reunion—the sounds of a wayward child coming home.

For a moment, place yourself in Revelation 18. Ask yourself, "If all my security, lifestyle and hopes were destroyed because of a defective worldview, how would my weeping sound to God? Would my tears sound like an angry, scared child who is still rebellious? Or would they sound like a child whose will has been broken, whose sins have been forgiven, and whose life feels loved and secure in the arms of God?"

HEAVEN SINGS "NEVER AGAIN"

In Revelation 18:20–24, John describes a completely different reaction in heaven. Earth may be weeping, but heaven is singing. If a title could be given to their anthem, it would be "Never Again." The heavenly choir is assembled and charged in verse 20.

> [20] "'Rejoice over her, O heaven!
> Rejoice, saints and apostles and prophets!
> God has judged her for the way she treated you.'"

> [21] Then a mighty angel picked up a boulder the size of a large millstone and threw it into the sea, and said:

> "With such violence
>   the great city of Babylon will be thrown down,
>   never to be found again.
> [22] The music of harpists and musicians, flute players and trumpeters,
>   will never be heard in you again.
> No workman of any trade

will ever be found in you again.

The sound of a millstone

will never be heard in you again.

[23] The light of a lamp

will never shine in you again.

The voice of bridegroom and bride

will never be heard in you again.

Your merchants were the world's great men.

By your magic spell all the nations were led astray.

[24] In her was found the blood of prophets and of the saints,

and of all who have been killed on the earth.'"

Since deceiving Adam and Eve, Satan has worked to alter everyone's worldview. He offers religion, ambition, power, rewards, addictions, and more to divert our attention away from the reason we were created. We were created for a relationship with God.

Now in the end times, Satan organizes his greatest deception. He creates a one-world religion, government, and worldview all emanating from one city. It stands as Satan's strongest effort, but God topples and breaks it. And heaven breaks out and sings "Never Again." Five times in verses 21–23, heaven sings that any sign of life from Satan's worldview will be heard or seen "never again!"

A WORLDVIEW WITH NO FOUNDATION

Author, speaker, and apologist Dr. Ravi Zacharias was invited to speak at Ohio State University. While being driven to the lecture hall, they passed the Wexner Art Center. His driver said, "This is a new art building for the university. It is a fascinating building designed in the post-modernist view of reality." Looking at it, Dr. Zacharias saw that the building had no pattern. He saw staircases that went nowhere and pillars that supported nothing. Dr. Zacharias then asked his driver, "Did they do the same thing with the foundation?" The driver laughed, for even he knew the building couldn't stand if the architect had treated the foundation the same way.[73]

You may have an appealing, well-thought-out, and even successful building, but it won't be able to stand if it's built on a faulty foundation. There are many worldviews that are appealing, well-thought-out, and have even proved to be successful in some areas of life. However, Revelation 18 makes a strong point. If your worldview is not God's worldview, it will not stand. Ultimately it will fall and you will fall with it. Why? Because any worldview other than God's worldview will be as fragile as eggshells to God's touch. You might as well go ahead and call your worldview "Humpty Dumpty."

73   Ravi Zacharias, "If the Foundations Be Destroyed," Preaching Today, tape no. 142.

CHAPTER 21

YOU'VE ALREADY WON!
REVELATION 19

IMAGES IN THE BOOK OF Revelation make it easy to forget that this book is actually a letter. Though we discussed it when studying Revelation 1, it's important to remember who God had in mind when He inspired John to write this letter, and what the recipients were experiencing at the time.

Revelation 1:11 says that John wrote to the seven churches in Asia Minor, around 94–96 AD. Emperor Domitian reigned, and the persecution of believers that Nero had started, Domitian perfected. As the believers suffered and died under Domitian's rule, possibly some thought,

This isn't worth it.

It's better to compromise a little or at least keep my faith to myself.

I might as well accept the fact that as a believer, this is as good as it's going to get.

I want to quit.

When reading scripture, we read about God's truths and people's lives in the past, in order to gain wisdom and strength for today. It enables us to fulfill the proverb, "Look backward with gratitude and forward with confidence."[74] Yet the book of Revelation reverses that proverb. John writes to believers who have lost their spiritual self-confidence. They've lost their confidence in God, their faith, and themselves. To restore their confidence, John doesn't tell them what God has done in the past, as much as he describes what God will do in the future.

Revelation 19 is a chapter for every believer struggling with poor spiritual self-confidence. If you feel the pressure of your peers is too strong for you to keep your faith, if you think you don't have enough within you to do what God asks, if you would say to God, "I've suffered too long to stand strong anymore," or if you are constantly saying under your breath, "I quit," then Revelation 19 is for you. In this chapter, God does not have you "Look backward with gratitude and forward with confidence." He gives you a picture of the future so you can "Look forward with gratitude and backward with confidence." By seeing God's victory in the future, you can look back upon any challenge you are facing and know "I've already won!"

Therefore, you might as well join in with heaven and begin singing.

SING IT!

In Revelation 18, God has just destroyed Satan's greatest effort of persecuting believers and deceiving the world. As a result, a jubilant heaven breaks into song. In Revelation 19:1–8, one particular word echoes throughout heaven—"Hallelujah!"

Hallelujah is a Hebrew word meaning "Praise God." William Barclay writes, "The series of Psalms from 113–118 were called the

---

74   Vern McLellan, *The Complete Book of Practical Proverbs and Wacky Wit* (Wheaton, IL: Tyndale , 1996)

Hallel, the *Praise God,* and were part of the essential education of every Jewish lad."[75] The Jews knew their spiritual self-confidence was directly tied to singing praises to God. They knew this because their songs of praise to God were directly tied to great experiences with God. Recalling those great experiences with God in their past gave them the spiritual self-confidence needed to stand strong with God in the present.

If you want to see if your spiritual self-confidence is high or low, check two things. First, see if you're singing, and second, listen to what you are singing. If you've lost your song, you've probably lost your spiritual self-confidence. If you have a song, but it's the wrong song, you still might have poor spiritual self-confidence. If you're singing "gloom, despair, and agony on me," you might have a song in your heart, but it's not the song your heart needs.

When I attended seminary, the students were polled to discover their favorite songs of worship. The two favorite songs were "Victory In Jesus" and "How Great Thou Art." (Yes, I'm old.) I believe those songs were meaningful to us because if we were experiencing strong spiritual self-confidence those songs let us express it, and if our spiritual self-confidence was low, those songs helped lift it.

If your spiritual self-confidence is low, you need to get back to singing praises to God. A great song to sing is the one in Revelation 19. This is the only chapter in the New Testament where you will find the word "hallelujah." It appears four times in the first eight verses, and when you hear it, it sounds as though you are listening to four stanzas of one praise song—a praise song entitled "Praise God!"

---

75   William Barclay, *The Revelation of John Volume 2,* revised edition (Philadelphia: Westminster Press, 1976), 169.

Praise God! He's Won!

Revelation 19:1–2 is the first stanza of heaven's praise song. In it you hear heaven sing, "Praise God! He's Won!"

> [1] After this I heard what sounded like the roar of a great multitude in heaven shouting:

> "Hallelujah!
> Salvation and glory and power belong to our God,
> [2] for true and just are his judgments.
> He has condemned the great prostitute
> who corrupted the earth by her adulteries.
> He has avenged on her the blood of his servants."

Verse 1 identifies "a great multitude" singing this song. The only other time this great multitude is mentioned in Revelation is in Revelation 7:9–10. There the multitude virtually sings the same song as here in Revelation 19, and the ones singing are the believers who were martyred during the tribulation.

Thus you can understand why, in verse 2, they sing praises to God for avenging their blood. Yet the praise these martyrs sing in Revelation 7 and now repeat in Revelation 19 is *"Salvation belongs to our God!"* Though they thank God for avenging them, what they truly praise Him for is winning salvation for them. Avenging is retaliation. But God did more than retaliate, He won their salvation. You sense what this means to them as they start their second stanza.

Praise God! Satan's Done!

Revelation 19:3 records the lyrics to the second stanza of heaven's praise song. It is short but strong.

³ And again they shouted:

"Hallelujah!

The smoke from her goes up forever and ever."

Thus far, we hear two stanzas of heaven's praise song. They are "Praise God! He's Won!" and "Praise God! Satan's Done!"

The smoke in verse 3 refers to the smoke rising from the fall of Satan's one-world religion, government, and worldview. It's the fall of Babylon the Great described in Revelation 18. We notice the verse explains *"The smoke from her goes up forever and ever."* The smoke never ends, from a fire that never goes out. Babylon the Great will never be rebuilt. Satan will never regain his dominance over the earth.

If heaven had allowed me to pen this verse to their praise song, the martyrs would have sung, "Praise God! He's won! You can put a fork in Satan: he's done!" It's over!

Praise God! Everyone Sing!

Satan may be done, but heaven's singing is not. Revelation 19:4–5 tells the third stanza. With it, the volume grows louder as more are invited to sing.

⁴ The twenty-four elders and the four living creatures fell down and worshiped God, who was seated on the throne. And they cried:

"Amen, Hallelujah!"

⁵ Then a voice came from the throne, saying:

"Praise our God,

all you his servants,

you who fear him,

both small and great!"

As was explained in the study of Revelation 4, it is likely that the twenty-four elders represent the entire heavenly priesthood (1 Chron. 24; 1 Pet. 2:4–5, 9–10). That means Old Testament saints, New Testament believers, and Tribulation martyrs are now singing side-by-side with the angels. The four living creatures are part of God's angelic order. Therefore, all of heaven is now singing "PRAISE GOD!"

Stop for a moment and imagine what it would be like for you to "PRAISE GOD!" beside your heroes of the faith. For me,

I'd weep with Jeremiah...and sing!

I'd raise my hands with Moses...and sing!

Though I've never danced, I'd dance before God with King David...and sing!

Though He'd probably be pushing the beat, I'd keep up with Peter...and sing!

I'd close my eyes with Paul...and sing!

I'd stand arm and arm with my dad, listen to him sing for a while, then join him...and sing!

With full lungs I'll join in with all of heaven and sing "Praise God! He's Won!" "Praise God! Satan's Done!" "Praise God! Everyone sing, because God's taken care of everything!"

Praise God! He's Taken Care of Everything!

By Revelation 19:6–8, the sheer numbers of and emotion from within the singers cause the song's crescendo to become a roar. Listen to the fourth stanza of heaven's song:

⁶ Then I heard what sounded like a great multitude, like the roar of rushing waters and like loud peals of thunder, shouting:

"Hallelujah!

For our Lord God Almighty reigns.

⁷ Let us rejoice and be glad

and give him glory!

For the wedding of the Lamb has come,

and his bride has made herself ready.

⁸ Fine linen, bright and clean,

was given her to wear."

(Note: Fine linen stands for the righteous acts of the saints.)

Verses 7–8 allude to the wedding between the Lamb and His bride. John 1:29 and 3:29 say that Jesus is the Lamb of God, and the bridegroom; Ephesians 5:22–32 announces that the church is His bride.

In every culture, a lot goes into preparing for a wedding. The bride and groom have to deal with challenges from difficult people, as well as with getting themselves ready. That's often why they employ a wedding coordinator.

If you have surrendered your life to Jesus, before you can enjoy this heavenly moment with God, you first have to deal with difficult people. The statement *"Let us rejoice and be glad"* in verse 7 reminds you of this. The only other time the Greek verbs for "rejoice and be glad" appear together in scripture is in Matthew 5:11–12. Jesus uses them when He says,

¹¹ "Blessed are you when people insult you, persecute you, and falsely say all kinds of evil against you because of me. ¹² Rejoice

and be glad, because great is your reward in heaven, for in the same way they persecuted the prophets who were before you."

When you add your voice with all of heaven and sing "HALLELUJAH!" "PRAISE GOD!", you realize you are there because God took care of everything to get you there. He helped you overcome the difficult people in your life and the difficulties of your life.

Verse 7 also states that the *"bride has made herself ready."* Verse 8 explains that she's now dressed in *"fine linen, bright and clean."* Throughout Revelation, white linen represents the apparel of righteousness.

When you sing with others in heaven, you sing emotionally because you realize you don't deserve to be there. Isaiah 64:2 states that our righteousness is as filthy rags to God. Because of Jesus' sacrifice on the cross for our sins, when you surrendered your life to Jesus, God removed your rags and gave you His righteousness. You don't stand singing in heaven because you earned it; you are there because God took care of it. Because He has taken care of everything, you can't help but sing "Praise God."

Words and Music

I once read of Mark Twain losing his temper at his home. Looking for a shirt to wear, he couldn't find one without a button missing. Furious over this, he began cussing. His wife stepped in the room and thought his cussing was childish, so she began mimicking him. When she finished her cussing fit, Twain was calm, even smiling. Mrs. Twain felt she had proved her point, until Twain said, "Honey, you may know the words, but you don't know the music."

Many read Revelation 19:1–8 and say, "I already knew this." Yet your low spiritual self-confidence tells you, "You many know the words, but you've lost the music." If you want to reclaim the music, if you want to restore your spiritual self-confidence, stop and consider the words to the song.

You don't have to wait until heaven to sing the song of heaven. If you have surrendered your life to Jesus, the song of victory in heaven is one you can sing now. You can sing that God has won your salvation, and that you will one day sing with the saints, angels, and loved ones. You can sing it as loud as you want, because you know there's nothing Satan can do about it.

Therefore, when difficult people drain you, when difficult circumstances challenge you, when these plus your own spiritual weaknesses deflate your spiritual self-confidence, sing! Don't just remember the words, reclaim the music. Sing it the way you will sing it in heaven.

PRAISE GOD! HE'S WON!

PRAISE GOD! SATAN'S DONE!

PRAISE GOD! EVERYONE SING!

PRAISE GOD! HE'S TAKEN CARE OF EVERYTHING!

Sing it with conviction, because you know, regardless of what you face or feel, Revelation 19 tells you that "You've already won!"

PICTURE IT!

Obviously, not everyone is moved by music. However, most everyone is moved by what they see. Furthermore, what you see can sometimes move you to sing. Therefore, God not only lets you hear what heaven sings in verses 1–8, but in verses 11–21 He lets you see what the earth sees in Jesus' victorious return.

Seeing Jesus as More than You Thought

Revelation 19:11–16 provides a tightly packed description of Jesus. Opening these verses, the images pour out. Though you might have thought you had a good picture of Jesus, verses 11–16 shows that He's more than you thought.

> [11] I saw heaven standing open and there before me was a white horse, whose rider is called Faithful and True. With justice he judges and makes war. [12] His eyes are like blazing fire, and on his head are many crowns. He has a name written on him that no one knows but he himself. [13] He is dressed in a robe dipped in blood, and his name is the Word of God. [14] The armies of heaven were following him, riding on white horses and dressed in fine linen, white and clean. [15] Out of his mouth comes a sharp sword with which to strike down the nations. "He will rule them with an iron scepter." He treads the winepress of the fury of the wrath of God Almighty. [16] On his robe and on his thigh he has this name written:
>
> KING OF KINGS AND LORD OF LORDS.

These verses list four names given to Jesus. You are allowed to know three of them. In verse 11, He is called *"Faithful and True."* What a contrast to the unfaithful and deceptive ways Satan always used and especially employed during the tribulation. Verse 12 adds that Jesus' *"eyes...like blazing fire"* allow Him to burn away every lie. This enables Him to judge and act justly. Thus, with His robe dipped in the blood of the martyred saints, when He avenges them, it will be right because He is *"Faithful and True."*

He is also called *"the Word of God"* in verse 13. This is not new. God inspired John to give Him this same title in the introduction of the Gospel of John. John 1:1, 14 refers to Jesus stating,

> ¹ In the beginning was the Word, and the Word was with God, and the Word was God.

> ¹⁴ The Word became flesh and made his dwelling among us. We have seen his glory, the glory of the One and Only, who came from the Father, full of grace and truth.

When Jesus first came to earth, He gave us a chance to see God live among us and hear Him speak to us. That's why Jesus is called "the Word of God."

However, when Jesus returns to earth, the earth sees Him as heaven always has. He will be more than anyone ever thought. That's why the third name given Him is so fitting. Verse 16 calls Jesus *"KING OF KINGS AND LORD OF LORDS."*

Reciting the names given to Jesus makes me think of titles given to royalty on earth. Though he is seldom fully introduced, if he were, this would be the full title used for Prince Charles of England. He would be called,

> His Royal Highness The Prince Charles Philip Arthur George, Prince of Wales and Earl of Chester, Duke of Cornwall, Duke of Rothesay, Earl of Carrick, Baron of Renfrew, Lord of the Isles, Prince and Great Steward of Scotland, Knight Companion of the Most Noble Order of the Garter, Knight of the Most Ancient and Most Noble Order of the Thistle, Great Master and First and Principal Knight Grand Cross of the

Most Honourable Order of the Bath, Member of the Order of Merit, Knight of the Order of Australia, Companion of the Queen's Service Order, Honorary Member of the Saskatchewan Order of Merit, Chief Grand Commander of the Order of Logohu, Member of Her Majesty's Most Honourable Privy Council, Aide-de-Camp to Her Majesty.[76]

Though this says a lot about Prince Charles, verses 12 and 16 say much more about Jesus, while using fewer words. Verse 12 points to *"many crowns"* on Jesus' head, which is why verse 16 labels Him as *"KING OF KINGS AND LORD OF LORDS."* The single message of these two verses is that, regardless of the length of your titles or bloodline, there is no king greater than the King of kings, no ruler greater than the Lord of lords.

Therefore, when the size of your challengers and challenges buckles your spiritual self-confidence, stop and compare them to the size of Jesus. Though they may be great, they will never be greater than Jesus. Revelation 19 reminds you that Jesus will always be more than you ever thought, and will do everything you ever hoped.

Seeing Jesus Do Everything You Hoped

In Revelation 19, verses 11–16 give you a picture of the way Jesus is, while verses 19:17–21 give you a picture of what He can do. It should inspire you to see that in these remaining verses, Jesus does everything you hoped He would.

> [17] And I saw an angel standing in the sun, who cried in a loud voice to all the birds flying in midair, "Come, gather together for the great supper of God, [18] so that you may eat the flesh of kings,

---

76   Provided by Wapedia. "Wiki: Charles, Prince of Wales (4/7)" http://wapedia.mobi/en/
Charles%2C_Prince_of_Wales?t=8.#10.

generals, and mighty men, of horses and their riders, and the flesh of all people, free and slave, small and great."

[19] Then I saw the beast and the kings of the earth and their armies gathered together to make war against the rider on the horse and his army. [20] But the beast was captured, and with him the false prophet who had performed the miraculous signs on his behalf. With these signs he had deluded those who had received the mark of the beast and worshiped his image. The two of them were thrown alive into the fiery lake of burning sulfur [21] The rest of them were killed with the sword that came out of the mouth of the rider on the horse, and all the birds gorged themselves on their flesh.

The world's best moviemakers could not capture the magnitude of these verses. King Jesus returns to earth backed by the armies of heaven, armies comprised of countless believers and angels.

Though the sight of heaven's armies impresses, you can't miss seeing Jesus. All of heaven's troops are wearing the fatigues of righteousness: fine linen, white and clean (v. 14). Jesus is the only one whose uniform stands out: it's been dipped in the blood of the martyrs (v. 13).

There are times in battle when troops are asked not to salute a higher-ranking officer, for fear of putting him at risk. Jesus stands out fearlessly in His blood-stained robe, for He knows what He is about to do, that He is the only one who can do it, and that there is no one or anything that can stop Him.

Though the Antichrist (the beast) and the false prophet have amassed a worldwide army to face Jesus, they are the first He captures.

Verse 20 chronicles Jesus taking them and throwing them in hell. This should clear up any confusion. Jesus talks about it in the gospels and utilizes it in Revelation. THERE IS A HELL!

Regarding the worldwide army that gathers to fight God, it won't be much of a fight. Verse 21 points to Jesus as the only one fighting. Those fighting God learn that the very same power God used to create the universe, He uses to destroy them. With a word from His mouth, God spoke the universe into existence (Genesis 1), and with a word from His mouth, Jesus speaks, and a worldwide army is dead.

Out of Sight, Out of Mind

One of the reasons I believe God places this bigger-than-life picture of Jesus in Revelation 19 is because we often forget all that Jesus is and all has He promised to do. We live life personally scared instead of spiritually confident, because somehow when we face challenges in life, we put Jesus out of sight and out of mind.

It's like the story of the family who had moved to a new house. It was the first night that four-year-old Tommy was sleeping in his new room. In the middle of the night Dad hears Tommy crying. Running into Tommy's room, Dad turns on the light asking, "Tommy, what's wrong?" "I got scared." "What scared you?" Dad asked. Wiping his tears, Tommy explained, "I thought I heard something outside my window. Then I saw shadows on the wall and didn't know what they were. I tried to hide under my covers, but I just got more scared."

Kneeling by Tommy's bed, Dad hugged him then said, "Tommy, remember tonight when I shut and locked your window before tucking you in?" "I forgot." "And Tommy, don't you remember me showing you where the light switch was by your bed in case you needed to see something?" "I forgot." "But, Tommy, don't you remember me telling you that Mom and I are in the room next to yours, and if you needed anything just let me know?" "Daddy, I forgot." Then suddenly Tommy eyes lit up with an idea. He said, "Daddy, why don't you stay in my room with me? I know if I see you, I won't get scared, because I won't forget."

How many times do we live life like Tommy? Instead of living life with strong spiritual self-confidence, the shadows and sounds of what might happen cause us to hide from life. We pull the covers over our heads hoping everything will go away. But, instead of becoming calm, we just grow more scared.

In Revelation 19, God draws lovingly close to us and says, "Remember, I've already taken care of everything. I've secured your salvation. I've defeated Satan. There's no one or anything bigger than me." And if we say to God, "But I forgot," God gives us this picture of Jesus in Revelation 19 to keep with us always. It reminds us that Jesus is more than we ever thought, and has done and will do everything we hoped. Therefore when challenges in life threaten our spiritual self-confidence, we can face it fearlessly and say, "Because of Jesus, I've already won."

ACCEPT IT!

The two verses separating how Jesus is seen in heaven and how He will be seen when He returns to earth address the common plight of poor spiritual self-confidence. Verses 9–10 explain that the problem many have with poor spiritual self-confidence is not that we have forgotten the greatness of Jesus and all He's already done, it is that we have trouble accepting it. Verses 9–10 read,

[9] Then the angel said to me, "Write: 'Blessed are those who are invited to the wedding supper of the Lamb!'" And he added, "These are the true words of God."

[10] At this I fell at his feet to worship him. But he said to me, "Do not do it! I am a fellow servant with you and with your brothers who hold to the testimony of Jesus. Worship God! For the testimony of Jesus is the spirit of prophecy."

Trouble Accepting what God has Offered

The first group living with poor spiritual self-confidence represents those who have never accepted God's invitation for a relationship with Him through Jesus. Verse 9 expresses this when saying, *"Blessed are those who are invited to the wedding supper of the Lamb."*

Jewish weddings had four phases. Phase one was the *BETROTHAL*—a formal word describing two sets of parents arranging the marriage of their children. Phase two was the *PRESENTATION*—festivities lasting a week prior to the ceremony. Phase three was the *CEREMONY*—the exchanging of vows. Phase four was the *WEDDING SUPPER*—a meal celebrating the marriage of the bride and groom.

Please understand, many today live with poor spiritual self-confidence because you have never accepted God's invitation to the wedding supper. That means you've never acknowledged God's sincere *BETROTHAL*, that He has always wanted a relationship with you. Furthermore, you have fought the *PRESENTATION*, the activities of God preparing you to share life with Him. That means you've never experienced the *CEREMONY* with God. You've never made a vow to surrender your life to Him alone, forever. Therefore there is no WEDDING SUPPER for you. There is no celebration of who Jesus is, all He has done, and the life you have with Him now and forever. No wonder your spiritual self-confidence is low. The only one you truly rely on in life is you.

Trouble Living with All God has Given

I, on the other hand, fall into another group of individuals struggling with low spiritual self-confidence. It's not because I haven't accepted God's offer for a relationship with Him. I have. My problem is that I have trouble accepting the fact that I have actually received everything God promised me in a relationship with Him.

Because of my relationship with God through Jesus, I have everything I will ever need. And yet, at times, I find myself living as though I have nothing in life to help me face and overcome life's challenges.

The late Dr. Adrian Rogers helped me with this. For thirty-three years he served as Senior Pastor of Bellevue Baptist Church in Memphis. Before his retirement in 2005, the church had grown to over 29,000 members.

I was with a small group of pastors who heard Dr. Rogers say that the secret to his long ministry was that he learned to pace himself. For Dr. Rogers, P.A.C.E. was an acronym describing his regular morning routine with God. He explained,

"P" stands for "PRAISE"

I lift my hands to heaven and say, "God, I praise you!" Then I list all the attributes and accomplishments of God as I praise Him.

"A" stands for "ACCEPT"

Next, I cup my hands before God and say,
"Lord, I accept everything your Word says I have."

"C" stands for "COMMIT"

Then, I hold my hands up as though I'm being held up and say,
"Lord, I commit to do everything you want me to do today."

"E" stands for "EXPECT"

Finally, I extend my arms out before God and say,
"Lord, I expect a great day with you today."

Maintaining such a PACE with God, it's no wonder God accomplished all that He did through Dr. Rogers. He lived each day realizing that no matter the challenge, because of his relationship with Jesus, he had already won.

Dr. Rogers lived with strong spiritual self-confidence and I'm now striving to do the same. In doing so, Revelation 19 helps me understand the following. When I live with strong spiritual self-confidence, I don't fight each day in order to be victorious in Christ. I live it in the confidence that I already am. I know that because Jesus has already won the ultimate battle, I've already won any battle I will face. However, Revelation 19 also reminds me that if I ever forget this, stop for a moment and "Sing It!" "See It!" "Accept It!" and then get back to "Living It!"

CHAPTER 22

A SECOND CHANCE AT EDEN
REVELATION 20

AFTER READING THROUGH REVELATION 20 several times, I found myself saying, "This sounds familiar." Upon deeper study, I found out why. In several ways, reading Revelation 20 is like reading Genesis 1–3. At first, I felt as though God was taking me back to the Garden of Eden. But then realizing that Revelation 20 takes place in the future, it sounded as though God eventually gives us a second chance at Eden.

The reason this chapter captivated me was because it allowed me to ask myself some important hypothetical questions. They are the "what if...?" questions we usually keep somewhere in the back of our mind. I've written them below, and it's likely when you read them, you'll say, "You know, I've thought that before as well."

WHAT IF Satan had no influence on earth? What would life be like?

Wouldn't we like to see what life would be like if Satan was out of the picture, and if God's influence and leadership went uncontested? How would the earth look physically without famines, floods, or disease? What would the lead stories be on the evening news in a world without any of Satan's influence?

WHAT IF I could walk with Jesus on earth the way Adam and Eve walked with God in the Garden of Eden? Would I cherish it, or, after a while, take it for granted?

I've always been a little jealous of Peter, James, and John. They were the three people on earth who probably spent the most time with Jesus. I would love to do that. Yet I remember that when Jesus was arrested, neither of them stood up for Him. James left Him, Peter denied Him, and John remained silent about Him. So again I wonder, "If I could walk with Jesus on earth, would I cherish it, or over time would I take it for granted?"

WHAT IF I were Adam or Eve? Would I have stood strong, or would I have been deceived?

If I had a closeness with God the way Adam and Eve did, and if I had access to all of Eden the way they did, would I have been deceived by Satan the way they were, or would I have stood strong?

Though they are only hypothetical questions, these are important questions to ask, because according to Revelation 20 God provides a second chance at Eden. Therefore, we need to take these "What if...?" questions seriously as we look at Revelation 20.

A WORLD WITHOUT SATAN

God saw all that he had made, and it was very good. And there was evening, and there was morning—the sixth day.

— GENESIS 1:31

Genesis 1–2 records that it took God six days to create the heavens and earth. Satan doesn't enter the picture and begin his influence until Genesis 3. Thus for a while, Adam and Eve experienced Eden as a world without Satan.

According to Revelation 20:1–3, God removes Satan from the earth and seems to provide a second chance at Eden.

> [1] And I saw an angel coming down out of heaven, having the key to the Abyss and holding in his hand a great chain. [2] He seized the dragon, that ancient serpent, who is the devil, or Satan, and bound him for a thousand years. [3] He threw him into the Abyss, and locked and sealed it over him, to keep him from deceiving the nations anymore until the thousand years were ended. After that, he must be set free for a short time.

"And I saw!" This three-word phrase appears nine times in Revelation (Rev. 5:2; 8:2; 9:1; 13:1; 15:2; 19:17; 20:1, 4, 12). Each time John uses it, he is introducing a new vision. I'm sure, after all John has seen of God's wrath and Satan's ravaging on earth, he is thrilled to have this new vision in verses 1–3.

In John's new vision, Satan is bound and thrown into *"the Abyss."* The Abyss is mentioned in four chapters in Revelation (Rev. 9, 11, 17, 20). It refers to "a temporary place of incarceration for certain demons."[77] Reading verse 7, we learn that God has sentenced Satan there for a thousand years.

A Thousand Years without Satan

During the thousand years in which God removes Satan from the earth, He fulfills the promises He made through the Old Testament prophets—promises of establishing His kingdom on earth. Below is a brief list of those promises. They give a detailed picture of what

---

77   MacArthur, *Time*, 297.

God's kingdom on earth will be like. It's a picture of the kind of life all people long to have.

WITH SATAN REMOVED FROM THE EARTH

- There will be peace under Christ's authority (Isa. 9:6–7)
- War is replaced by joy (Isa. 65:18–19)
- Holiness characterizes the Kingdom and its subjects (Zech. 14:20–21)
- Comfort is given by the King ((Isa. 66:13)
- Perfect justice is administered by the King (Isa. 9:7)
- Perfect social order is established by the King (Isa. 65:21–23)
- Knowledge of divine truth is widespread (Isa. 11:2; Jer. 31:33–34)
- Physical infirmity and sickness are gone (Isa. 35:3–6; Ezek. 47:12)
- Longevity of life is restored (Isa. 60:20)
- Economic abundance is enjoyed (Isa. 30:23–26; Amos 9:13)
- The whole earth worships Jehovah (Isa. 45:22–24; Zechariah 14:16f)[78]

Now that's the type of life we expect God to provide! Stop for a moment and picture the earth prior to Revelation 20. Under the influence of Satan's one-world government, religion, and world-view, the earth could be viewed in 3-D—full of DECEPTION, DESTRUCTION, and DEATH.

---

78   Charles F. Pfeiffer, Howard F. Vos, and John Rea editors, *Wycliffe Bible Encyclopedia* (Chicago: Moody, 1975), 119.

Revelation 20 enables us to see what God does to the earth with Satan gone. It's like being in Eden again. Therefore, I think it's time we started casting blame where blame is due, and started blaming Satan for the hard experiences we have on earth.

Casting Blame where Blame is Due!

In my many years as a pastor, I've had late night phone calls, early morning hospital visits, and emotional conversations in my office with people in severe pain. A child is terminally ill, a young mother unexpectedly dies of a heart attack, a young man takes his life, another has his life taken, and the list goes on. In these conversations, I've seen many turn to God for strength, and others turn against God and blame Him.

When I think of those who turned against God and blamed Him for their pain, one encounter comes to mind. I was in my mid-twenties, and pastoring a church that an adolescent and her parents began attending. You couldn't miss them. It wasn't a big church, and when the daughter entered in her wheelchair, she stood out. Her mom called me one day, saying that her daughter really needed to talk with me, so her mom brought her to my office, and then left.

The conversation was light and warm at first. Then, I asked her about her relationship with God. It was as though I had thrown a switch. Her countenance immediately changed from sweet to bitter. She talked about her wheelchair, life without much use of her legs, and wondered how a loving God could do this to her. I let her do most of the talking that day, but did show her Genesis 3. I showed her how Adam and Eve lived in a perfect world with God, but because of Satan's deception and their sin they were driven out. I told her we are not living in a world God wanted, but one that Satan altered. I also told her that God hasn't abandoned us, but offers us a relationship with Him, so we can get through this altered world with His help.

She came back to my office a few more times, and eventually surrendered her life to Jesus. I had the joy of baptizing her. It wasn't long after her baptism, however, that her mother called to say she was now in a rehab center. She had somehow hidden from her parents her dependency on alcohol.

I visited her in the center. Though the experience was hard for her, I didn't see the same bitterness. After a week in the center, the mom called to tell me why her daughter had formed the addiction. A rehab counselor learned that years earlier a teacher in her school sexually molested her and threatened her if she told anyone.

I still get sick recalling this story. Sick over the challenges of a young girl in a wheelchair; sick that a teacher would take advantage of her and threaten her, and sick that for years she found more comfort in a bottle than from God. Yet, I tell her story because her mom and dad told me to. It was because she stopped blaming God and surrendered her life to Him that she truly began getting the help she needed.

This was not the world God wanted for her, nor were these the experiences He wished for her. Satan altered this world and set all this in motion back in Eden. But God did offer the opportunity to have a personal relationship with her and to never abandon her. He offered to help her through this world altered by Satan.

Revelation 20 seemed to be the perfect time to tell her story, for it reminds us this is not the world God wanted. But, with His help, we can get through it and ultimately experience a world without Satan. For in the second Eden experience, we physically walk with Jesus.

WALKING WITH JESUS

Then the man and his wife heard the sound of the LORD God as he was walking in the garden in the cool of the day.

— GENESIS 3:8

When reading Genesis 3:8, I sigh with longing. I've always wanted what Adam and Eve had—the privilege of physically walking with God on earth. According to Revelation 20:4–6, we get that chance when God gives us a second chance at Eden.

> [4] I saw thrones on which were seated those who had been given authority to judge. And I saw the souls of those who had been beheaded because of their testimony for Jesus and because of the word of God. They had not worshiped the beast or his image and had not received his mark on their foreheads or their hands. They came to life and reigned with Christ a thousand years. [5](The rest of the dead did not come to life until the thousand years were ended.) This is the first resurrection. [6] Blessed and holy are those who have part in the first resurrection. The second death has no power over them, but they will be priests of God and of Christ and will reign with him for a thousand years.

These verses explain how Jesus sets up His kingdom on earth. The question is, "Who will be on earth under His rule?" Here's the breakdown of those with Jesus as He starts His thousand-year reign on earth.

Those who Returned with Jesus

Revelation 19:11–16 describes Jesus' triumphant return to earth. Coming with Him are the armies of heaven. Within the ranks you have Old Testament saints (Zech. 14:5), New Testament believers (Col. 3:4), and souls of the Tribulation martyrs (Rev. 19:14). They remain on earth to be a part of Jesus' thousand-year reign.

Those Resurrected by Jesus

1 Thessalonians 4:13–18 explains that the bodies of the Old Testament saints and New Testament believers are resurrected by God during the rapture. At that time, their souls and bodies become one. Now, as Jesus establishes His kingdom on earth, Revelation 20:4–6 explains that the bodies of the Tribulation martyrs are resurrected and reunited with their souls, which were with Jesus in His triumphant return. Thus, the Old Testament saints, New Testament believers, and Tribulation martyrs live body and soul on earth with Jesus.

Those not in the Worldwide Army against Jesus

If you recall, the only ones struck dead in Jesus' triumphant return are those representing the armies of the Antichrist (Rev. 19:17–21). That means those not in that great army are still alive when Jesus establishes His kingdom.

There are two groups who were not in the great army of the Antichrist. One includes the believers who were not martyred and who survived the Tribulation. The other group represents nonbelievers who were not a part of the battle of Armageddon. Not every nonbeliever was in that great army.

Thus, in summary, here are those who will be under Jesus' rule when He begins His thousand-year reign on earth. You have the bodies and souls of Old Testament saints, New Testament believers, Tribulation martyrs, and Tribulation survivors, both believers and nonbelievers. They all get to walk the earth with Jesus and live under His rule.

A Change in Leadership

Stop and think how different it will be to live on earth under Jesus' rule. I believe it was Ralph Waldo Emerson who said,

Every great institution is the lengthened shadow of a single man.

His character determines the character of the organization.[79]

Since Eden, and until Jesus establishes His kingdom on earth, Satan has been the CIO of earth—the Chief Influencing Officer. Second Corinthians 4:4 labels him *"The god of this age."* Satan's character has determined the overall character of the earth.

However, Revelation 20 announces a dramatic change in leadership. For the first time since Eden, Jesus is now the CIO of the earth. Verse 4 announces that Jesus appoints judges and gives them His authority to rule. Verse 6 explains that believers serve as priests of God and reign with Him forever. The earth represents the lengthened shadow of a single man. Jesus' very character becomes the character of the earth.

THE SERPENT IS BACK

Now the serpent was more crafty than any of the wild animals the LORD God had made. He said to the woman, "Did God really say, 'You must not eat from any tree in the garden'?"

– GENESIS 3:1

---

79   John C. Maxwell, *Developing the Leader within You* (Nashville: Thomas Nelson, 1993), 39.

In the initial Eden experience, Satan slithers in, deceiving Adam and Eve. Instead of standing strong, Adam and Eve disobey God, ending the Eden experience. Revelation 20:7–10 reads as though this happens all over again at the end of Jesus' thousand-year reign. We are given a second chance at Eden, and again some will fail.

> [7] When the thousand years are over, Satan will be released from his prison [8] and will go out to deceive the nations in the four corners of the earth—Gog and Magog—to gather them for battle. In number they are like the sand on the seashore. [9] They marched across the breadth of the earth and surrounded the camp of God's people, the city he loves. But fire came down from heaven and devoured them. [10] And the devil, who deceived them, was thrown into the lake of burning sulfur, where the beast and the false prophet had been thrown. They will be tormented day and night, forever and ever.

Some passages in scripture I have to read and re-read, and then pray and re-pray over to gain understanding. This is one of them, for initially I had two troubling questions.

Two Troubling Questions

First, I wondered, *"WHY WOULD GOD RELEASE SATAN AND ALLOW HIM TO THREATEN THIS SECOND CHANCE AT EDEN?"* Then I remembered that God allowed Satan to threaten the first Eden experience. And when you look at both accounts, God allows Satan in to cast insincerity out. Though God allows Adam and Eve to walk in His Garden and allows masses to live in Christ's Kingdom, God still wants to make sure their hearts are fully His. He wants to be certain that they are surrendered to Him and not the system, culture, routine, or way of life He provided. God wants to know, "If given a choice of a different life, which life would they choose?"

Second, I wondered, *"IF OUR ETERNITY AS BELIEVERS IS SECURED IN CHRIST, HOW COULD ANYONE BE DECEIVED BY SATAN AND DESTROYED BY GOD AT THE END OF JESUS' THOUSAND-YEAR REIGN?"* I believe in Jesus' promise in John 10:25–30 that when we sincerely surrender our lives to Him, we are placed in His hand and He will never let us go. We are assured of eternity with Him in heaven. Then how could so many, a countless number, like "the sand on the seashore," be deceived by Satan and destroyed by God?

It was then I remembered that not all experiencing the thousand-year reign of Christ were believers. The initial make-up of the citizens will include Old Testament saints, New Testament believers, Tribulation martyrs, as well as Tribulation survivors—believers and nonbelievers alike. Furthermore it is believed that during the thousand years, you still have marriages and families. Children are born to believers and nonbelievers. A large number of people will apparently be comfortable with the culture of the kingdom, but will fail to fully surrender to Christ the King.

As in the first Eden, God allows Satan to slither in to test the hearts of those who were given a second chance at Eden. He tests the hearts of nonbelievers who survived the tribulation, and the generations born during Jesus' thousand-year reign on earth. Tragically, masses fail the test.

Two Humbling Lessons

You may have already considered this. The answers to these troubling questions actually produce two humbling lessons.

The first lesson is *"THE MORE THINGS CHANGE, THE MORE THEY STAY THE SAME."* A lot of time elapses between Genesis and Revelation. Even today, many say we are more advanced. We are well traveled, better educated, and with advancements in technology we are even healthier.

Yet when you look at the three main characters in both Eden experiences, nothing has changed: God is the same, Satan is the same, and humanity is the same. God creates a utopian experience for us, wanting a relationship with us. Satan wants to deceive us, keeping us from that relationship with God. Whether or not we experience that Eden-like experience or are separated from God depends on our choice. It all depends on whether we choose to surrender to God alone, or listen to Satan's lies to satisfy ourselves.

The second lesson is *"THERE IS NO SUCH THING AS SALVATON BY ASSOCIATION."*

Nonbelievers who survive the Tribulation will probably think they are safe, because they are now a part of Jesus' thousand-year reign. They will likely think that being associated with Old Testament saints, New Testament believers, Tribulation martyrs, and survivors who are believers is enough. Yet many, tragically, will learn that association is not the same as salvation.

Many people born to believers during Jesus' thousand-year reign may think that, because their families are believers and the culture around them is Christian, therefore they are safe. They, too, will tragically learn that there's no such thing as salvation by association. It's only salvation by full surrender to God.

There are many today who think that because they attend church they are safe with God. They too are relying on salvation by association. But it doesn't work. Just look at your car. Evangelist Billy Sunday taught, "Going to church doesn't make you a Christian any more than going to a garage makes you an automobile."[80]

Furthermore, there are many today thinking that, because they were raised in a Christian home, they are safe with God. Now think about an airplane. I can go get my ticket, go through security, point to my wife Loree or my boys and say they are with me, but they are not getting on that plane unless they have their own ticket.

There is no such thing as salvation by association. It's only salvation by surrender. And the message in Revelation 20 is, "Surrender now or be cast out!"

CAST OUT!

So the LORD God banished him from the Garden of Eden to work the ground from which he had been taken.

— Genesis 3:23

Genesis 3:23 cites the end of the first Eden experience. God judges Adam and Eve for their sin and casts them out. A legend in Scotland states that when Adam and Eve were put out of Eden, they settled in Scotland, because Scots believe that Scotland is the next best thing to paradise.[81] Though their offspring would eventually reach Scotland, Adam and Eve were sentenced to an experience far harsher than Eden.

---

80   Draper, *Quotations*, entry 1286.
81   Robert C. Shannon, *1000 Windows* (Cincinnati, OH: Standard, 1997).

They were driven out to experience the hardships and pain of earth outside Eden.

In Revelation 20:11–15, God offers a second chance at Eden. Again some, like Adam and Eve, fall to Satan's deception and sin against God. This time when God judges and convicts them, they experience something far worse than earth without Eden.

> [11] Then I saw a great white throne and him who was seated on it. Earth and sky fled from his presence, and there was no place for them. [12] And I saw the dead, great and small, standing before the throne, and books were opened. Another book was opened, which is the book of life. The dead were judged according to what they had done as recorded in the books. [13] The sea gave up the dead that were in it, and death and Hades gave up the dead that were in them, and each person was judged according to what he had done. [14] Then death and Hades were thrown into the lake of fire. The lake of fire is the second death. [15] If anyone's name was not found written in the book of life, he was thrown into the lake of fire.

As Americans, we look to the United States Supreme Court as our final court of judgment. Yet each year the Supreme Court refuses to hear one to two thousand cases. Verses 11–15 clarify who God judges, the books He will use, the sentencing at stake, and the fact that no one case is refused. Everyone receives a hearing before God. Everyone is judged.

Who will be Judged?

The Apostle Paul addresses believers in 2 Corinthians 5:10 saying, *"we must all appear before the judgment seat of Christ."* This particular judgment is for believers only. Verse 11, however, describes a judg-ment for nonbelievers. It's the Great White Throne Judgment. Those assembled to be judged include all the unbelievers who have died and gone to Hades. Hades is mentioned ten times in the New Testament, and is the place of punishment for unbelievers until their final sen-tencing to hell.[82]

Verse 9 teaches that God destroys the last of earth's unbelievers by fire. Then verses 11–15 divulge that all unbelievers who have died and gone to Hades stand before God to be judged at the Great White Throne Judgment. There God judges them according to the books at His disposal.

The Books of God's Judgment

Just as all judges render their verdicts according to the law, and just as the law and its precedents are kept in books, God refers to His books when He judges unbelievers.

Among His books is the Word of God—His written and unchang-ing law. Legislators today continue adding new laws and amending old ones. They do so saying, "We can do this because we see the constitution as a 'living document,' one that can change with the times." Yet God says no one is to add, subtract, or amend anything of His Word, because His Word is truly alive (Matt. 5:18; Heb. 4:12; Rev. 22:18–19). We add, subtract, and amend laws to fit our times because we see them as the words of dead men on paper. We do not change the Word of God, because the One who wrote them is alive, and still speaks through His Word. Because God will never die, His law judges lives for all time.

---

82   MacArthur, *Commentary*, 308.

Also among His books we find the records of our life. These volumes hold everything we said (Matt. 12:37), everything we thought—our conscience (Rom. 2:15), everything we did publicly (Matt. 16:27), and everything we did privately (Rom. 2:16). And if anyone thinks that the record of their life is good enough to get into heaven, God reaches for one more book. Verse 12 identifies it as *"the book of life."*

The Book of Life is mentioned six times in Revelation (Rev. 3:5; 18:8; 17:8; 20:12; 20:15; 21:27). It refers to the record of those who, while on earth, sincerely surrendered their lives to God through Jesus.

You may have lived an exemplary life. You may have been good to your family, honest, and hard working. You may have been good to others, and respected them. You may have even joined a church, faithfully attended, and served in some capacity. Yet if you never sincerely surrendered your life to God through Christ, you can tell God about the good life you lived, but He already knows it. In fact, He could tell you, "You're right. You did live a good life. I have all the records in my other books. But the one record I don't have is the most important. I have no record of you sincerely surrendering all of your life to me. There is no record of you in the Book of Life." At that point you'll hear Jesus say what He promised in Matthew 7:32. All not found in the Book of Life hear Jesus say, *"I never knew you. Away from me, you evildoers!"*

The Sentence

Hearing God say, *"Away from me, you evildoers!"* is the same as hearing a judge today say, "Bailiff, take the guilty party away." With those words, you know your sentence has begun.

The sentence for those with no record in God's Book of Life is given in Revelation 20:14–15. They are thrown into the lake of fire. That's God's description of hell. Jesus gave a similar picture when teaching about hell. The word He used most to describe hell was "*gehenna*." The Valley of Gehenna was the trash dump southwest of Jerusalem. Not only did people dispose of their waste there to be burned, but often the corpses of criminals where thrown onto the fires. Thus when Jesus called hell "*gehenna*," people saw it as a place of perpetual fire, billowing the stench of burned flesh.

The harsh reality of God's sentencing is that those not found in the Book of Life are sent to hell—to the lake of fire. They do not go as lifeless corpses, but alive. They feel it, and continue feeling for eternity

LIFE BETWEEN TWO EDENS

According to the books of Genesis and Revelation, life on earth began with an Eden and ends with an Eden. Both Eden experiences have similarities. Both allow those living on earth to enjoy walking with God without Satan around. Even the Scots would say of both experiences, "It's even better than Scotland."

Furthermore, in both Edens, Satan is allowed in to do what comes naturally for him—deceive. Adam and Eve fell to his deception and disobeyed God. They were cast out of Eden to endure the hardships of an earth altered by Satan. The same happens when Satan is allowed to influence the second Eden experience. Only then, those who fall are joined with all who never surrendered to God, and God casts all out to experience hell for eternity.

Hearing this, it is clear. You can neither go back to the first Eden experience, nor are you living in the future Eden experience. Therefore, what should you do as you live life between the two Edens?

Say to God, "Thy will be done!"

The first thing to do is make sure you have sincerely said to God, "Thy will be done." This comes from C. S. Lewis who wisely said, "There are only two kinds of people in the end: those who say to God, 'Thy will be done,' and those to whom God says, in the end, 'Thy will be done.'"[83] If you say to God, "Thy will be done" and fully surrender your life to Him, then you will experience the second Eden and you will experience eternity with Him in heaven.

However, if you fail to surrender your life to God, there will come a time when you hear God say to you, "Thy will be done." You didn't want a relationship with Him, therefore you will spend an eternity without Him. Grievously, you'll hear Him say, "Away from me." Then you will know your sentence in hell has begun.

Make sure you say to God "Thy will be done" and surrender your life to Him, before you hear Him say to you "Thy will be done... Away from me."

Serve God Today as Your King

If you have surrendered your life to Christ, then my encouragement to you is don't wait until the second Eden to walk with Jesus as your King. If you have surrendered your life to Jesus, He is already your King. That means today and every day you live and serve at His pleasure. As you do, you reveal to others who your King is, what His character is like, and what life is like when lived under Jesus' rule.

---

83   Tony Dungy, *Quiet Strength* (Carol Stream, IL: Tyndale, 2007), 53.

You will also be surprised at how many people are watching, needing to see the difference.

A few years before the Soviet Union fell, *Christianity Today* published an article retelling the experiences of a former criminal named Kozlov. He described the difference he saw between himself and other prisoners who were believers. He said,

> Among the general despair, while prisoners like myself were cursing ourselves, the camp, the authorities; while we opened up our veins or our stomachs, or hanged ourselves; the Christians (often with sentences of 20 to 25 years) did not despair. One could see Christ reflected in their faces. Their pure, upright life, deep faith and devotion to God, their gentleness and their wonderful manliness became a shining example of real life for thousands.[84]

Kozlov later became a believer and church leader, because he saw in others the hope of a different life.

The day will come when we will have a second chance at Eden. It is a day when Satan is gone and Jesus is the Chief Influencing Officer of the world. But until then, Satan is still the one whose character is influencing the overall character of the world. That is why it is so important that we believers live our lives today with Jesus as our King. There are too many people in our homes, businesses, schools, and neighborhoods needing hope that there is a different life than they are experiencing. By living with Christ as our King, we send the message that "Life with Christ is an endless hope, without Him a hopeless end."[85]

---

84   "Bible Illustrator 3.0" (Parsons Technology, Inc.: Hiawatha, Iowa). The *Christianity Today* article referenced was published June 21, 1974.

85   Draper, *Quotations*, entry 5938.

CHAPTER 23

WHAT WOULD YOU PAY FOR HEAVEN?

REVELATION 21

THOUGH I KEEP TELLING MYSELF not to be surprised by people, it still happens. I read of a survey where the wealthiest one percent of Americans were asked, "How much would you pay for a place in heaven?" The survey itemized the different amenities of heaven and what the respondents were willing to pay. The survey was taken back in 1998, which means the amounts listed would be more today. Still, it gives an insight into the mindset of this elite group. Here's the breakdown of what they would pay:

> To experience the beauty of heaven – $83,000
>
> To acquire a special talent in heaven – $285,000
>
> To have a great intellect in heaven – $407,000
>
> To receive true love in heaven – $487,000

I'm assuming that the ones surveyed were allowed to create their own heavenly package, because the average sum they were willing to pay for a place in heaven was $640,000.

Where did they come up with the amount of $640,000? What type of heavenly package were they creating? Possibly, some were willing to sacrifice their brains for love. Others may have wanted to spend eternity without talent, as long as they were given a beautiful location.

Though it did surprise me that they were able to come up with a dollar amount, what surprised me most was that the dollar amount they gave was only 25% of their net worth on earth. The average net worth of this group was 2.5 million dollars, and yet they felt having a place in heaven was worth only $640,000.[86]

Those dollar amounts speak volumes. This particular group believes that what they have amassed in life is more valuable than what God can provide for them in eternity. The numbers they give scream that they have no clue what heaven will truly be like.

Now to make sure this message isn't just for the one percent with a large net worth on earth, it's evident the rest of us don't have a clue what heaven will be like either.

Randy Alcorn reminds us in his book *Heaven*,

> ...3 people die every second, 180 every minute, and nearly 11,000 every hour. If the Bible is right about what happens to us after death, it means that more than 250,000 people every day go either to Heaven or Hell.[87]

By the way most people put off any discussion about heaven or hell, it's clear that many are clueless about both. Revelation 20 ends with a description of hell that should cause everyone to avoid it at all cost. Now, Revelation 21 gives a picture of heaven that should motivate everyone to make sure they are there no matter the cost—even if it costs you more than $640,000.

---

86   McHenry, *McHenry's Stories*, 141. The original source cited by McHenry was *Homelife*, July 1998, p.66.

87   Randy Alcorn, *Heaven* (Carol Stream, IL: Tyndale, 2004), xix.

Therefore, let's look at God's description of heaven in Revelation 21. As we do, ask yourself, "What would I be willing to pay for a place in heaven?"

WHERE EVERYTHING IS NEW

Revelation 21:1–5 reads as the summary of a house on the market. It gives a general idea of all the amenities, and then in bold print it states, "EVERYTHING'S NEW!"

> [1] Then I saw a new heaven and a new earth, for the first heaven and the first earth had passed away, and there was no longer any sea. [2] I saw the Holy City, the new Jerusalem, coming down out of heaven from God, prepared as a bride beautifully dressed for her husband. [3] And I heard a loud voice from the throne saying, "Now the dwelling of God is with men, and he will live with them. They will be his people, and God himself will be with them and be their God. [4] He will wipe every tear from their eyes. There will be no more death or mourning or crying or pain, for the old order of things has passed away."
>
> [5] He who was seated on the throne said, "I am making everything new!" Then he said, "Write this down, for these words are trustworthy and true."

When God says, *"I am making everything new!"* He means it. The word "new" appears three times in the first two verses. In the Greek, this means that God creates an entirely new quality of life. Verses 1–4 summarize what this will be like.

New Surroundings

In verse 1, John sees *"a new heaven and a new earth, for the first heaven and the first earth had passed away."* It's important to remember that 2 Corinthians 12:2 indicates there are three uses for the term "heaven" in the Bible. At times, it refers to the clouds and atmosphere hovering the earth. On other occasions, it speaks of the stars and universe. Or, as in 2 Corinthians 12:2, it points to God's home.

In Revelation 21:1, the Greek word used for "heaven" identifies earth's clouds and atmosphere. You see that same word in 2 Peter 3:10, where Peter explains, *"But the day of the Lord will come like a thief. The heavens will disappear with a roar; the elements will be destroyed by fire, and the earth and everything in it will be laid bare."* The Greek word for "elements" is the same word translated as "heavens" in Revelation 21:1.

The reason God destroys the earth and its very atmosphere is that God is replacing everything touched and altered by Satan and sin (Eph. 2:1–2). The new earth and atmosphere will be the way God always intended.

What would you pay to live on a new earth, under a new atmosphere, where there is no evidence of Satan or sin? It's all God's. Before setting a price, look at what else is new.

A New Capital City

In verse 2, John sees *"the Holy City, the new Jerusalem, coming down out of heaven."* Abraham longed to see this, as Hebrews 11:10 states: *"For he was looking forward to the city with foundations, whose architect and builder is God."*

Some characterize this new Jerusalem as God's capital city of the new heaven and new earth. Verses 9–21 provide a detailed overview of God's blueprints for His new capital city. Therefore, before assessing what to pay to be a part of this, get more facts.

When adding up the value of heaven, look at more than just the cost of building materials. Have in mind the value of the experiences you will have, as well.

New Experiences

Verse 3 announces, *"Now the dwelling of God is with men, and he will live with them."* This has not happened since Adam and Eve's experience with God in the Garden of Eden (Gen. 3:8). Yes, we had God walk among us for thirty-three years as Jesus, and yes, every believer since Jesus' ascension has had God's Holy Spirit living within them (John 14:17), but this is different. We will live and exist with God himself. Most would say that experience alone is priceless. But there's more.

Not only is the opportunity to live with God in a new heaven and new earth a priceless experience, but it also creates other priceless experiences. Verse 4 explains that in your new experience with God, *"He will wipe every tear from their eyes. There will be no more death or mourning or crying or pain, for the old order of things has passed away."*

Verse 4 explains that God wipes away every tear because He dispels every source of our tears—death, mourning, crying, and pain. At this point, it's helpful to remember that not all pains are physical. God knows that. That's why, 800 years prior to John's vision, God inspired the prophet Isaiah to announce in Isaiah 65:17, *"Behold, I will create new heavens and a new earth. The former things will not be remembered, nor will they come to mind."*

How much would you spend to forget a mistake in your life? How much would you pay to forget old painful roads?

When my son Lee was 10, we moved from Weatherford, Oklahoma, to Richmond, Virginia. Even though we knew we were being obedient to God, the move was still painful, especially for Lee. In Weatherford, he had developed a close circle of friends. They were now gone, and Lee entered a fifth-grade class full of new faces.

As I drove Lee to school each morning, the rides were often quiet. Occasionally I'd try to lighten the moment with humor. A few times, Lee would ask me to drive around the block once more to give him time to dry his eyes. As Lee moved on to middle school and high school, I was glad to take different roads to school. Still, I found myself avoiding the old road I used to take when dropping off Lee in the fifth grade.

When Lee was a freshman in college, he came home on fall break and asked, "Dad, can we go play basketball outside at my old elementary school?" Driving that old road, I told Lee how painful it was to me. He said, "I know, Dad; this is at least the third time you've told me."

Every one of us has old roads of painful experiences we want to forget. On those roads we hurt someone close, or said something we wish to take back. They can be painful roads of obedience to God, or mournful roads of disobedience to God. Though my family knows I'm directionally challenged and often forget which roads to take, when it comes to painful experiences, I seldom forget those roads. Yet, Revelation 21:4 says that one of the values of heaven is that *"the old order of things has passed away."* The Greek word for "passed away" means "to put behind you." Isaiah 65:17 states that God puts those painful roads so far behind us that they *"will not be remembered."*

What would you pay to forget all your painful roads and have a fresh start with God? Verses 6–8 explain that you will never know if you settle for second best.

WHERE THE BEST IS SAVED FOR LAST

The late Adrian Rogers said, "The devil gives the best first and the worst last, but the Lord saves the best for last."[88] John underscores this in verses 6–8.

> [6] He said to me: "It is done. I am the Alpha and the Omega, the Beginning and the End. To him who is thirsty I will give to drink without cost from the spring of the water of life. [7] He who overcomes will inherit all this, and I will be his God and he will be my son. [8] But the cowardly, the unbelieving, the vile, the murderers, the sexually immoral, those who practice magic arts, the idolaters, and all liars—their place will be in the fiery lake of burning sulfur. This is the second death."

Those who ultimately appreciate the full value of heaven are individuals brave enough not to settle for second best.

Verse 6 applauds those who are thirsty but refuse to settle for anything less than *"the water of life."* They are like the woman Jesus met at a well in John 4. He knew her story. She had been married five times and was now living with a man. Thirsty for fulfillment, she tried quenching it through relationships with men. It didn't work because she was settling for second best. After surrendering her life to Jesus, the true "living water," she realized she would never thirst again (John 4:14).

---

88   *Adrianisms: The Wit and Wisdom of Adrian Rogers* (Memphis, TN: Love Worth Finding Ministries, 2006), 161.

Verse 7 continues the applause by cheering for those who inherit heaven by overcoming the urges to settle for something less than being a child of God. The charge to overcome appears eight times in Revelation (Rev. 2:7, 11, 17, 26; 3:5, 12, 21; and 21:7). Seven appear when John addresses the seven churches in Asia Minor. The culture pressured people into settling for second best, instead of surrendering all to Jesus.

Though dates may change, human nature hasn't. Our culture today, like John's, pressures us to choose a way of life that is second best. That makes God's words in verse 7 priceless. With the old heaven and earth gone and the pressures of a godless world gone as well, those enjoying the new heaven and earth held out for what was best, when everyone else told them to settle for less.

A close look at verses 6–8 uncovers three great rewards for those refusing to settle for second best on earth. FIRST, when surrendering to Jesus, you experience fulfillment with God on earth and with Jesus for eternity. You never thirst again. SECOND, you inherit all of heaven as your home. Refusing to settle for anything less than life with God on earth, you live with Him forever in heaven. And THIRD, you hear the greatest "I told you so!" in history. It's implied in verse 8. Here, God calls everyone who settles for second best "cowards." Believers have always known it requires far more bravery to surrender to a life with God than to settle for what the world says is right. Thus in verse 8, God says only the brave get to enjoy the best with Him—the best that He's saved for last.

TO LIVE IN A GOLDEN PLACE

When God saves the best for last, His best is beyond imagination. Not only is it impossible to price, I know firsthand that it is impossible to describe.

In 2006, I was being prepped for surgery. A biopsy revealed skin cancer on my nose that needed to be surgically removed. I had never been put under anesthesia before, so when the anesthesiologist gave her instructions, she had my attention. She said that, occasionally, some patients wake up in the middle of surgery, and if I did, to let her know and she would knock me out again. If that happened, I was ready to scream, "Knock me out!"

Yet something did happen in the middle of surgery. I saw something that, until my study of verses 9–21, I ineptly described as a golden door with gold radiating from behind it. I later told Loree that in that moment I felt a love like I had never known, and that suddenly everything in life became clear and simple. I have endearingly called what I saw and experienced, "The Golden Place."

While still experiencing The Golden Place, I became aware that I was on the surgical table, and the love I experienced was then directed to those in the room. I had a burning desire to speak to them. The surgical team later told me much of what I said, and how God addressed many of the specific needs in their lives—needs I never knew existed. The anesthesiologist confessed that when she heard me talking, it wasn't the usual mumbling or gibberish of someone under anesthesia. She thought I was really waking up, so she gave me more drugs to knock me back out. But I would not stop talking.

Waking up in the recovery room, the surgical team came in one at a time, moved by the experience. Though years have passed, I will never forget the Golden Place. Because of what I saw, and because of the challenges even to this day to find words to describe it, I have a deeper appreciation for John's challenges at describing what he saw in verses 9–21.

> [9] One of the seven angels who had the seven bowls full of the seven last plagues came and said to me, "Come, I will show you the bride, the wife of the Lamb." [10] And he carried me away in the Spirit to a mountain great and high, and showed me the Holy City, Jerusalem, coming down out of heaven from God. [11] It shone with the glory of God, and its brilliance was like that of a very precious jewel, like a jasper, clear as crystal. [12] It had a great, high wall with twelve gates, and with twelve angels at the gates. On the gates were written the names of the twelve tribes of Israel. [13] There were three gates on the east, three on the north, three on the south, and three on the west. [14] The wall of the city had twelve foundations, and on them were the names of the twelve apostles of the Lamb.
>
> [15] The angel who talked with me had a measuring rod of gold to measure the city, its gates and its walls. [16] The city was laid out like a square, as long as it was wide. He measured the city with the rod and found it to be 12,000 stadia in length, and as wide and high as it is long. [17] He measured its wall and it was 144 cubits thick, by man's measurement, which the angel was using. [18] The wall was made of jasper, and the city of pure gold, as pure as glass. [19] The foundations of the city walls were decorated with every kind of precious stone. The first foundation was jasper, the second sapphire, the third chalcedony, the fourth emerald, [20] the

fifth sardonyx, the sixth carnelian, the seventh chrysolite, the eighth beryl, the ninth topaz, the tenth chrysoprase, the eleventh jacinth, and the twelfth amethyst. [21] The twelve gates were twelve pearls, each gate made of a single pearl. The great street of the city was of pure gold, like transparent glass.

These verses describe God's capital city on earth. Someone did the math for verse 16 and said that, at its base, the Holy City, New Jerusalem, would cover roughly 1,750,329 miles.[89] That's around three-fourths the size of the United States.[90] Yet it's not the size of God's capital city that captures our attention—it's the beauty.

A Place that is Beautiful

Four walls surround God's New Jerusalem. They stand twenty stories tall, seventy yards thick, and are made of jasper (v. 18). Jasper is like a clear crystal. The walls rise supported by twelve foundations. Each foundation is comprised of different gems (vv. 19–20). Each wall has three gates and each gate is cut from a single pearl (vv. 10–14).

Heaven's buildings and streets are made of transparent gold (vv. 18, 21). I read that mining companies still work in locations that yield only one ounce of gold for every one ton of dirt displaced. If all the gold ever mined was melted down, it would barely fit into a cube measuring twenty yards on each side.

God described His New Jerusalem as three-fourths the size of the United States, with facilities and streets made of transparent gold. Because of the transparent gold, the great walls of jasper, and with the glory of God radiating in heaven, I believe that John has described in these verses the Golden Place I saw. That became even clearer to me

89 Jeremiah, *Escape*, 224.
90 Wiersbe, *Be Victorious*, 149.

when I read John MacArthur's translation of the Greek word "brilliance" found in verse 11.

> The Greek word translated "brilliance" refers to something from which light radiates. To John, the heavenly city appeared like a giant lightbulb, with the brilliant light of God's glory streaming out of it. But that light did not shine through the thin glass of a lightbulb, but through what looked to John like a very costly stone of crystal-clear jasper.[91]

Though John does a far better job than I have, neither of us do justice to the beauty of heaven. The beauty is priceless, and so is the clarity and simplicity of life experienced there.

A Life that is Clear and Simple

Looking away from God's heaven, life becomes cluttered and confused. But when we turn our eyes toward heaven, it becomes clear and simple again.

For years, at gravesides and funeral services, I've told the story of Dr. A. N. Hall and have seen its calming effect upon believers. Dr. Hall's story helps us look toward heaven and simplify our lives.

Just before Christmas in 1940, Dr. A. N. Hall, the esteemed pastor of the First Baptist Church in Muskogee, Oklahoma, unexpectedly died of a heart attack. After the emotional services of a heartbroken church, Mrs. Hall went to the church to clean out her husband's study. On his desk she found the outline of what would have been Dr. Hall's last sermon. The week he died, the seventy-five-year-old pastor was thinking about "My First Five Minutes in Heaven."[92]

---

91   MacArthur, *Time*, 321.
92   W. A. Criswell, *Standing on the Promises* (Dallas: Word Publishing, 1990), 157.

Using Revelation 21 and the title of Dr. Hall's unpreached sermon, I have comforted countless family members with a picture of their loved one's first five minutes in heaven. Let me do it for you now. Let me give you a glimpse of your first five minutes in heaven.

As you approach heaven, you notice how strong you are. If you have suffered any form of illness or handicap on earth, you won't have it in heaven. You are awed by the four walls surrounding heaven: they are twenty stories tall and made of jasper.

Each wall has three gates and each gate is cut from a single pearl. As you walk through the open pearl gate, you turn around and notice that it remains open. In fact, it never shuts. While on earth you may have locked the doors and windows of your home at night to protect you from intruders, but you don't have to worry about that in heaven. There will never be an intruder in heaven. Only those who accepted God's invitation and surrendered their lives to Him while on earth will enter.

As you continue your walk in heaven, you find yourself walking on transparent streets of gold, beside buildings of transparent gold. As the glory of God reflects off these, you realize there will never be any night here, only day.

Then you notice the different sounds in heaven. First, there's the absence of weeping, mourning, crying, and pain. These are such familiar sounds on earth that it's almost strange not to hear them in heaven. However, you don't miss them for long, because you love the singing you hear. God is a music lover. Seventy times in the Psalms it calls us to sing to the Lord. I don't know what songs we will sing in heaven, but I doubt anyone will complain over the style of the music.

Though the sights and sounds of heaven are wonderful, they can't compare with the reunions you enjoy with loved ones already there. In John 13, Jesus tells His followers that He would go to Jerusalem and die. They didn't like hearing that so He comforted them by saying, in John 14:1–3,

> [1] "Do not let your hearts be troubled. Trust in God; trust also in me. [2] In my Father's house are many rooms; if it were not so, I would have told you. I am going there to prepare a place for you. [3] And if I go and prepare a place for you, I will come back and take you to be with me that you also may be where I am."

If you have surrendered your life to Jesus, you are reunited with others who have as well. You embrace spouses, children, parents, siblings, and dear friends. You recognize heroes of the faith who you have read about and admired. And, of course, the greatest experience of all is seeing Jesus.

With this picture of heaven still fresh in your mind, let me ask two questions. First, "How clear and simple does life seem to you now?" It's remarkable how such a picture calms your life, making it simpler and clearer. Second, "How much would you pay to have an experience like that for eternity? How much would you pay to call heaven home?"

TO CALL IT HOME

Reading the remaining verses of Revelation 21, we see the priceless gift God offers. He gives us the opportunity to call heaven home. Look at verses 22–27:

> [22] I did not see a temple in the city, because the Lord God Almighty and the Lamb are its temple. [23] The city does not need

the sun or the moon to shine on it, for the glory of God gives it light, and the Lamb is its lamp. ²⁴ The nations will walk by its light, and the kings of the earth will bring their splendor into it. ²⁵ On no day will its gates ever be shut, for there will be no night there. ²⁶ The glory and honor of the nations will be brought into it. ²⁷ Nothing impure will ever enter it, nor will anyone who does what is shameful or deceitful, but only those whose names are written in the Lamb's book of life.

Throughout the Bible, God makes His presence available to us in many ways. In the wilderness, God's presence was acknowledged in the tabernacle and then later in the temple. In John 1:14, John describes Jesus saying, *"The Word became flesh and made his dwelling among us. We have seen his glory, the glory of the One and Only, who came from the Father, full of grace and truth."* This time, instead of us meeting with God in a tabernacle or temple, God puts on flesh and blood to walk the earth with us.

That's why I love John's statement about the new heaven and earth in verse 22. He writes, *"I did not see a temple in the city, because the Lord God Almighty and the Lamb are its temple."* John says that Christ Himself will be with us in heaven—God in flesh. However, John also states that God will not limit Himself to being with us in the flesh only. He is with us as He was with Adam and Eve (Gen. 3:8). We get to enjoy our new heaven and new earth living with our Heavenly Father. Being with our Heavenly Father makes heaven a home.

REASSESSING THE VALUE OF HEAVEN

I wish those who had taken the survey in 1998 had understood Revelation 21 before giving their answers. They would have seen how silly it was to try to place any dollar amount on securing a place in heaven.

You Can't Afford It

When you stop and reassess heaven and the experiences there, you realize it's priceless. No one can afford it. That's why it surprises so many to learn that their place in heaven has already been paid for in full. Romans 6:23 records God's payment for our sins by saying, *"For the wages of sin is death, but the gift of God is eternal life in Christ Jesus our Lord."*

Though it's been paid in full, that doesn't mean everyone receives God's gift of eternal life. Romans 10:9–10 says you have to ask for it and accept it. The Bible says, *"That if you confess with your mouth, 'Jesus is Lord,' and believe in your heart that God raised him from the dead, you will be saved. For it is with your heart that you believe and are justified, and it is with your mouth that you confess and are saved."*

Asking for God's gift of eternal life involves first confessing that you have sinned against God and asking for His forgiveness. Then you surrender your life to Him. That means whatever He asks, you do for the rest of your life. Doing this, you receive a gift you could have never worked hard enough or long enough to earn. You get to call heaven home.

You Can Look Forward to It

When you get to call heaven home, you discover a new reason why it's so valuable: you get to look forward to it. That's one of the reasons God inspired John to write the book of Revelation. God knew that the initial readers, the members of the seven churches in Asia Minor, were struggling to remain faithful to God in their culture. It was hard being a believer around 94 AD.

In fact, there has never been a generation of believers that hasn't found it hard to live their faith in the day in which they lived. That's why we need to read Revelation 21 as John's initial readers did. We need to read it and see heaven as something to look forward to, as well as an encouragement to stay faithful until we are there.

I was reminded of this while reading about Samuel Morrison. After serving twenty-five years in Africa as a missionary, his failing health forced him to return home to the United States. Also traveling home on the same ocean liner was President Teddy Roosevelt, who had been on a three-week hunting expedition. When the ship pulled into New York harbor, music sounded, people cheered, and streamers filled the air: all to welcome the President home.

In the middle of the fanfare, Morrison quietly disembarked, and weaved his way anonymously through the crowd. Walking away from the ongoing cheers for the President, Morrison's heart became bitter. He prayed, "Lord, the President has been in Africa for three weeks, killing animals, and the whole world turns out to welcome him home. I've given twenty-five years of my life in Africa, serving you, and no one has greeted me, or even knows I'm here." Morrison stopped for a moment. Then his eyes brightened and a smile slowly kept growing as he looked toward heaven with a thankful gaze. Morrison tells that in that moment he felt the gentle touch of God, as he sensed God's spirit telling him, "But, Samuel, remember. You're not home yet."[93]

When life is hard as a believer, when you've been faithful and haven't seen the fruit you expected, when you've worked hard to honor God but it seems no one sees, when you would like just a little appreciation for all you've done, but it seems others get it for doing things that don't even pertain to God or godliness, just remember: you're not home yet. The day will come when you will be home in heaven. Then you will enjoy and experience more than you ever imagined, more than you or I will ever deserve.

---

93   McHenry, 143.

CHAPTER 24

HANG ON, I'M COMING!

REVELATION 22

GOD USED MY BOYS MANY times to show me how I treat Him. I especially remember when they were young, around the pre-kindergarten and early elementary years, and needed help with something. A toy or game was out of reach, they couldn't get a box open, or there was some great dilemma that needed to be resolved. Whatever it was, there was no lag time between their need and their hollering "DAD!"

And they didn't simply say, "DAD!" I was always impressed with how much they could squeeze into that one breath and yet keep it all the same volume. With one breath they not only called my name at a volume neighbors heard three houses away, but they also gave an extensive explanation of their need. They'd say something like:

> Dad, I can't reach the game at the top of my closet, and Mom got onto me last time for standing on a chair, can you come and get it down for me? I want to take it to my friend's house so a bunch of us can play. I promise I won't leave it there like I did last time. OK?

Because I was usually working on something, and if their cry for help didn't involve someone bleeding, I would often say, "I'll be right there." Yet if my response wasn't fast enough, I'd hear something like,

"Dad, are you coming?" "Yes, I'll be there in a minute" was my usual reply. I know that 2 Peter 3:8 says, *"With the Lord a day is like a thousand years,"* but in my boys' minds, Dad's minute felt like a thousand years. It wasn't long until I heard desperation in their voice, and they had reduced everything down to simply calling my name, "DAD!!!" With that last plea, I'd begin moving from where I was and would tell them, "Hang on, I'm coming."

It was during one of these "Dad, are you coming?" moments that God showed me something rather humbling. When my boys called to me announcing their need and asking for help, I immediately knew that it was something I was able to do and that I was going to do it. But because they didn't see any immediate action, they began to panic. Even though they knew from previous experience that when I said I would do something for them I did it, they still panicked.

That's when God stopped me and showed me that I treated Him the same way my boys treated me. My prayers to God had the same cry for help followed by a lengthy explanation of why I needed it. When it didn't seem that God was acting fast enough, I'd bring it up again. And if it still seemed as if He wasn't helping, I'd simply call His name in prayer thinking, "You know what I need." Even though God had met my needs many times in the past, I still panicked that He wouldn't come through.

I am fairly confident that I've just described moments when you've acted that way with God as well. Though your needs may have been different, the tone and panic in your voice was probably the same. Like me, you were wondering, "God, you know what I'm going through. I've asked for Your help. Are You coming?"

This is exactly what the initial recipients of the book of Revelation were wondering as well. It was around 94 AD. Emperor Domitian has been aggressively persecuting Christians. Faithful believers have watched their friends and family members being discriminated against, persecuted, and martyred. I'm sure they called out to God for help. When they received what God told John to write in the book of Revelation, it was God's way of letting them know, and letting us know today, "Hang on, I'm coming."

I'LL TAKE CARE OF EVERYTHING

If you are panicking over something right now, then I pray that God's final words in Revelation 22 will comfort and assure you as they did those who read it for the first time. Hopefully you are comforted to hear God say, "Hang on, I'm coming, and I'll take care of everything." You hear this in verses 1–5.

> [1] Then the angel showed me the river of the water of life, as clear as crystal, flowing from the throne of God and of the Lamb [2] down the middle of the great street of the city. On each side of the river stood the tree of life, bearing twelve crops of fruit, yielding its fruit every month. And the leaves of the tree are for the healing of the nations. [3] No longer will there be any curse. The throne of God and of the Lamb will be in the city, and his servants will serve him. [4] They will see his face, and his name will be on their foreheads. [5] There will be no more night. They will not need the light of a lamp or the light of the sun, for the Lord God will give them light. And they will reign forever and ever.

Verses 1–5 read not only as a continuation of Revelation 21, but Revelation 21–22 also show how God ultimately resolves every problem caused by the sin in the Garden of Eden. Warren Wiersbe reveals this by placing the accounts of Genesis 1–3 beside Revelation 21–22.

GENESIS	REVELATION
Heavens and earth created, 1:1	New heavens and earth, 21:1
Sun created, 1:16	No need for the sun, 21:23
The night established, 1:5	No night there, 22:5
The seas created, 1:10	No more seas, 21:1
The curse announced, 3:14–17	No more curse, 22:3
Death enters history, 3:19	No more death, 21:4
Man driven from the tree, 3:24	Man restored to paradise, 22:14
Sorrow and pain begin, 3:17	No more tears or pain, 21:4[94]

Every problem and pain in life can be traced back to the curse given in the Garden of Eden in Genesis 3:14–19.

After Satan's deception caused Adam and Eve to sin against God, God curses the serpent, Adam, Eve and the earth. God's curse reflects what sin had done to God's plan for us. Instead of living in harmony with God and each other, our sinful nature causes us to rebel against God and to be harmful to each other. As a result of our sin and God's curse, pain marks our existence. We are born under cries of labor pains, and then we labor painfully to make ends meet as we battle disease until we die.

Though God's curse was because of our sin, His ultimate cure comes solely from Him. Revelation 22 reads as God's checklist for making everything right. It announces that for believers, life will be

---

94   Wiersbe, 145.

restored (v. 5), hurts will be healed (v. 3), wrongs will be made right (v. 3), and right actions rewarded (v. 12). God tells His believers, "I will take care of everything. Trust me."

YOU CAN TRUST ME

Yet even as a believer, your trust in God may become smaller as the parade of troubles grows longer. Job describes that feeling when saying, *"Man born of woman is of few days and full of trouble."* (Job 14:1) In Hebrew, the phrase *"full of trouble"* indicates an ongoing line of troubles—one after another.[95] Job confesses, "My line of troubles seems longer than my life." At this stage in his life, he wonders if God will ever hear his cry and meet his needs.

Most of us have felt like Job. At times we've watched the growing line of troubles cause our trust in God to shrink. Because God is everywhere and knows everything, He knows when our troubles drain our trust. He knows when it's hard for us to believe Him when He says, "Hang on! I'm coming, and I will take care of everything." That's why He says what He does in verses 6–11. Here, God gives you three reasons why you can trust Him even when your parade of troubles grows long.

I've Kept My Word Before

The first reason God says you can trust Him is because when He gives His word, He keeps it. Verses 6-emphasize this by saying,

> [6] The angel said to me, "These words are trustworthy and true. The Lord, the God of the spirits of the prophets, sent his angel to show his servants the things that must soon take place."

---

95   Paul W. Powell, *How to Survive a Storm* (Annuity Board of the Southern Baptist Convention, 1994), 63.

> [7] *"Behold, I am coming soon! Blessed is he who keeps the words of the prophecy in this book."*

God says you can trust this promise, because He's made it before through the prophets.

As was said in chapter one, the book of Revelation has over 550 Old Testament references.[96] Specifically, the prophets Isaiah (Isa. 24–27), Ezekiel (Eze. 38–39), Daniel (Dan. 7–12), and Zechariah (Zech. 9–14) spoke of the events revealed in Revelation hundreds of years before John was born.[97] God has been making this promise for thousands of years.

Yet when you've been hurting for several years, you wonder if God will fulfill the promise He's repeated for thousands of years. Therefore, look at the promises God made concerning the first time Jesus came to earth—prophesies about the coming of the Messiah.

Some identify 456 messianic prophesies fulfilled by Jesus. Mathematician Peter Stoner calculated the probability that just 48 of those prophesies being fulfilled by one man as 1 in 10^{157}. That's a 10 followed by 157 zeros.[98] It's the same likelihood of scientists identifying a single star in the universe, putting a blind man at the controls of a spaceship, and having him find that star on the first try. It's impossible. Yet Jesus didn't fulfill just 48, He fulfilled all 456.

When you look at how God kept every promise about Jesus coming the first time, you should be confident that He will keep every promise He's made about Jesus coming the second time. God kept His

---

96   Draper, *The Unveiling*, 12.
97   Hindson, *Revelation*, 1.
98   "Mathematical Probability that Jesus is the Christ," http://www.biblebelievers.org.au/radio034.htm.

word before, and He will do it again. So, hang on! Jesus is God. He is coming again and He will take care of everything.

I Know What You're Going Through

Considering who God chose to write Revelation, you discover another reason to trust all that God says. Verses 6–7 remind you to trust God because you can trust His message. Verses 8–9 add that you can trust God because you can also trust His messenger.

> [8] I, John, am the one who heard and saw these things. And when I had heard and seen them, I fell down to worship at the feet of the angel who had been showing them to me. [9] But he said to me, "Do not do it! I am a fellow servant with you and with your brothers, the prophets, and of all who keep the words of this book. Worship God!"

A Spanish proverb says, "Talking bull is not the same as being in the bullring."[99] We usually give little attention to those who talk bull, but we want to hear everything someone has to say if he or she has actually been in the bullring. The Apostle John had been in the bullring.

God chose John to pen Revelation. Revelation 1:9 states what the initial readers already know about John, particularly that he's been a *"companion in the suffering."* Just as they have suffered, John truly has.

As was shared in chapter 1, tradition says Roman authorities tried to execute John by placing him in a pot of boiling oil. But he did not die. Therefore, they exiled him on the island of Patmos. He's the sole survivor of Jesus' original twelve disciples. The readers of Revelation know John has suffered as much, and probably more, than

---

99   Powell, 51.

they have. Still, he writes—with unrestrained confidence—God's encouragement to believers: "Hang on! I'm coming and will take care
of everything."

Too often, believers think that when you surrender to Jesus, God
places you in a protective bubble. In that bubble, you never lose your
health, wealth, or job. You live shielded from temptation, deception,
and heartache. But that's not true.

Chinese author and church leader Watchman Nee understood
this. He spent the last twenty years of his life persecuted and held
captive in a Communist prison. From his experiences he wrote, "To
hold on to the plough while wiping our tears—this is Christianity."
He gleaned this from Matthew 28:19. There, Jesus didn't say to His
followers, "I will quarantine you from life's pains." He said, "I will be
with you through life's pains—always!"

Now John has written the book of Revelation. One who experienced pain as a believer tells other believers in pain, "Hang on! Jesus is
coming, and He will take care of everything." Furthermore, in verses
10–11 John adds, "And He's closer than you think."

I'm Closer than You Think

Not only does pain cause you to question God's promise to come
again and take care of everything, but impatience stirs up doubt as
well. We are by nature an impatient people. Paul Powell confesses this
in his book *How to Survive a Storm*. His confession emerges from his
efforts to change the timepieces in his house for daylight saving time.

> I started adjusting the timepieces in our house and realized I had
> 22 of them to change. I started in the garage and reset the two
> clocks in our automobiles, the timer on our sprinkling system

and our front yard lights, and the wristwatch I keep in my golf bag. I then went to the kitchen and set the clock on our microwave. In the den, I changed the time on a TV, the VCR and our mantel clock. In the bedrooms, I reset three bedside clocks, a clock radio, and another VCR. Then in my closet, I reset our five wristwatches and my travel clock. Finally, I went to the backyard and set the timer on our backyard lights and our swimming pool sweep.

By the time I got through, I had lost the hour I had saved! And, I was a nervous wreck. Have you ever tried to get 22 clocks all set on exactly the same time? As someone said, "The man who has one watch knows what time it is. The man who has two is never sure."[100]

One of the reasons we wonder if God will keep His promise to come and take care of everything is because we have too many timepieces. We have timepieces and schedules for when we want to graduate, marry, have children, be in a certain size of house, and retire. Though we can set, adjust, and live by our timepieces, we forget that God has His own. He acts and moves according to His time, not ours. However, verses 10–11 indicate that it's about time for God to come and take care of everything. Through these verses God says, "I'm closer than you think."

> [10] Then he told me, "Do not seal up the words of the prophecy of this book, because the time is near. [11] Let him who does wrong continue to do wrong; let him who is vile continue to be vile; let

---

him who does right continue to do right; and let him who is holy continue to be holy."

God's statement in verse 10 magnifies two clues that His coming is closer than we think.

First, God reminds us that *"the time is near"* for His coming. These are the same words God tells John to write in Revelation 1:3. As was explained in that study, the phrase *"time is near"* uses the Greek word *kairos* for time, instead of *chronos*. If God used *chronos*, He would be referring to a measurement of time. But by using *kairos*, God points to epochs of time. Epochs in history act like seasons in a year. You know a change is coming because the signs are evident. However, it's not until it's over that you can accurately date it.

The second statement in verse 10 indicates that we are in the last season before Jesus returns. John is told, *"Do not seal up the words of the prophecy of this book, because the time is near."* This is opposite of what God told Daniel in Daniel 12:1–4. There God gives to Daniel the same vision of the end times He gives John. However, in Daniel 12:4 God tells Daniel to *"seal the words of the scroll until the time of the end."* Daniel is told to seal the words until the end time, but John is told not to seal them up, because we are near the end of time.

The season of Daniel and the prophets has passed, as has the season of Jesus' ministry on earth. We are now in the season of the church, a season where Jesus' followers go into all nations telling everyone about Him. This is the last season before Jesus' return. The wait is over. In the next season, Jesus returns.

That's why the message in the book of Revelation is so strong. God says to believers: "Hang on! I'm coming and will take care of everything. You can trust me. I'm closer than you think."

I WILL REWARD AND BLESS

In verses 12–15 God provides two added incentives to hang on until He comes. He reminds us that when He comes He will reward and bless.

> [12] "Behold, I am coming soon! My reward is with me, and I will give to everyone according to what he has done. [13] I am the Alpha and the Omega, the First and the Last, the Beginning and the End.

> [14] "Blessed are those who wash their robes, that they may have the right to the tree of life and may go through the gates into the city. [15] Outside are the dogs, those who practice magic arts, the sexually immoral, the murderers, the idolaters, and everyone who loves and practices falsehood.

> [16] "I, Jesus, have sent my angel to give you this testimony for the churches. I am the Root and the Offspring of David, and the bright Morning Star."

One of the joys I have as a pastor involves traveling to other churches to preach revival services. I remember my dad doing that. It not only excited him, but it excited my brother and me as well. Just before leaving, Dad would pull Chuck and me close and say, "Boys, Dad's going to be gone for a few days. While I'm gone, I need you to do something for me. I need you to be good and do everything your mom says. If you do that for me, when I return I'll have a surprise for both of you."

Dad usually returned while Chuck and I were still in bed. Mom would tell us the next morning, "Daddy's home." I can still see both of us running into the bedroom and waking him up. Sure, we were glad Dad was home, but what we really wanted to see was what he had to give us.

That feeling returned to me as I studied verses 12–16. It's as though God has been telling us throughout Revelation, "I want you to be faithful to me until I return. Now if you are faithful to Me, when I return I'll have two surprises for you." However, they are not surprises in the truest sense, because God tells us what they are in verses 12 and 14.

Your Reward

In verse 12, God says, *"Behold, I am coming soon! My reward is with me, and I will give to everyone according to what he has done."* These words brought to mind Jesus' statement in Matthew 6:1–6. In my paraphrase, Jesus said,

> "I know there are some who act good and godly just to have a good reputation. If that is all they want, then that is all the reward they'll get—a good reputation on earth." Then Jesus adds, "But I see what others miss. I see the sacrifices you make, the care you give, the love you show on my account. I see it when your heart breaks for me and others when you pray—not at church or in a group, but when it's just you and me."

All of us receive various rewards and recognitions in life. We receive a diploma as we shake the hand of a principal or dean after graduation. Yet because that principal or dean doesn't know us well, or had little to do with our accomplishment, the handshake and exchange isn't as meaningful as expected.

Then there are those times when someone close to us, who truly knows us and all we have been through, acknowledges us. It might be with a card, a gift of appreciation, or a sincere statement, yet because it's from them, it means so much more. Now think what it will mean for the One who truly knows us and all we have done to greet and reward us. In verse 12 God assures, "Hang on! I'm coming. I've seen everything you've done in your faithfulness to me. I can't wait to reward you." When I picture that experience with God, for me, it's worth the wait.

Your Blessing

In verse 14, God identifies a second incentive. It's one that you can experience now and when He comes. God promises in verse 14, *"Blessed are those who wash their robes, that they may have the right to the tree of life and may go through the gates into the city."*

The key word in verse 14 is "blessed." Jesus uses it nine times citing the Beatitudes in Matthew 5:1–12. John uses it eight times in Revelation.

Though the Greek word literally means "happy," when Jesus uses it in Matthew, one could probably translate it "unusually happy." In His beatitudes, Jesus says believers can be happy when poor, hungry, thirsty, or in mourning. We can also be happy when meek, merciful, and when persecuted as a peacemaker. What's unusual is that we experience happiness in these kinds of experiences. But in Christ, we can.

However, when reviewing the eight references of God's blessing in Revelation, our happy experience moves from unusual to understandable. It's understandable because, when reading and taking to heart the words of this book (1:3; 1:3; 22:7), we avoid the tribulation to come (14:3; 16:15), experience all the blessings of eternity with God (19:9; 20:6; 22:14–15), and experience an understandable happiness. Thus when Revelation 22:14 describes us wearing a white robe, walking through a pearled gate reaching for fruit from the tree of life, we stop and think,

> That's what God has promised me. It will all be mine when He comes. Therefore, I can hang on and be faithful to Him until He comes, because when I consider everything He has promised me for eternity, there is no doubt, I AM SO BLESSED!

TILL I COME . . .

The images of eternity with God are so strong in Revelation 21–22 that we might forget we're not there yet. In fact, you might forget the purpose of this letter is to inspire believers to remain faithful to God until He comes. That's why the last five verses in the book of Revelation are important. They are God's clear charge of what He wants us to do until He comes.

Share the Message!

God first charges us to share the message. Verse 17 states:

> [17] The Spirit and the bride say, "Come!" And let him who hears say, "Come!" Whoever is thirsty, let him come; and whoever wishes, let him take the free gift of the water of life.

Three times in this final chapter, God repeats to believers *"I am coming soon"* (Rev. 22:7, 12, 20). Yet even God knows that we can become so focused on our challenges, and long so much for His return, that we forget our purpose. Verse 17 reminds us that until God's return, we are to work with the Holy Spirit compelling people to come to Christ.

I remember a time when life's frustrations robbed my focus. I was serving a challenging church. The challenge was that the community was changing, but the church refused to see it and meet its needs. It seemed every suggestion I made was either contested in a committee or on the floor of the church. On a couple of occasions, votes passed or failed by one vote. The whole experience was so draining that I considered leaving the ministry.

Something happened, though, that restored me spiritually. I experienced a joy and vitality I had not felt in a long time. I led a young man to Jesus. In that rejuvenated moment, I could see with fresh eyes what had actually drained me. I had become so frustrated over the challenges in my life as a pastor, that I had lost focus on the purpose of my life as a believer. My purpose was to help people surrender to Jesus. I learned that it didn't matter if a church wouldn't follow my lead. What was important was that I never stopped helping people surrender to Jesus.

The charge in verse 17 is the charge of the book of Revelation. As a believer, you will face many challenges in life. Don't become so frustrated by your challenges that you lose focus on your purpose. Your purpose is to share the message of Jesus and help others surrender to Him. I've learned that when you are faithful at fulfilling your purpose, you are filled with more than you need to handle life's frustrations.

Guard the Message!

The second charge God gives appears in verses 18–19. There, He says, "Be sure to guard the message until I come."

[18] I warn everyone who hears the words of the prophecy of this book: If anyone adds anything to them, God will add to him the plagues described in this book. [19] And if anyone takes words away from this book of prophecy, God will take away from him his share in the tree of life and in the holy city, which are described in this book.

As others have experienced, one day I had three clean-cut polite young men come to my house. They wanted to read from their bible. When I said there was no need, they asked why. I knew the founder of their beliefs said that Jesus gave him new insights with which to amend the Bible. So I told them, "Because I believe when God inspired John to say that no one is to add or take anything away from His Bible, He meant it." They added, "But those verses only pertain to the book of Revelation." Again I disagreed, and here's why.

Though verses 18–19 specifically refer to *"this book"* of Revelation, a thorough study of the book of Revelation reveals that this one book covers all books of the Bible. Furthermore, Jesus said in Matthew 5:18, *"I tell you the truth, until heaven and earth disappear, not the smallest letter, not the least stroke of a pen, will by any means disappear from the Law until everything is accomplished."*

The reason I was so emphatic about this was because their salvation depended on an unchanged Word of God. Verse 18 states, *"If anyone adds anything to them (the words of this book), God will add to him the plagues described in this book."* Remember, unbelievers are the ones left behind to experience the plagues described in the book of Revelation. Verse 19 announces, *"And if anyone takes words away from this book of prophecy, God will take away from him his share in the tree of life."* Again, unbelievers are the ones who will not see or experience the tree of life. I was emphatic about this with those young men, because if anyone changes the message of the Bible they remove any chance of salvation with God.

For this reason my prayer for years has been, "Oh, Lord, please help me not to say anything more or less than You have said in Your Word." As believers, we must guard the message of this book, for only the unchanged message of this book leads to salvation.

Rely on My Grace!

The third charge from God assures us we can faithfully share and guard His message until He comes. God says in verses 20–21, "Rely on My grace."

> [20] He who testifies to these things says, "Yes, I am coming soon."
> Amen. Come, Lord Jesus.
> [21] The grace of the Lord Jesus be with God's people. Amen.

I love how verses 20–21 flow together and form a single statement. You hear God saying, "Yes, I'm coming soon, but until then, my grace will be with you. Therefore, rely on my grace."

I read that, during the Civil War, a group of Union soldiers were under attack at Allatoona Pass. General Sherman saw this from Kennesaw Mountain and sent word to the soldiers, "Hold the fort, I am coming." Years later that story was told to evangelist and hymn writer P.P. Bliss. He wrote the following lyrics to inspire believers:

> "Hold the fort, for I am coming,"
> Jesus signals still.

> Wave the answer back to heaven,
> "By thy grace we will."[101]

The visions John transcribes in the book of Revelation are visions of the future. They were given to John to inspire believers then and us today that, though it's hard to live out our faith, be faithful. In Revelation 22, God encourages us by saying, "Hold on, I'm coming." My prayer is that we will answer God with the words of Bliss' hymn, "By thy grace we will."

TILL I CARRY YOU HOME

The book of Revelation encourages us to remain faithful to God, by giving us a picture of His personal return. Though God will return personally, I'm also strengthened by the truth that as a believer He is with me spiritually. His spirit is within me, which means He will help me hang on through the challenges of life until He comes. God reminded me of this through another experience with one of my boys.

Lee was only three, and for some reason the doctor said they would need to draw blood from him. Lee didn't know what that meant, but I did. I sat in the chair with Lee on my lap. He watched closely as they placed a rubber strap around his arm. He would have been far more nervous about this if I hadn't been there. I was his security. In his mind was the thought, "Daddy won't let me go through anything painful."

Then they stuck that needle in Lee's arm to draw blood. In a matter of seconds his little face said, "Hey, I'm scared. Ouch, that hurt!" Then, while crying, he turned to me and gave me a look that said, "Daddy, why did you let that happen?" I knew it was something Lee

---

101   R. Geoffrey Brown, "Look! A Great White Horse!" Preaching Today, tape no. 111.

had to go through, but at that moment I couldn't explain it in a way he could understand. So I just held him close, to comfort him through it. Besides, I knew that in just a little while I would carry Lee to the car. We'd go home together, and everything would be all right.

I know there have been times that you and I have looked at God the way Lee looked at me. You feel that you've been acting good in His lap, and then suddenly an experience in life causes you to feel like Lee. You're scared. You're hurt. With tears in your eyes you look to God as if to say, "Father, why did you let this happen?"

The book of Revelation reminds us that every believer will go through painful experiences in life. Some painful experiences are because of a world altered by Satan and sin. Other painful experiences come because we are living our faith in a rebellious world. Sometimes, God can explain to us why we had to go through those experiences, and other times He won't, because at that moment there's no way we could understand.

But we can be assured of this. If we have surrendered our life to Jesus, we will never go through a painful experience away from the lap of God. Though He may not keep us from it, He will hold us through it. Besides, He knows that when we have gone through everything we need to go through, He's going to carry us home, and everything's going to be all right. But until then, keep sharing the message, keep guarding the message, and keep relying on God's grace. Hold the fort until God comes and makes everything right.

For more information about
Mark Becton
&
A Confident Peace
please visit:

www.groveave.net
www.wordsofvictory.net

....

For more information about
AMBASSADOR INTERNATIONAL
please visit:

www.ambassador-international.com
@AmbassadorIntl
www.facebook.com/AmbassadorIntl